Scribe

ALSO BY BOB RYAN

Wait Till I Make the Show

Celtic Pride

The Pro Game: The World of Professional Basketball

Hondo: Celtics Man in Motion (John Havlicek autobiography)

The Boston Celtics: The History, Legend,
and Images of America's Most Celebrated Team

Cousy and the Celtic Mystique (with Bob Cousy)

Forty-Eight Minutes: A Night in the Life of the NBA

Drive: The Story of My Life (Larry Bird autobiography)

The Four Seasons

The Road to the Super Bowl

When Boston Won the World Series

The Best of Sport (editor)

SCRIBE

My Life in Sports

BOB RYAN

B L O O M S B U R Y
NEW YORK • LONDON • NEW DELHI • SYDNEY

Published by Bloomsbury USA, New York
Bloomsbury is a registered trademark of Bloomsbury Publishing Plc

All papers used by Bloomsbury USA are natural, recyclable products made from wood grown in well-managed forests. The manufacturing processes conform to the environmental regulations of the country of origin.

LIBRARY OF CONGRESS CATALOGING-IN-PUBLICATION DATA HAS BEEN APPLIED FOR.

ISBN (cased edition): 978-1-62040-506-2
ISBN (exclusive signed edition): 978-1-63286-057-6

First U.S. Edition 2014

1 3 5 7 9 10 8 6 4 2

Typeset by Hewer Text UK Ltd, Edinburgh
Printed and bound in the U.S.A. by Thomson-Shore Inc., Dexter, Michigan

To Elaine, who misses the original Boston Garden as much as I do
(I think).

Contents

CHAPTER 1

Shootaround: "Do You Mind If I Call Red First?"

The Boston Celtics' morning shootaround was over on October 1, 1980, and I was back in my hotel room around noontime speaking on the phone to my old friend Paul Silas, who was starting his third season with the Seattle Supersonics and his fourth after leaving the Celtics for financial reasons in 1976.

We were in Terre Haute, Indiana, a site carefully chosen for a good reason. For Terre Haute was the location of Indiana State University, alma mater of Larry Bird. The Celtics had booked an Indiana exhibition trip, scheduling games in Indianapolis, Terre Haute, and, after this particular evening, Evansville. As coach Bill Fitch would say—and he was the first person I ever heard express the sentiment—scheduling preseason exhibition games in Indiana when you have Larry Bird on your team is a no-brainer.

I heard a knock on the door.

After asking Silas to wait a sec, I opened the door. There stood Dave Cowens, still in his green practice uniform with the number 18 jersey. He was holding a small sheaf of papers.

Cowens had been a member of the Celtics since the 1970–71 season. He had been a co–Rookie of the Year, an MVP, the center on two championship teams, and a player whose intense playing style had turned his name, for some, into a pejorative. To refer to any college player as "Cowens-like" was to identify the young man as a ferocious competitor. But more than that, he was the single most fascinating personality I had yet encountered during my then-dozen years as a working sportswriter. He had an unrivaled dossier of iconoclastic, principle-based behavior, both on and off the court. There was a much better chance of finding a player who resembled Cowens than of finding a person like him.

"Come in," I said. "I'm talking to your old buddy Silas. Want to say hello?"

The two chatted briefly. I wrapped up the call and said, "Okay, what's up?"

"Here," he said, handing me the papers, "read this."

I began to read, but after several paragraphs I realized something. The pages were out of order. I wasn't quite sure what the purpose of it was until I started at the top.

It didn't take long for it to hit me. Oh my God, I thought. This is a *retirement* statement.

Retirement? Why? Okay, he hadn't had a good game the night before in Indianapolis, but in an account of a preseason game in Milwaukee played five days earlier I had noted that "Cowens was again the best Boston player." That's right: "again."

But here it was. "I used to treasure the individual confrontations with Kareem or Bob McAdoo, and relished the fact we were playing against teams like the Knicks of the early seventies and the old Chicago Sloan-Love-Walker quintets, who made you reach for everything you had in order to compete with their type of play. These challenges were exciting and real; they were invigorating and exhausting.

"However, I can no longer play that caliber of basketball, and it is unbelievably frustrating to remain in an occupation which is wearing and in which one has seen better days."

Further on he wrote: "The primary reason I will not remain on the roster of the Celtics or any other professional basketball club is due to the fact that I have a highly-weakened and worn-out set of feet and ankles, and their respective anatomical members."

How many players would address their body parts as "anatomical members"? It was classic Cowens.

He addressed the fact that he would be forfeiting his salary from the final year of a five-year contract, stressing that he didn't think he could earn it. "Therefore," he wrote, "I don't want preferential treatment from the coach due to my status as a seasoned veteran, because then I wouldn't be able to expect maximum efforts from my teammates. Fairness goes hand in hand with dedication, especially when one is involved in a group participation effort."

"So what do you want from me?" I said.

"Two things," he said. "Help me put it in order. You know, give me some professional help. And tell me what you think." Then came the punch line: "And I'd like to have this printed in the paper." I told him I thought the *Boston Globe* could accommodate him.

The truth is it was very nicely and powerfully written, which did not surprise me because this was not the first time I had recognized his writing ability. I felt I could improve it without making it anything less than the World According to Dave Cowens.

"I'll need some time," I told him. "Maybe an hour."

He was heading out the door when he turned around. "Do you mind if I call Red first?" he inquired.

Excuse me? Do I, Bob Ryan, mind if he, Dave Cowens, calls the hallowed Red Auerbach, Mr. Celtics, on my phone to inform him he is retiring from active duty in the National Basketball Association, effective immediately?

I gave him my blessing.

The conversation was brief. It went through Mary Faherty, Red's longtime secretary.

"Hello, Mary. It's Dave. Is Red in? Red, it's Dave. Remember what we talked about the other night? Well, I'm doing it. Okay, see you when I get back."

And he returned to his room.

After phoning the *Globe* office to alert them to a pretty nice exclusive story, I began working on the statement. He had begun by writing it longhand on yellow legal-pad paper but had then decided to do it on a typewriter. The statement consisted of four and a half pages of copy, and the finished product was about 80 to 85 percent Cowens and 15 to 20 percent Ryan. I was able to edit it in an old-fashioned handwritten way, suitable for dictation.

The story did not end there.

Sometime around three thirty or four o'clock, the team assembled on the bus for the trip to Evansville, where they would be playing the Chicago Bulls. Cowens boarded with his mates to break the news. He briefed them on the whys and wherefores of his decision, and he told center

Robert Parish, acquired from Golden State in a draft-day deal the spring before but off to a very poor start with his new team, that he was sure Parish could do the job.

According to multiple sources, resident team comedian M. L. Carr piped up.

"Are you done now?" he asked. "Is that it?"

"Yes," Cowens replied.

"Then get the [naughty word] off our bus!"

The bus pulled away, and there I was, standing with Dave Cowens.

"What happens now?" I asked.

He told me he'd be going back home to Newport, Kentucky, for a few days. But there was a problem. He didn't have his credit cards, and he was low on cash. This was 1980. There were no ATMs.

So I went to the nearest Avis office, rented a car, and handed him the keys. Off he went.

I then got into my car for the drive to Evansville and the game with the Bulls. I seem to recall coach Bill Fitch leaving Robert Parish in after he picked up four fouls in the first quarter, as if to say, "Okay, pal, you're on your own. You'd better figure it out." Anyway, the Celtics won, and the post-Cowens era had begun.

I never went to journalism school, but I doubt there is a J-school anywhere that can prepare any sportswriter for a day like that.

CHAPTER 2

"The Sportster"

The column's name was "The Sportster." It had a circulation of one. It was a typewritten sheet, on standard eight-by-eleven paper.

The columnist was opinionated. After all, he was a columnist. The main topic was an assessment of the Mercer County Parochial Basketball League's 1957–58 season, at least to that point, which was sometime in December of 1957. The fact that the columnist was actually a participant in that league gave the opinions additional gravitas. The columnist's view expanded near the end, as he offered an analysis of the NBA season's status, focusing on the play of the Boston Celtics. The columnist was particularly enamored with Bob Cousy, who, the columnist declared, "quarterbacks the club masterfully."

I was eleven.

That was the genesis of a sportswriting career that has lasted forty-six years and taken me to just about every state, plus many foreign countries. It was a career focused on, but not limited to, coverage of basketball and baseball. I covered the Boston Celtics for the *Boston Globe* in three separate chunks, totaling thirteen and a half seasons over a span stretching from 1969 to 1988. College basketball had been my basic orientation, but I developed a deep love of the NBA, which I saw grow from what could accurately be termed a mom-and-pop operation into an international conglomerate. No one could rightfully dispute the premise that basketball is now the second-most popular team sport in the world, after soccer.

When I began with the *Globe*, I never even considered the prospect of covering an Olympics. I wound up doing eleven of them as a columnist, six summer and five winter. I cannot imagine my career without them. Flawed and bloated as they are, the Olympics remain a fascinating laboratory for anyone who loves good sporting competition and just plain people watching.

The laundry list of the things I was fortunate enough to cover as both a reporter and a columnist also includes World Series; baseball playoffs; Super Bowls; NFL playoff games; NBA playoff games and finals; Stanley Cup playoffs and finals; World Basketball Championships; college bowl games; college football championship games, by whatever name; NCAA basketball tournaments (including twenty-nine Final Fours); college hockey Frozen Fours; golf majors; Ryder Cups; a limited diet of NASCAR events; a few Belmonts; major boxing matches; a lone Davis Cup; and, yes, the ultimate résumé booster—a dog show. My boss even forced me to cover an Ultimate Fighting Championship affair in August of 2011, and I was smart enough to retire before he could coerce me into another one. That doesn't include all the local stuff, or the feature stories, some of which led to some of my most memorable experiences, journalistically or otherwise.

I don't think there is a remote doubt that I was destined to do this. Sportswriting is a two-part word, and my entire life has been devoted to both aspects. Any time I was taken by my father to a local sporting event—say, for example, a Friday night Trenton Catholic high school basketball game—I did not consider the experience to have had any validity until I read about it the following day in the morning *Trentonian*, a tabloid published in my hometown of Trenton, New Jersey. Part of it was making sure I saw what I thought I saw. The other part was the writing. Words mattered to me.

I always was a reader. I read the *Trentonian* from back to front, sports first, just as I read the afternoon *Trenton Times* in a more conventional manner. But reading the newspapers was just the beginning.

By the time I was nine people knew that the thing to give me at Christmas and birthday time was a book on sports. For Christmas in 1955 someone gave me a copy of a book by Paul Richards entitled *Modern Baseball Strategy*. Richards made quite a name for himself managing the White Sox and Orioles, and he was known for innovative strategy such as placing a pitcher in the field for a batter or two in order to create a favorable pitching matchup before returning the original guy to the mound.

The book was a basic primer, with such chapter headings as "Handling Pitchers," "Base-Running Strategy," "Signs and Signals," "Back-up and Cut-off Plays," and the one I most remember, "Batting Order." I really took that one to heart. From then on, I studied lineups and pretty much figured that anyone who could bat third or fourth in a major-league lineup was a god, no questions asked.

I couldn't read enough about baseball. I was the only kid on my block who could recite the Infield Fly Rule, and I was also the only kid on my block who knew which team had won the 1921 World Series. The way I looked at it, any idiot knew about the 1927 Yankees. Knowing something about John McGraw's 1921 New York Giants was another matter.

One invaluable element of my baseball education were a pair of league histories put out by Grosset & Dunlap in 1955, entitled *Sport Magazine's Book of Major League Baseball Clubs*. Each of the then-sixteen major-league teams had a history written by a prominent sportswriter, and I when I say "prominent" I am not engaging in hyperbole. They included Fred Lieb, Harold Kaese, Frank Graham, Grantland Rice, Shirley Povich, and H. G. Salsinger. That is a twentieth-century roster of Who's Who in American Sportswriting. My mother bought these books for me at the famous Gimbel's department store. They were $1.41 apiece (I still have the book flap with the sticker price). Who knows how many times I read, reread, and re-reread them. I treasured those books then and I treasure them now. When people ask me how I got in the business, I tell them I started preparing from the time I was five or six. By the time I began reading these league histories at age nine I was already a veteran reader.

That nine-year threshold must have represented some sort of reading epiphany, because in the same year I became enraptured by both *SPORT* magazine and the *Sporting News*, which, after my parents gave me subscriptions, became the twin cornerstones of my sports education.

Reading *SPORT* was an absolute must for anyone taking sports even semi-seriously in the fifties. Founded in 1946, its first editor was Ernest V. Heyn, and he was able to attract such writing luminaries—I hesitate to label them as strictly "sportswriters"—as Rice, Salsinger, Jack Sher, and Tom Meany. New York Giants manager Mel Ott submitted a first-person appreciation of John McGraw. It was postwar America, and the appetite for sports was proving to be insatiable.

No previous attempt at a national monthly devoted solely to sport had been a success. *SPORT* would prove to be the first, and by the time I was introduced to it as a nine-year-old it had become the go-to spot for information, analysis, previews, and personality profiles. In addition to the expected coverage of the Big Three—that is to say, baseball, boxing, and thoroughbred racing, the three most important sports in the first half of the twentieth century—a reader would find over the course of a twelve-month period articles on football, basketball, golf, tennis, track and field, auto racing, wrestling, fishing, hunting, and even powerboat racing (I'm sure I've omitted a few). There were book reviews, quizzes, cartoons, beauty queen contests, and a must-read front-of-the-magazine section entitled "SPORTalk," which was essentially a notes column. I especially loved the historical pieces. Each issue was capped off by a lengthy piece called the "SPORT Special," and the last page always contained a sober-minded editorial.

The Sporting News should need no introduction for any legitimate sports fan over the age of forty. The masthead proclaimed it to be "the Base Ball Paper of the World" (yes, "Base Ball," not "Baseball"), and it was universally referred to as the "Baseball Bible," which was no exaggeration. *TSN* began pumping out extensive baseball coverage on a weekly basis in 1886, and by the time I was introduced to it the publication was in full flower. *TSN* was the unquestioned, unchallenged heavyweight champion of All Things Baseball. Any baseball writer who was anybody was part of the *Sporting News* stable.

TSN was famed for its catchy headlines. I could provide dozens of examples, but here are two. Try this one from the May 28, 1958, edition: EARLY L.A. LAG LAID TO LIMPING PACE OF DODGERS' CODGERS. Or this one from the September 30, 1959, edition: TEEPEE TEMPEST TURNS TO TEA; FLASH, FRANK BURY BRICKBATS. The former is self-explanatory, perhaps, but the latter may need the aid of a translator. It seems that Cleveland Indians general manager Frank Lane had changed his mind, first firing and then rehiring Indians manager Joe "Flash" Gordon. Reading *The Sporting News* meant that, by definition, a fan was bilingual, conversant in both English and Baseballese.

In *The Sporting News*, official team nicknames were clever and colorful.

Experienced readers became familiar with the Bums, or sometimes Dem Bums (the Dodgers), the Flock (the Orioles), the Tribe (the Indians), and the Corsairs or Bucs (the Pirates). Later on, after expansion, we would all learn about the existence of the Halos or Seraphs, otherwise known as the Los Angeles Angels.

TSN did pay seasonal attention to other sports, but even in December and January the focus was on the National Pastime. As I entered adolescence, and became increasingly aware of my own athletic mortality, I began to fantasize about someday writing for either or both *TSN* and *SPORT*. Those wishes were later fulfilled, although in the case of *The Sporting News* my involvement was as an NBA columnist.*

When I wasn't reading *SPORT*, *The Sporting News*, or the daily newspapers, I was reading books on sports. I loved biographies and autobiographies, and thus devoured *Babe Ruth* by Tom Meany, *Lucky to Be a Yankee* (Joe DiMaggio, with an uncredited collaborator), and Bob Feller's *Strikeout Story*, written with Gordon Cobbledick. I recall reading and rereading a wonderful paperback, *Baseball's Greatest Players*, that profiled players from the turn of the century to Roy Campanella. I still recall tidbits from the entries, specifically one involving Rogers Hornsby, who, after retirement, was putting on a batting exhibition in which he was calling the direction of his blows. The storyteller was pitching, and when Hornsby said his next one would be hit up the middle the pitcher said he'd better get someone else on the mound because *he* sure wasn't going to be standing there!

All this reading didn't interfere with either playing or watching television. I always seemed to have time for everything that mattered to me. I was just a normal kid with an abnormal interest in the printed word. Sooner or later I was going to try some actual writing, and thus was born "The Sportster." I would later write for both my prep school and college papers, but "The Sportster" represented my baby steps as a writer. You know those Blake Griffin Kia commercials in which he confronts the younger hims? I wonder what would have been my reaction had a future me informed the eleven-year-old author of "The Sportster" that

* I did achieve a milestone involving *SPORT* when I was asked by the fine people representing Sport Media Publishing Inc. to be the guest editor of an anthology entitled *The Best of "SPORT"* in 2003.

he would someday become a friend of, and coauthor a book with, that Celtics guard whom he so pompously declared "quarterbacks that club masterfully"?

In some ways that eleven-year-old kid from 214 Ellis Avenue in Trenton, New Jersey (phone number EX 3-9965), still exists. If aging is supposed to lead one away from so-called childish ways, in my case defined as an extreme interest in sports, then I guess I've never grown up. My knowledge of sports has grown and my understanding has deepened, but what has always mattered most to me—more than the individuals involved—is a never-ending interest in games. After all, isn't that what it's all about? It's about competition. It's about strategy. It's about execution. And when you've been around sports long enough, you can bring history, both yours and in general, into the equation. I don't care if you're talking about the Super Bowl, Game 7 of the World Series, the championship game of the World Cup, or the Thanksgiving Day high school football game between Town X and Town X East on the field down the street from your house. Everything in sports revolves around the game, the match, the meet, or whatever it is you call the competition in whatever sport you're talking about.

I believe if you were to poll my colleagues about what they most associate with me and the way I have gone about things for forty-six years as a writer for the *Boston Globe*, a TV reporter, and a TV talking head, I'd be willing to bet it would be my enthusiasm. I've never lost the passion for competition, on the field, the court, the rink, wherever it takes place. Give me a good game, and I'll be happy. That's the way it was when I was eleven. That's the way it is now.

CHAPTER 3

Trenton Born

I'm from Trenton, New Jersey, which, I've often kidded, is a good place to be from, not in. It's a cheap shot, trying for a quick laugh, and I should know better. The fact is, I am proud of my hometown.

Trenton is now a typical decaying Eastern city. New Jersey is full of them—Newark, the state's largest city; Jersey City; Passaic; Clifton; Paterson; Camden, to name a few. The glory days of all these cities are long past, Trenton included. This is hardly exclusive to New Jersey; it's a scenario many urban areas in the United States can relate to.

Trenton is rich in Revolutionary War history. Washington famously crossed the Delaware there in order to defeat those dastardly Hessians on December 26, 1776, and no account of the war is complete without mention of Trenton. It has been the state capital since 1790, and it was actually the capital of the entire United States of America in the months of November and December in 1784 before the permanent capital was located farther south.

Trenton is as centrally located as any state capital can be. It is in the belly button of New Jersey, the geographic center of the state being five miles southeast of the city. Pennsylvania sits across the Delaware River, specifically the towns of Morrisville and Yardley. There are three bridges leading from Trenton to Pennsylvania, plus a railroad bridge on which hangs a sign that has generated conversation of varying kinds since its installation in 1917. There isn't a train traveler between New York and Philadelphia who hasn't taken notice of this sign: TRENTON MAKES THE WORLD TAKES.

Times change, and by the sixties Trenton wasn't making so much anymore. As Trenton deteriorated, that sign was a convenient target. When I arrived at the Lawrenceville School—a prep school located equidistant between Trenton and Princeton—in 1959, I learned that the, shall we say, cosmopolitan student body, which came from all over the country and the world, and which represented a fairly altitudinous social class, had a different slogan for Trenton, one I would hear a few hundred times over the next five years: "What the World Refuses, Trenton Uses." Ho-ho.

As is the case with so many American cities, Trenton once had a flourishing manufacturing economy. Lenox china, a product with great cachet, was made there. The steel cables for the Brooklyn Bridge had been made there. When the sign was put on the Lower Free Bridge, Trenton manufactured such items as wire rope, cigars, ceramics, and rubber. It wasn't until my adolescence that I discovered Trenton actually manufactured *two* kinds of rubber. Yes, indeed, there was also a condom factory no one talked about.

Trenton was still feeling good about itself when I was born in what was then McKinley Memorial Hospital on February 21, 1946, and that good feeling continued throughout my childhood. Trenton's population in the 1950 census was 128,009. How much have things changed? The 2011 population was officially listed at 84,899. Do the math on that one.

I am sad about that, and today I drive through a depleted downtown that had four movie theaters, two hotels (the Stacy-Trent and the Hildebrecht), and such department stores as Yard's, Dunham's, and Arnold Constable. Downtown Trenton in my youth was a destination.

A kid has no idea about a lot of things, and not until adulthood did I realize how lucky I was to have grown up in Trenton at that particular time. In terms of stockpiling someone with certain aptitudes, with the kind of experience he would need to maximize his potential, I seriously doubt I could have grown up in a better place.

What are my two great loves? 1) Sports. 2) Music.

Trenton was a great sports town. The first time anyone was paid to play basketball was on November 7, 1896, when the Trenton YMCA defeated the Brooklyn YMCA by a 15–1 score at the Trenton Masonic

Temple. The players were paid a rather impressive $15 apiece. By the time I was born, fifty years later, Trenton was a baseball town, a basketball town, and a soccer town. The Trenton Giants competed in the Class B Inter-State League. The Mercer County Parochial Basketball League had been founded by my father, Bill Ryan. Semiprofessional soccer was played all over the place. There was great high school interest in Trenton High and Trenton Catholic teams. Sports ruled.

Trenton's geography played a big role in this. It is located approximately forty miles northeast of William Penn's statue in downtown Philadelphia and approximately sixty miles southwest of New York City. Most important, Trenton had two newspapers. For many years the afternoon *Trenton Times* had the market all to itself. But in 1946 some forty disgruntled members of the International Typographic Union broke away from the *Times* to form their own morning newspaper, calling it the *Trentonian*. Lord knows where they obtained the financing, but they did, and the amazing fact is that the two papers remain in cutthroat competition, making Trenton, New Jersey, by far the smallest market in America (I'd peg the metropolitan area as in the vicinity of 250,000 people) containing two truly competitive newspapers. There is no Joint Operating Agreement, as exists between other competitive newspapers. As a true multi-newspaper town, Trenton sits alongside such urban locales as New York, Chicago, and Boston.

With two papers, you get competition. With two papers, you get coverage. Thus, every aspect of sports rated intense coverage. I got all the major-league reporting I could ever want. College football mattered because Princeton was eight miles up the road. In the summer American Legion baseball commanded attention. And by the time I was ready to compete, every box score from every Little League baseball game and every contest in the Mercer County Parochial Basketball League was published in the two Trenton papers. If you'd like to see the box score from my twenty-point game against Saint Francis, I'm halfway ashamed to say I've still got it.

When I was two, the Trenton Post 93 Schroths won the national American Legion championship. I don't remember it, of course, but I sure heard a lot about it growing up. When I was nine, Morrisville won the 1955 Little League World Series in Williamsport. Yes, the team was from Pennsylvania, but Morrisville is but a sacrifice fly across the

Delaware from Trenton and its exploits were covered by the Trenton papers and by Trenton radio station WBUD. Bus Saidt, the voice, and later the pen, of Trenton sports in those days, broadcast the games. He also brought home the news for Trenton High, Trenton Catholic, and the Post 93 Schroths in their big games, and was as well the play-by-play man when the Trenton Colonials brought Eastern League basketball to Trenton in 1961. Throw in Princeton basketball and football, and Bus Saidt was constantly on the air.

The Morrisville team might as well have been a Trenton team. When it returned home from Morrisville via train, the players arrived at the Trenton station. My father and I were among the estimated ten thousand who came to greet them.

We didn't have to wait long for our next celebration. The Trenton representative won the 1956 Babe Ruth League World Series by defeating host Portland (Oregon) and its standout left-hander Mickey Lolich. The winning pitcher was Al Downing. They both became successful major-league pitchers, Lolich winning 217 games in 16 seasons, mostly for the Detroit Tigers, including three in the 1968 World Series, while Downing won 123 in seventeen seasons for the Yankees and Dodgers. His name also lives on in baseball history because he was the victim of Hank Aaron's record-breaking home run number 715.

The Babe Ruth League had its beginnings in Trenton. In 1951 a group headed by Marius D. Bonacci started a baseball league for thirteen-, fourteen-, and fifteen-year-olds called the Little Bigger League. The headquarters remain in Lawrence Township, barely a quarter mile north of the spot where once stood Dunn Field, the home park of the Trenton Giants. The league would change its name to the Babe Ruth League in 1954, but not before the first two Little Bigger League World Series had been played at Wetzel Field in Trenton. Stamford, Connecticut, won them both.

The year 1957 was a memorable one for Trenton Catholic basketball and its great coach Father Clarence O'Shea. The Golden Wave won both the New Jersey Parochial A championship and the prestigious Eastern States Catholic Invitational Tournament (ESCIT) in Newport, Rhode Island. There was no bigger deal in East Coast high school basketball during the fifties than the ESCIT, and I say that with all due respect to the Knights of Columbus tournament in Washington, D.C. Four years later Trenton High won the New Jersey Group IV, or large school, state title in basketball.

The wait for yet another Trenton championship was brief. The 1962 Trenton Babe Ruth League All-Stars matched the success of the 1956 team, winning the Babe Ruth League World Series with a wild 7–6 victory over that same Portland representative. Trenton had a 7–2 lead, and the seventh run was a big one. It was courtesy of first baseman Vince Anapete, who scored from third on an infield grounder and would have been out from here to Uranus had he not executed a head fake and gorgeous fadeaway slide to elude the Portland catcher's tag. The *Trenton Times* had the photo, and I was there.

Given its proximity to both Philadelphia and New York, Trenton may very well have been the television capital of America. Most Americans in the fifties had the three network channels, period—the local NBC, CBS, and, if you were lucky, ABC affiliates. ABC had a tortured history, not being on anything resembling equal footing with NBC or CBS until 1953. That was the extent of television's offerings for the vast preponderance of Americans in the fifties and sixties and even the seventies.

Not us. Those of us living in Trenton and Mercer County got everything provided by both New York and Philadelphia, plus the fledgling public television station in Newark. We got something on every channel on the dial from 2 to 13, with the exception of 8. As a result, we got to see more major-league baseball on television than any fans in the country. In those days the Dodgers were on channel 9, the Yankees and Giants were on channel 11, and the Phillies were on channel 6. And I watched a lot of it.

That's a lot of exciting stuff for one sports-mad boy to take in. I didn't realize how great all this was. I took it all for granted. It was the only life I knew.

Trenton was also the perfect place to be when rock 'n' roll broke out.

I was always into music. There were 78 RPM records around the house, and we watched variety shows such as *The Ed Sullivan Show*, in which all kinds of music was presented. Radio was a constant presence, and by age seven or eight I was listening to the available Top 40 music, whether it was "Shrimp Boats" by Jo Stafford, "The Wayward Wind," by

Gogi Grant, or "The Little White Cloud That Cried" by Johnnie Ray. WBUD personality Jack Pinto had a daily program at noon entitled *The Big Top Ten*, and I was a regular summer listener.

There is eternal debate over what was the first rock 'n' roll song or when exactly rock was born, but for the sake of argument let's give Bill Haley and the Comets and Elvis credit for kicking off the era. Just as we had a chance to sample television from both New York and Philly, so, too, could we experience radio from both cities. I was a huge fan of disk jockey Dan Ingram at WABC in New York, and of Joe Niagara at Philadelphia's WIBG.

Sports and music have always guided my life, and they have always gone well together, whether it was Red Sox fans adopting a popular Broadway tune called "Tessie" as a theme song to use in the 1903 World Series against the Pirates, or the "Sweet Caroline" Fenway Park phenomenon of recent years. I have always maintained that while every music fan is not necessarily a sports fan, only one in a million sports fans is not a music fan.

I grew up in what people in most other locales call a duplex, but which we in Trenton called a "semidetached" house. My grandfather Patrick Halloran owned the left side of the dwelling. Henry Nelson owned the right side.

I had no idea I was growing up in what would come to be known as an "extended," as opposed to a "nuclear," family. My father never owned a house. He married Mary Halloran in October 1944 while he was on leave from stateside active duty in the army, and when he returned home they moved into the house on Ellis Avenue. Also living there were my mother's two younger sisters, Margaret, known as "Peg," and Catherine. It was a three-story house with an unfinished basement and an attic where the sisters Halloran had bedrooms. In time we got a dog, an Irish setter named Terry. As was the custom of the day, Terry resided outside in a doghouse. Would anyone even *think* of doing that today?

The centerpiece of all our childhood neighborhood activity was an expanse of land we simply called "the Lot." What I am about to describe is a way of life I believe has pretty much vanished from this country.

With two exceptions, the housing on our side of Ellis Avenue consisted of semidetached dwellings. All the houses had a backyard and many had a garage at the end. In our case it was a three-car garage, although others were for just one or two. The people on Princeton Avenue, parallel to Ellis, had backyards only, no garages. But in between the garages on Ellis Avenue and the backyards on Princeton Avenue was a large dirt rectangle stretching for most of an entire block. This we called "the Lot," and there I spent thousands of hours playing baseball, touch football, basketball, and kids' games such as ring-a-levio for the entire decade of the fifties until we moved to Lawrence Township, a mile or so outside the city limits, in 1960.

These were the fifties. There were no play groups, only us and our daily desires. Games were passed on from generation to generation. You didn't need adults to supervise. On a typical summer day, I was outside by eight thirty or nine with my friend Ricky Green, who lived at 1428 Princeton Avenue. We would start off playing a one-on-one game we called "swift pitching." A batter stood in front of one of the garages, the favorite one being Alma McStravick's. Not every garage owner was okay with his or her garage being used as a backstop for our games, but Mrs. McStravick was fine with it because two of the regular participants were her grandson John and granddaughter Patty.

The ground rules were simple. The strike zone was called by the pitcher. Anything hit past the pitcher was a single. If it hit the fence at the end of a Princeton Avenue house it was a double. Into the yard was a triple. Off the house itself was a homer. On occasion, we toughened the rules up a bit, making into the yards a double, off the house a triple, and onto the roof a homer. The ball was either a tennis ball or a small rubber ball (but not one of those famed New York "Spaldeens"; we did not have them in Trenton).

You had to identify yourself as a particular team (one was almost invariably the Yankees) and you had to bat either right-handed or left-handed, depending on who was up in the lineup you chose. There were only sixteen major-league teams and we knew many, if not all, the players well enough to construct very plausible batting orders. That speaks to the dominance of baseball in the fifties.

Swift pitching was just the start of our day. In time more and more neighborhood kids would drift in, and so we would begin playing three-on-three, four-on-four, or more depending on how many participants we had. If we accumulated enough players on a given day, we would head a few blocks up to Extension Field, where there was a backstop and a diamond. There we would play six-on-six or seven-on-seven hardball, with balls hit to the right side by right-handed hitters being considered foul balls. When we had enough people and were in the mood, we would play tackle football, instead of our daily autumn games of touch.

So we'd be playing baseball in summer in some form or another from eight thirty until midafternoon, and if someone happened to have a Little League game that night he would go home around three thirty or four, put on his uniform, and either hop on his bike (which I usually did) or get a ride to the Little League field.

The immediate neighborhood was loaded with kids, and we all congregated at the Lot. We were coed, too, and no one thought anything about that. Patty McStravick was a good left-handed hitter, just about as good a player as her brother, John. Patty Wszolek also played with us. The times being the times, neither one was allowed into the North Trenton Little League, which, of course, was ridiculous.

A hierarchy did exist on the Lot. The regulars were divided into the Big Guys and the Little Guys. The Big Guys had first dibs on everything, of course. If they needed a body in order to fill out one of their games, they would ask one of the Little Guys to play. It was a big deal. The Little Guy in question had to understand he wasn't going to get a chance to do much. If the game happened to be basketball, the Little Guy had better not actually take a shot. That would be his last game for a while. But Big Guys felt it was their obligation to mentor, even if the word had never been heard of or uttered. My next-door neighbor Marty Nelson was one of the Big Guys. And I can distinctly recall his teaching me how to catch a football by looking it into my hands.

I must make a confession nearly sixty years after the fact. I lied to get onto my Little League team. Or my mother did.

I did not start my nine-year-old year on a Little League team, and after all these years I'm still not sure why. Shortly after the season began Denny Morris, who along with Ricky Green was one of my two best friends even though he was two years older, made a push to get me on the North Trenton Little League team coached by his uncle Pat McCormick. An impromptu tryout was held, at which McCormick hit me a few fly balls. I caught enough of them to get his approval, and I was given a uniform, but not before Mrs. Ryan did a little fudging.

The North Trenton Little League had National and American divisions, and the Beacon Finance team coached by Pat McCormick was in the National Division. The only problem was I lived at 214 Ellis Avenue, and that fell in the province of the American Division. My mother found a solution. She had a relative named Mary O'Toole who lived on Princeton Avenue, in the jurisdiction of the National Division. She submitted that address for me, and I became a member of the Beacon Finance juggernaut.

Pat McCormick put me in the next game's lineup in the most appropriate place for a nine-year-old cheater: I was batting ninth and playing right field. In my first Little League at-bat I hit a dribbler somewhere. I hustled toward first, and to this day I can see the ball beating me by a half step. The ump's call: "Safe!" Not only was I a cheater, I was a *lucky* cheater. I was batting 1.000.

At the season's end I was batting .067. I was 0 for the rest of the season. There was some poetic justice after all.

I played two more years for Pat McCormick. He was loud and boisterous and somewhat scary, but he knew I was his nephew's friend and he treated me pretty well. The best thing he did for me was to provide a five-minute tutorial the following season on how to play first base. He showed me the footwork and I'd like to say I mastered it. I've seen major leaguers in the last fifty-plus years who I swear never had that valuable lesson. It was the perfect position for someone who was slow and did not have a good arm but who had pretty good hands.

By my eleven-year-old year I made the all-star team. Not only that, but I was put into the starting lineup for our opening game against the West Trenton Little League. The North Trenton Nationals had gone a long way in state competition the year before, losing out to a Delaware Township team that would go to the championship game in Williamsport. We didn't quite go that far.

In the bottom of the second we had the bases loaded with two outs. I was due up, batting ninth. But the manager, Joe Cramarz, had another idea. He pinch-hit for me—with his own son. Yeah, who could make this stuff up? My replacement struck out on a pitch above his nose. I know I would never have done that because I was so afraid of that kid on the mound I would have given myself a permanent take sign. Still, you have to ask why I was put in the starting lineup in the first place.

Three years later Casey Stengel would pinch-hit for the Yankees' Clete Boyer before his first scheduled plate appearance in Game 1 of the 1960 World Series. Someday, in that big clubhouse in the sky, Clete and I must have a drink and share notes. I'll buy.

When I wasn't playing ball, reading a sports magazine, watching television, or listening to the radio, one other thing was occupying my time—tap dancing.

We were related to Ellen and William O'Toole, who had founded the Trenton Conservatory of Music in 1920. Bill was a piano teacher and concert performer. Ellen was a piano teacher as well as an expert in early childhood education. The rambling property on East State Street in Trenton was also the site of the Wee School, a nursery school where I had been enrolled at age two and a half. My picture was in the paper proclaiming me to be the "youngest student in Trenton," or some such thing.

I was able to receive free piano and dance lessons. I gave up the piano for the simple reason that we didn't own one and I needed to be transported to the conservatory in order to practice. But I kept up the tap dancing for several years. In addition to performances at the school, our troupe traveled to nearby sites for shows. There is no question I was the best tap-dancing first baseman in the North Trenton Little League. And that early experience is no doubt the reason I have always maintained an interest in dance, starting with those glorious Fred Astaire–Ginger Rogers musicals. I am among many who think the greatest dance number in movie history was Astaire and Eleanor Powell tap-dancing to "Begin the Beguine" in *Broadway Melody of 1940*. By the way, I can still do a sprightly soft-shoe.

I played my twelve-year-old Little League season in an entirely different league. I had been recruited—the only word for it—by family friend Patrolman Mickey McGuire to play in the Trenton Police Athletic

League. The PAL leagues were not part of Little League Baseball Inc. They set up their own all-star games against other PALs, but that hardly mattered to me since we weren't going to Williamsport any time soon. My team was the PAL Yankees and we weren't very good. We won just one game and I did drive in the winning run. My other distinction was making the final out in Bobby Czumbil's no-hitter.

But that was the end of my baseball career. With no speed and no arm, the move to the ninety-foot diamond was more than I could handle. I didn't even bother trying out for the Babe Ruth League. From that point on, my participant sport would be basketball. But my love for baseball would endure.

That love of baseball was inspired by my father, Bill Ryan. I was his only child, and we were undeniably a sports family. He had been in the army and after marrying my mother was heavily involved in the local sports scene, whether working for the Trenton Giants, or in the athletic department at Villanova in Philadelphia, or dreaming up sports promotions or institutions, such as the Mercer County Parochial Basketball League. In the picture of me that appeared in the *Trentonian* when I was two, I was wearing a Dodgers uniform—why the Dodgers is a puzzlement, given my father's Giants affiliation, but perhaps it was symbolic.

Willie Mays made his organized baseball debut in Trenton during the 1950 season, and from what I was told, I was there not just that night, but plenty of others besides. I spent the summer of 1951 in Columbus, Georgia, where my father was the business manager of the Columbus Cardinals of the Sally League. Many a Friday and Saturday night during the winters of 1952–53 and 1953–54, while my father was at Villanova, we attended college basketball games at either the University of Pennsylvania Palestra or the Philadelphia Convention Hall, meccas of the college game then. In summers, I'd wake up many Sundays to learn my father was taking me to a baseball game in New York or Philadelphia. My father was an extrovert's extrovert and was friends with such contemporary Giants as pitcher Al Corwin, jack-of-all-trades Bobby Hofman, backup catcher Ray Katt, and of course the Say Hey Kid himself. He also knew some Philadelphia Phillies players, and one day he brought first baseman Marv Blaylock to our house in Trenton, where, in the backyard, I demonstrated my swing for him.

And then I awoke on the morning of May 10, 1957, hearing many voices in the house, to discover my father had passed away during the night. He had been ill as long as I could remember. He had a stomach ulcer, and my mother had fought a prolonged losing battle to establish his condition as service related. He had gone into the hospital for an operation and never came home. The cause of death was complications from pneumonia and peritonitis, among others.

A widow at thirty-nine, my mother never remarried, but she had already proven herself independent and capable of taking care of herself. She was a secretary by trade, and a very good one, initially to the business manager of the Lawrenceville School. When the headmaster's secretary retired, Mary Ryan was the obvious choice to succeed her. An extrovert like my father, she could make conversation with anyone, in any circumstance, and she became a central figure in the daily goings-on at the school.

With my father gone, my mother made it clear she would do her best to feed the sports monster that had been cultivated inside me. And she did. She came up with tickets to the Army–Notre Dame football game in the fall of 1957, the ballyhooed resumption of a rivalry that had captivated America throughout the 1930s and '40s. Monte Stickles kicked the game-winning field goal in the Irish's 23–21 victory. Over the years she surprised me with tickets to various games, and made sure that, in the years before I got my driver's license, I got to go wherever I needed. I cannot imagine how my life would have unfolded had she been ignorant of or, worse, hostile to sports.

CHAPTER 4

Trenton Made

I managed to thrive in grade school, despite being one of fifty, sixty, or even seventy students in a class, but that was a way of life at Saint Joseph's. I was number one in the class for eight years, captain of the Patrol Boys, supreme grand knight with the altar boys, and a starter on the basketball team, as well as president of the class. Nauseating, huh? The nuns loved me and as far as I know my classmates didn't hate me for it.

That would all change.

My mother had gone to work at Lawrenceville in 1956, and I'm pretty sure one reason she took the job was because qualified staff offspring might earn scholarships there. The Lawrenceville School was founded in 1810 by Isaac Van Arsdale Brown, a Presbyterian minister, and had evolved into one of the best prep schools. Throughout most of its twentieth-century existence it was regarded as a feeder school for Princeton. For a kid from a working-class Trenton background to attend such a school was a phenomenal opportunity.

I passed the admissions test and was accepted, and that should have been the end of the story, but it wasn't. The church wasn't happy. The pastor at Saint Joseph's Church put pressure on my mother to send me to Notre Dame High School. My mother was a staunch cradle-to-grave Catholic, and this was a very troubling issue for her. But she continued to resist and finally convinced the pastor to give his blessing.

The catch was that I was put into Lawrenceville's "first form," or eighth grade. The school was modeled on an English system, and thus, instead of calling the classes eighth grade, freshman, sophomore, junior, and senior, they were designated as first through fifth forms. I was only thirteen but had finished eighth grade at Saint Joseph's. I had begun to grade at age five, never having gone to kindergarten, and had been the youngest boy in my grade school class. By going back, the admissions office felt I could ease into Lawrenceville's academic life. But what was far more important in my mind was that it would save my basketball career.

The freshman, or "junior," basketball team that year was loaded. My friend Dee Megna, whose father was the varsity head coach, and I were the only eighth graders to make the team. We had a very strong starting five and went undefeated. Neither Dee nor I played any meaningful minutes, but I was on track. I would start on the "junior" team as a ninth grader (second form), start on the junior varsity (third form), come off the varsity bench as a fourth former, and start on the varsity as a fifth former. I would never have played if I had been forced to compete with the class ahead of me, and that would have shattered me.

Athletics aside, going to Lawrenceville was absolutely pivotal in making me the writer I would become. With all due respect to Notre Dame High School, or any other high school, I cannot imagine achieving anything close to what I have achieved had I not had the great gift of going to Lawrenceville. Mary Ryan knew what she was fighting for.

Everything that wasn't math or science was based on writing, and that included foreign languages. Either Latin or French was required, and I chose French. We walked into Chet Wagner's French I class and he began speaking French to us. No English—ever. We did not "translate." We were immersed in the "conversational" method, taught not just French words and grammar but to *think* in French. And I loved it from the first second. Learning to speak French made me feel like a whole new me.

Writing, writing, writing. Essays, essays, essays. That's the way it was in English, history, and any form of social studies. I was constantly writing, and even more so when I joined the school's weekly paper, the *Lawrence*, plunging in with enormous relish. I would eventually become sports editor, and some of my fondest memories of those years are the many Wednesday and Sunday evenings spent working on the paper.

It wasn't just the sheer accumulation of writing opportunities that made Lawrenceville such a valuable experience for me. I benefited from the general atmosphere of achievement and inherent competition. One hundred percent of the class would be going to college. Quarterly and midterm grades were posted outside each classroom's door. Everyone knew where everyone else stood in that regard. There was no dearth of extracurricular activities, whether it was a flourishing theater club known as the Periwig, or a French club known as the Parlons Français, or a literary discussion group called the Pipe and Quill, for which I was chosen despite a grade point average that did not appear to make me worthy. But I was kind of a lopsided oddball figure, known for being able to speak and write while being a complete doofus in math and science. For every 80 or 90 grade in something requiring writing there would be that 65 or worse in something pertaining to the other side of the brain.

I really did flunk geometry one year, and I didn't exactly sparkle when I took it over the next year. And I have always believed I flunked chemistry my fifth-form year. My final grade was 61 (60 was passing). But there was no way kindly Jack Devlin was going to prevent Mary Ryan's kid, "the Scribe," from graduating. He was a sports fan, and he also knew I was never going near a lab again.

"The Scribe." Head football coach Jack Reydel hung that nickname on me because I wrote for the *Lawrence*, and it stuck. I was his manager, and I was also the resident sportswriter presence, as well as a member of the basketball team. Most of the teachers, and even headmaster Bruce McClellan, called me "Scribe."

As you might expect, there were some colorful teachers. Chief among them was A. Graham Down, an Englishman who taught history and played the organ. I can still hear him uttering such phrases as "Oh, how the mighty have fallen." One day he spied a student in his class named John Earle with his eyes closed. "Life, young Earle!" he boomed. "Or I'll bang your head against the wall, and it will be wood against mortar!" Gotta love that.

Another memorable character was English teacher Jim Waugh, a published poet who had come to Lawrenceville, as I recall, in an exchange program with the Groton School in Massachusetts and never went back. Talk about small worlds: While at Groton he had taught Peter Gammons, who would become my fellow *Boston Globe* intern and lifelong friend.

Jim Waugh was engaging and witty, and he made me work harder than I wanted to. He was also the assistant basketball coach (and later the head baseball coach). He and head coach Ed Megna frequently commandeered my friend Tom Haney and me to play two-on-two with them after practice. The rule was that we couldn't touch them without it being a foul and they could do *anything* they wished to us without being called. Megna was about five nine and Waugh five six, but they were clever and they knew what they were doing. I'd still like to believe Tom and I won most of the time.

I carved out my niche at Lawrenceville and, I like to think, made the absolute most out of the opportunity, unless you think that high marks are all that matter. I'm going to guess I finished somewhere around 120 out of 160 in class standing, but I doubt anyone got more than he needed from the school than I did. All that reading and writing put me way ahead of the game when it came time to make a living. And as sports editor I got to put my own picture in the paper making a nifty three-point play against Princeton High. Shameless? Well, yeah. But it was a good photo. I told you I took advantage of my opportunities.

> We won the New Jersey Group IV prep school state championship when I was a fourth former, or junior. I scored twelve points in the title game, which looked good in the box score. The truth is I entered the game when we were up by twenty-five in the third quarter. It was all in garbage time. I went eight-for-eight from the foul line using my modified Bill Bradley free throw shooting style, complete with rump sticking out.
>
> We were knocked out of the tournament in my fifth form year by St. Benedict's and their star, Jim Delaney, the future commissioner of the Big 10. He guarded me the entire game, holding me to a farewell box score of 3-3-9 (we played a strict zone). That must have been why Dean Smith offered him a scholarship.

As much as I loved everything about Lawrenceville, I didn't want to lose contact with my world back home in Trenton. I attended as many high school basketball games as I could, both because I wanted to see the games and because I wanted to connect with my old friends, who had all gone to Notre Dame High. And then when the Trenton Colonials came into the Continental Basketball Association in 1961, I began going to their games with some regularity. I must have talked a lot about the Colonials. Each member of my Lawrenceville class has a quote underneath his yearbook picture, something that attempts to sum up the essence of that person. My quote was "What do you mean, study? The Colonials played last night."

I'm sure I also talked a lot about Nick Werkman. He was an All-State player from Trenton Catholic, and its successor, Cathedral High, who had gone to Seton Hall. He was a six-three scoring machine who finished third, first, and second nationally in collegiate scoring during his three years at Seton Hall. Nick was a complete player of his times. He posted up regularly and many of his shots were taken without looking at the basket. He had a well-developed over-the-shoulder shot, and I adopted it for myself. I was obsessed with Nick Werkman.

I had somehow made the acquaintance of his younger twin brothers, Phil and Mark. One memorable summer night I went down to their neighborhood for some pickup ball, when who should materialize but Nick himself. What happened next I will never forget.

The court we were playing on had chain nets, which is standard urban fare, since chains can withstand the elements. But the Great Man had brought his own silk nets! He ordered one of the locals to bring his bike over to the basket, and while that kid held his bike steady, Nick mounted the seat, removed the chain nets, and hung his silk ones in their place. Next thing you know I was playing in a game with my idol. It was if a humble parishioner had been visited by the pope.

Trenton remains a central part of me to this day. As for the Lot, it's still there, but it no longer serves as a gathering place for the neighborhood kids. Strangely, not once while I was growing up did I think about, or hear an elder talk about, just who owned the land. It was just public property. But somewhere along the way somebody put up a fence right in the middle of the Lot and now people park their cars there. No more ball playing. No more fun. And the garages are a mess. If someone threw a good fastball at one of them, it would probably fall down.

I grew up in a time, and in a manner, that has vanished. The Lot serves no good purpose and Extension Field, where we played hardball and tackle football, has been the site of a shopping center for a good forty years. I have no idea where the neighborhood kids would play any game of their choosing today.

Trenton has changed, and not for the better, but the sign is still there, although sometimes it is missing a letter or two.

TRENTON MAKES THE WORLD TAKES.

Let them laugh. I'll tell you one thing Trenton made—me.

CHAPTER 5

Boston College

Without denigrating Boston College, I was about as "educated" as I was going to be when I left Lawrenceville. I did what I had to do in order to fulfill the academic requirements to get a degree; history was my chosen path, and it was both fun and painless. But the truth is my greatest takeaways from BC were gaining more writing experience, this time at the student paper, the *Heights*; working on radio station WVBC; and earning my graduate degree in hoopology, the course being taught by Professor Robert Joseph Cousy.

The other good thing for me about BC was renewing acquaintance with the kind of people I had grown up with. The average BC dorm student in the midsixties came from the exact type of Catholic high school I would have attended. It didn't matter if they came from Monsignor Bonner in Philadelphia, Chaminade on Long Island, Notre Dame of Bridgeport, or Saint Ignatius of Cleveland, they were the people I knew back home.

Cousy was Mr. Basketball to all of America when I first met him in 1964. He had just retired from the Celtics a year earlier and had quickly been hired as BC's basketball coach. His Q rating, if there was such a thing fifty years ago, would have been off the charts. After a predictably shaky first season (10-11), his next five teams went to three National Invitation Tournaments (when that still meant something) and two NCAA tournaments, including a Final Eight appearance in 1967, when we lost to Dean Smith's first Final Four North Carolina team in the East Regional finals. The records in those five years were 22-7, 21-5, 23-3, 17-8, and 24-4. I'm here to tell you we were good.

Cousy had an early recruiting success in John Austin, a six-one guard from Washington, D.C., who averaged 27.1 points a game over his three-year career. He was limited to a cup of coffee in the pros, but in college he was a big-time scorer. His forty-nine points against Georgetown has been the BC standard for nearly fifty years. Other prominent players during my four years at BC included six-eight forward Jim Kissane and six-five forward Steve Adelman. But the best of them was Terry Driscoll, a six-seven center who had enormous hands and was completely ambidextrous inside. He was a stellar rebounder and threw magnificent outlet passes to trigger BC fast breaks. The Milwaukee Bucks made him the fourth pick in the 1969 draft, but he was never able to make a smooth transition to NBA forward. In college, however, he was as effective and entertaining a college center as anyone could want. While Boston College has turned out successful NBA players, such as guards John Bagley, Michael Adams, and Dana Barros, and current forward Jared Dudley, Terry Driscoll remains, in my judgment, the greatest BC player ever.

I tried out for the freshman team, but my timing was bad. This was Cousy's first full recruiting class, and he had hit the jackpot—six scholarship players, plus two additional scholarship-worthy players who had spurned offers from other good programs in order to play for him. Of the twelve available spots, eight were thus taken up by recruited players, leaving four spots for the seventy-five or so of us who tried out. I got by the first cut, but that was it. I would spend the next four years as an intramural player, as well as a referee, but the great benefit of my tryout was meeting Frank Power, Cousy's freshman coach. In terms of sheer basketball knowledge, Cousy practically looked up to *him*, and he became a friend of mine for life.

I had also fantasized about broadcasting baseball and basketball games, and on a Saturday morning in November 1964 I got my chance. Syracuse had brought its basketball team to BC for a full-scale game-condition "scrimmage," a somewhat common occurrence in those days. Student radio station WVBC, which then was heard only in the dorms, was conducting a tryout for the basketball play-by-play job in conjunction with the Syracuse scrimmage. The 'Cuse was a quality opponent, featuring a backcourt of Dave Bing and Jim Boeheim, the former a future Hall of Fame player and the latter a future Hall of Fame coach. Two or three of us tried out; I got the job and kept it for four years. I'm not sure I ever had more fun doing anything. With few exceptions, we only did home games. When we played in the Madison Square Garden Holiday Festival at Christmastime or in the NIT, I would tape a broadcast for later airing.

One night during the 1965–66 season, Red Auerbach's last as coach of the Boston Celtics, I looked up to see someone leading Red across the floor at BC's Roberts Center during halftime. He was in attendance to scout BC guard John Austin, a player Red was predisposed to like since he had gone to high school in Red's adopted hometown of Washington, D.C. I swear I do not remember anyone telling me about any plan to secure Red as a halftime guest, so when I saw him ambling toward us with that unmistakable gait of his I almost panicked. The only thing I remember about the interview itself was that I began with an innocuous question about the Celtics' position in the Eastern Division standings, vis-à-vis the Cincinnati Royals, and that Red dismissed it by saying his main concern was his team's readiness for the playoffs. As dreamlike as the interview was, photographic evidence exists to prove that it all happened.

If I loved broadcasting so much, you could well wonder why I didn't pursue it. I confess I'm not entirely sure myself. I knew I didn't have the best voice, for one thing, but I suppose the primary reason was my love of writing.

My vanity and ego had prevented me from going out for the *Heights* as a freshman. I had come from a kingpin position at Lawrenceville, and the summer before college I had worked as a copy boy at the *Trenton Times*, but I knew that first year I'd be stuck writing about soccer, swimming, or topics I felt would be beneath me. When my friend and eventual roommate Reid Oslin took control of the sports department in my sophomore year, I knew my journalistic ship had come in. I spent the next three covering basketball, football, and baseball, and writing columns. Thanks to all this, I was able to establish a good relationship with Bob Cousy.

We were all in awe of the Cooz, proud that he was coaching our team, and were impressed to hear that, as a sign of how seriously he took this job, he had informed the staff he would not accept any phone calls during practice. Practices were open to one and all, and were a basketball tutorial, particularly with regard to the fast break, which Cousy felt was an essential part of the game. BC had never been much of a player in basketball—its only NCAA appearance had been in 1958—but I became completely swept up in the excitement to the extent that in my junior and senior years I attended forty-seven of our fifty-one games, home and away.

My Boston College experience was immeasurably enhanced almost immediately, at the freshman "mixer" the second night of Orientation Week. Fairly late in the evening, I spotted a cute girl in a red dress and I asked her to dance. He name was Elaine Murray and she, like me, was an only child. We have been together ever since—check your circle of acquaintances and see how many couples are both only children. Her father was an ardent Boston College football and hockey fan, so I rounded out her sports education by bringing basketball and baseball into her life. The summer after our junior year would prove to be a historic one for Boston baseball fans, and we were caught up in it.

My first visit to Fenway Park had been in September of 1963, when I was in Boston looking at colleges, and, sports fanatic that I was, I dragged my aunt Peg to the park. The second, the following summer, was more memorable. My mother and I were checking out off-campus housing at BC and went to a game on Sunday, which happened to be Father and Son Day. Tony Conigliaro hit a game-winning three-run homer in the eighth off Angels reliever Bob Duliba. It was Tony's rookie year and the nineteen-year-old kid from nearby Swampscott was a media sensation.

While I didn't go to the park much during my time at Boston College, I nonetheless had something in common with a few million people in New England when the 1967 season began. That is to say I wasn't in any way prepared for what would become, and remains four decades later, the greatest fan rooting experience of my life.

The 1966 Red Sox had been markedly better during the second half of that season than they had during the first, but were still a 70-92 team, and no prognosticator had them pegged as a contender the next year. Their new manager, Dick Williams, had loudly proclaimed, "We'll win more than we lose," during spring training, but that was dismissed as silly braggadocio.

The Red Sox had struggled to maintain fan support following the 1960 retirement of Ted Williams. Attendance in 1965 slipped to a scary 652,201, the lowest since 1945. It rose to 811,152 the following year, but the town wasn't exactly engulfed in baseball fever. Fenway Park was not regarded as a civic treasure, either. Owner Tom Yawkey made it clear he wanted a new ballpark. Far from a baseball cathedral, it was more like that old couch at Grandma's house.

Ownership was so desperate to get bodies in the ballpark, they turned to the local colleges for help, inviting student representatives from the likes of Harvard, Boston University, Northeastern, and others to Fenway to brainstorm ideas about how to attract ballpark patronage from the thousands of college students in the Boston metropolitan area. I was the one dispatched from the Boston College paper, the *Heights*.

The season began and the Red Sox got off to a somewhat promising start. They were 22-17 when I took Elaine to the ballpark for the first time that year for a Memorial Day doubleheader. We sat in the bleachers, for a dollar apiece. The Red Sox beat Cleveland twice, 4–3 and 6–2. George Scott hit a game-winning homer in the opener. I was totally fired up. Those were the first two of the twenty-seven games I would attend that spring and summer, many of them with Elaine.

I may not know everything about baseball, or even baseball in Boston, but I do know one thing: 1967 was the dividing line in the history of Boston Red Sox baseball. The sport was in danger of losing its grip on a region that had been among the first to establish it as America's so-called National Pastime. There was massive ennui in the town, as if Ted Williams had spoiled them so they could never engage themselves that way in baseball again. The 1967 Red Sox reignited the flame and restored the passion. Today's ownership, accustomed to gates in excess of three million a season, could never thank the likes of Carl Yastrzemski, Jim Lonborg, Rico Petrocelli, George Scott, and Tony Conigliaro enough for everything that has happened to them. Absent 1967, it is hard to say what depths baseball would have plunged to in Boston.

The Red Sox then had a better television setup than most, but that still meant only fifty-some games were televised, the majority on Saturdays and Sundays. Evening telecasts were a capital-E Event. The primary means for fans to follow their team were radio and newspapers, but radio most of all. This may sound implausible, but you could keep track of a Red Sox game that glorious summer by driving around and hearing the broadcast booming out of the radio in the car next to you at a stoplight, or by walking around any Boston neighborhood and hearing the game from radios perched on front porches. The voices of Ken Coleman and Ned Martin were the sound of that summer.

We were all plugged into one of the great pennant races of all time, a four-team contest (actually five until the California Angels fell out around Labor Day) featuring the Minnesota Twins, the Detroit Tigers, the Chicago White Sox, and, of course, our Red Sox, the 100–1 preseason shot that had been nicknamed the "Impossible Dream" by its anchor radio station, WHDH. The entire station promoted the team, most notably its renowned morning man, Jess Cain, a gifted performer who wrote a song about the team's star, "Carl Yastrzemski, the Man They Call Yaz."

It was so great because it was so unexpected. Yaz was Superman, on his way to a Triple Crown while winning games with his bat, his glove, and his arm. Lonborg, a studious Californian who would have a second career as a dentist, was on his way to a Cy Young Award. Williams was the obvious candidate to be manager of the year. Tony C. was living at home and bashing homers for the team for which he grew up rooting.

The one big bump in the road came on the night of August 18, a steamy Friday night. Elaine was out of town with her parents. I didn't have a ticket beforehand, so I intended to buy a bleacher seat. A block from the park a guy offered me a box seat for face value. So that's where I was when Jimmie Hall of the Angels hit a foul ball in the first inning that rolled right under my seat (it's still encased in a plastic box in my home office). And that's where I was in the fifth inning when a Jack Hamilton fastball hit Tony C. in the face.

That was the end of Tony Conigliaro's 1967 season and the turning point in his life. When he stepped into the batter's box in the fifth inning of that scoreless game he was a carefree twenty-two-year old on his way to 550 or 600 career home runs and a berth in Cooperstown. When he awoke he had a battered face, a vision problem that would last the rest of his life, and a totally altered reality. Hamilton was blameless. It was a fastball that got away from him.

Tony made a historic comeback, knocking out 36 homers and driving in 116 runs in 1970. But he did it with one eye and that was not sustainable. His career was over by 1975. He was absolutely luckless after that, eventually suffering a heart attack/stroke combination and dying at age 44 in 1990. Believe me, not only the Conigliaro family was left asking, "Why?"

The 1967 season came down to the final weekend with four teams in contention. Chicago was eliminated on Friday night. The Red Sox came into Saturday against the Twins trailing them by one game. The Tigers had the toughest road of the three, because they had doubleheaders on both Saturday and Sunday with the Angels.

Detroit split with the Angels on Saturday. The Red Sox got a break in their game when Minnesota starter Jim Kaat had to leave with an injury. George Scott broke a 2–2 tie with a leadoff homer off Ron Kline in the seventh and Yaz "greeted," as we baseball writers love to say, starter-turned-reliever Jim Merritt with a three-run homer in the eighth. It was homer number forty-four. Harmon Killebrew matched that total with a two-run shot in the ninth, but the Sox prevailed, 6–4.

I missed that game because I was at a Boston College football game. But Elaine and I had tickets for that final Sunday. They were box seats behind the screen in Section 22, Box 133E, Seats 9 and 10. That I know because they are framed, along with the score book sheet of that game, in my home office. I had a summer job under the auspices of Boston College and on a payday late in July I had gone to Fenway to purchase some tickets. I noticed the Twins would be in town for the final game of the season, and I remember saying to myself, "Hey, that would be nice."

October 1, 1967. If the Red Sox won, the worst that could happen was a tie with Detroit, pending the outcome of their doubleheader with California. The Twins took a 2–0 lead into the fifth. Lonborg was leading off and he fooled everyone by dropping a perfect bunt down the third-base line. Jerry Adair singled to center past a diving Rod Carew. Dalton Jones singled to left, loading the bases.

Yaz was up. All season long he had been Mr. Clutch. I really do remember thinking that there wasn't the most remote chance he wouldn't get a hit. He ripped a shot up the middle for a two-run single. Before the inning was over three more runs were scored, and it had all begun with Lonborg beating out a bunt.

The score was still 5–2 Boston in the eighth. Minnesota produced a run and the great Tony Oliva was on first with two away when Bob Allison, invariably referred to as "the former Kansas football star," hit a bullet into the left field corner. But then he made a fateful decision. He tried to turn that single into a double, a dumb thing to do in this, the Year of Yaz. Allison was out from there to Lawrence, Kansas, 7–4 in your score book. Threat over. Inning over. Game effectively over.

A disbelieving Oliva stood on third, staring at Allison as the rest of the Twins took the field. I carried the sight of a furious Oliva glaring at his foolhardy teammate from 1967 until the moment in 1999 when I had the opportunity to confirm what I had seen. Oliva was one of many luminaries gathered in Boston for the All-Star Game, and I asked him if I had been correct, that he had been fulminating at Allison. "Oh, I don't know what I was thinking," he chuckled. "That was a long time ago." His words were one thing, but his tone said, "What do you think I was thinking?"

The Red Sox won, but the day wasn't over. They retired to the locker room to sit by the radio. Detroit, as it had done the day before, had won the first game of their doubleheader. WHDH had arranged to get a patched-in broadcast from Detroit, which would describe whether Boston had won its first pennant in twenty-one years or if there would be a one-game playoff the next day against the Tigers.

While that was going on we were heading back to Elaine's house on the trolley. There were transistors everywhere listening to Ernie Harwell's Tigers-Angels broadcast. Sometime around seven o'clock Detroit second baseman Dick McAuliffe, a tough contact hitter who had not hit into a double play all year, bounced into a 4-6-3 DP to end the game and the season with that one aberrational swing of the bat. Baseball and its endless contingencies and oddities. Dick McAuliffe hitting into a season-ending double play is one excellent example of what I mean when I say baseball has more conversational fodder than football, basketball, and hockey put together.

The Red Sox would lose the 1967 World Series to the Cardinals, four games to three. It was a disappointment but not a letdown. The Cards were worthy, with ace pitcher Bob Gibson at his peak. One could live with the Cardinals winning. Capturing the AL pennant as a true 100–1 shot was enough. The Sox had given us a complete season; they had brought joy and even contentment to our lives. The ballpark was quirky and charming again. Baseball had been put back in its proper place at the top of the local sports food chain. And when the Red Sox won it all in 2004 for the first time since 1918, some people, when asked where this ranked for them in their Red Sox experience, would say, "Oh, it's great, but it's not as great as 1967."

I knew exactly where they were coming from. I have never had a more exhilarating rooting experience. For years I could remember where I was during certain events of the season—standing in the shower after a day's work listening to Yaz end an oh-for-eighteen skid with a pinch homer in Yankee Stadium, or watching on a teeny-weeny black-and-white at Elaine's family trailer in New Hampshire when José Tartabull improbably threw out Ken Berry to preserve a victory in Chicago on the last Sunday in August.

I cannot begin to imagine what I would have thought if you had told me that in just under two years from that great final day at Fenway in 1967 I would be talking to Dick Williams in his kitchen about how it felt to be fired.

A lot would happen to me over the next two years. Following my graduation from BC in June 1968, I got a summer internship at the *Boston Globe*'s sports department after my roommate, Reid Oslin, turned down the opportunity. You never know when opportunity will strike. It was an eventful summer. I enlisted in the U.S. Army Reserve. And Elaine and I got engaged.

I stayed at the *Globe* until the end of October before heading to Fort Knox, Kentucky, for active duty in the reserves. Four months later I was discharged, fortunate not to have been sent to Vietnam, and Elaine and I were married. The *Globe* then took me back as an office boy with a verbal promise that I'd get the next opening on the staff.

A lot had happened to the Red Sox in those two years, too. Every team that wins a pennant always thinks it's the start of a dynasty, and the Red Sox were no exception. But things were never again as rosy under Dick Williams as they had been in 1967. Defense of the AL pennant had gotten off to a bad start when Jim Lonborg injured his knee in an off-season skiing accident. Tony C., no surprise, missed the entire 1968 season. That team went 86-76 and finished seventeen games behind the Tigers in the last-ever old-fashioned no-playoffs pennant race. The 1969 season was heading toward an 87-75 finish, twenty-two games in arrears of the Baltimore Orioles (and their kooky little manager, Earl Weaver), when owner Tom Yawkey and/or general manager Dick O'Connell fired Dick Williams on September 23, 1969, with nine games remaining in the regular season.

The *Globe* had an evening edition then and somebody had to get Dick Williams's reaction. That somebody was the Kid, the office boy sitting around waiting to get a spot on the staff. I drove to his apartment in Peabody, Massachusetts, and knocked on the door. He greeted me cordially. Sitting at his kitchen table was Larry Claflin, columnist for the *Boston Record-American* and a major player in the Boston journalistic scene. That intimidated me a bit, I must say. I figured he must have already gotten the good stuff.

I guess I did okay. The story was on the front page of the evening edition. Williams said that while he was "disappointed," he wasn't shocked. "I cannot say this was out of the blue," he said. "There has been too much in the papers. I was even making plans for next year."

For me to be involved in the story was a pretty big deal. Less than two calendar years from cheering the team on with all my heart on October 1, 1967, I was talking to Dick Williams on the day he was fired! That was almost overwhelming.

CHAPTER 6

Becoming a Reporter

I like to flatter myself by thinking that the National Basketball Association and I grew up together. And it's not just because the Basketball Association of America (BAA), which merged with the National Basketball League in 1949 to form the NBA, and Bob Ryan both came into the world the same year—1946.

The NBA was an established entity by the time I covered my first game in 1969. It's safe to say that any halfway-decent sports fan in America knew about Bill Russell and the Boston Celtics, who had just won the NBA championship for the eleventh time in the last thirteen years. The NBA was an established sports league, no question about it.

But a look at the 1969–70 *NBA Guide* does bring a smile to my face. The NBA I encountered as a working sportswriter was headquartered then, as now, in New York City. The address was 2 Pennsylvania Plaza, Suite 2360. That also happened to be located just above the latest Madison Square Garden, a fact that led more than one NBA person to growl about alleged favorable treatment afforded the New York Knicks, and forget about the fact that the Knicks had yet to win an NBA title. Appearances were appearances.

Walter J. Kennedy was starting his seventh year as commissioner. He had held many jobs following his 1934 graduation from Notre Dame, among them public relations director of the BAA back in 1946. So he knew where some of the prominent BAA/NBA bodies had been buried.

The entire NBA staff consisted of eight people. Including the commissioner, they were:

Administrative Assistant to the Commissioner—Carl Scheer
Director of Public Relations—Nick Curran
Supervisor of Referees—former star player Dolph Schayes
Chief of Staff of Officials—Mendy Rudolph
Secretaries—Helenmarie Burns, Constance Maroselli, Carol Mathison

That's it. Eight people ran the NBA. Individual team operations were similarly sleek. There were no listings in the 1969–70 *NBA Guide* for Basketball Operations, Events & Attractions, Finance, Human Resources, Legal, Marketing & Corporate Communications, Player & Basketball Development, Sports Communications Group, Publishing Ventures, Sports Media Relations, or Team Operations—all departments in today's NBA offices.

There were no listings for NBA Properties, which now has its offices in Manhattan; Secaucus, New Jersey; and Toronto. Nor were there listings for Licensing Apparel or Licensing Non-Apparel, or for NBA Store Merchandising Group, Sales Development & Marketing Programs, Information Technology, IT Application Development & Support, Customer Service, or Marketing Partnerships. Needless to say, departments like NBA Store or U.S. Media Programs didn't exist, nor did NBA Entertainment, Broadcast Operations, Programming & Broadcasting, International Television & Business Development, NBA Photos, Interactive and Electronic Licensing, or Creative Services.

Of course, there weren't yet any listings for NBA international offices, now in such locales as Paris, London, Barcelona, Hong Kong, Melbourne, Tokyo, Taipei, and Mexico City, plus an office in Miami devoted to Central American, South American, and Caribbean affairs.

And don't forget the Women's NBA.

The *NBA Guide* ceased publishing a complete list of NBA employees with the 2000–01 edition. Then, 589 people were named, and it is reasonable to assume that the list has grown some since then.

That 1969–70 season was all so many expansions, Olympics, World Championships, McDonald's Opens, regular-season games, exhibition games, global clinics, and international stars ago. I look at the NBA today and see a global conglomerate that represents the second-most popular team sport in the world. I think back to the 1969–70 NBA and I see Mom and Pop standing in the doorway.

Nonetheless, some all-time great players were on the floor then. The game has changed in many ways, but I firmly believe I could construct a twelve-man roster comprised of players who played at least five years of their NBA careers in the 1960s that could easily compete with a roster of the best players of the early twenty-first century.

Here's an impressive roster:

Centers—Bill Russell, Wilt Chamberlain
Forwards—Elgin Baylor, Bob Pettit, Rick Barry, Dave DeBusschere, Jerry Lucas
Guards—Oscar Robertson, Jerry West, Sam Jones, Hal Greer
Swingman—John Havlicek

And I'm leaving off Nate Thurmond, Willis Reed, and Lenny Wilkens, for starters.

Talent was never an issue in the NBA. *Packaging* was. For years the league had to answer to charges it was a "bush league." It was a hard charge to refute, because as late as the 1955–56 season the league was an eight-team circuit with three of its member cities in Fort Wayne, Syracuse, and Rochester. Significant franchise movement and expansion soon occurred, so that by the time I was involved in its coverage the NBA had become a fourteen-team league with franchises in both the Pacific Northwest (Seattle) and the Southwest (Phoenix), these being the first "major league" franchises in these locations for any of the four major American sports leagues. That very fact gave the NBA some new-found cachet.

When I began covering it I was not an NBA aficionado. I was a conscripted college man. That didn't mean I wasn't eager to learn. It meant I had a *lot* to learn, and not just because, at twenty-three, I was age-appropriate enough to ask Miss NBA out on a date.

In the fall of 1969, I was still working as a Monday-through-Friday office boy with a verbal promise that I would get the next opening on the *Globe*'s staff. One day in October *Globe* morning sports editor Fran Rosa sauntered over to where I was sitting and said, "You probably think I forgot about you, but your time has come. Bob Sales is leaving the sports department to go into the city room and you're getting his spot." This wasn't just *any* spot. Bob Sales had been covering the Celtics for the previous four or five years.

"Oh, one more thing," said Fran Rosa. "You're covering the Celtics opener Friday night."

People may not remember, but in Boston, in 1969, the winter sports currency was hockey, not basketball, never mind all those Celtics championships. There was no young eager beaver, middle-aged eager beaver, or even aging eager beaver dying to get the Celtics beat. There were just these kids, Bob Ryan and Peter Gammons, and the Ryan kid seemed to like basketball. That's about how it went. Talk about being unprepared!

First of all, the Celtics may not have had anything approaching the Bruins' fan base, but they did have a cult following and a daily audience of travelers and academicians reading the paper.

Bob Sales was very good at what he did. He could write the hell out of a basketball game and he seemed to have had a very good rapport with Bill Russell. He had just gotten bored. I remember him telling me there were only so many times he could watch the Celtics playing the same teams and it was all getting repetitive.

Second, I had zero preseason preparation. I had not been to one practice nor seen one exhibition game. I knew no one and had never spent any regular time around professional athletes. I wasn't too worried about the basketball part. The fact is I did have a better-than-average knowledge and feel for the game. In that sense, I had gone to the right college and studied under the right coach. I was confident I could write a decent basketball story. But covering a team is something entirely different than writing about a sport. There is no manual. I've never discovered a course anyone can take. It is the ultimate trial-and-error experience.

The 1969–70 Celtics were a team in complete transition. Bill Russell and Sam Jones had each retired, so that alone was cataclysmic. Russell had also been the player-coach. The new coach was thirty-five-year old Tom Heinsohn, five years removed from his own Hall of Fame playing career. He had spent the previous five years winning company awards as a demon insurance salesman, in addition to working on Celtics telecasts.

It was probably just as well he was unaware that in the November 11, 1967, edition of the *Heights* I had written the following:

> Everybody talks about [Celtics radio announcer] Johnny Most, and nobody watches Celtics games on TV without listening to him on the radio. That's too bad, because if you really want a laugh you should listen to Tommy Heinsohn, who is so partisan he makes Most sound like Walter Cronkite. Most is essentially a reporter, however ridiculous he may sound on occasion. Heinsohn is not; he is simply an ex-Celtic and a fanatic with no conception of professionalism on the air. He is the best argument for banning ex-athletes from the mike you are ever going to hear.

Celtics president and general manager Red Auerbach had just enjoyed success (back-to-back championships) with Russell as a player-coach, so it obviously didn't faze him that his new coach had never spent one second coaching anything, not even one of his sons' youth games. Heinsohn was also going to be the first Celtics coach in thirteen years not to enjoy the soothing presence of Bill Russell as his starting center.

The initial game in the post-Russell era was at home against the Cincinnati Royals. They also had a new coach—none other than Bob Cousy. He had left Boston College after the 1969 college season, and unexpectedly the Royals had offered him a job over the summer. So I knew at least one person would be able to answer some of my questions.

The Royals won, 110–108, and I remember three things about the evening. The first was the gasping of the home crowd when new Celtics center Henry Finkel, a seven-footer whose style of play was not exactly a carbon copy of Bill Russell's, went to the foul line and made the three little Jesus-Mary-Joseph signs of the cross on his forehead, lips, and chest before attempting his first free throw. The Celtics' traditional large base of Jewish fans were in shock—the University of Dayton grad was a Catholic!

The second was interviewing Royals überlegend Oscar Robertson after the game and thinking to myself as I was doing it, Oh my God! I'm talking to Oscar Robertson!

The third was discovering that I took too long to craft my precious prose and had missed my very first deadline. Writers' Rule Number One, first, last and always, is make deadline. Get the darned thing in the paper. I promise you it never happened again.

Peter Gammons also got a shot at the Celtics job. He and I split the first six home games or so. But Fran Rosa just kept giving me more and more games and gradually it was understood that I was covering the Celtics. Peter was always a baseball guy, anyway. He would eventually get the Red Sox beat and do more with it than anyone had, putting him in the Baseball Writer's Wing of the Hall of Fame because nobody ever wrote baseball better than Peter Gammons. His Sunday notes columns are the stuff of journalistic legend.

Covering the Boston Celtics for the *Boston Globe* in those days was not quite the same job it would become. We did not cover regular-season road games—truthfully, few newspapers did then. Road playoff games, yes, but not during the regular season.*

If road games were televised, I would go to the office, watch the game, and write the story, without quotes from the players, of course. Games not on TV—and back then the coverage was not very extensive—were handled by listening to the radio. However, Celtics announcer Johnny Most did not exactly announce the games in what we might call an impartial manner. He knew his basketball, no question. But he bled green and he had a voice that he himself described as sounding as if he had "gargled with razor blades." When he got excited his voice took on a strange quality. He could reach a high-pitch range that culminated in a faint whisper I called "dog whistle." In certain big moments Johnny got so hysterical you really didn't know what was going on. One night in Chicago, for example, in either a one-point or tie game, there was a climactic block-charge play as John Havlicek scored what would have been the game-winning basket and Johnny was in dog whistle. Basket good? Charge on Havlicek? Block on Jerry Sloan? Who knew?

If the Celtics lost, you definitely had to be careful how you presented the story. Listening to Johnny, you might think law enforcement people

---

* Not many newspapers covered NBA road games in those days. One that did was the Philadelphia *Bulletin*, whose George Kiseda, nicknamed "the Silver Quill" for his snow-white mane, was perhaps the single wittiest man who ever covered the NBA. If I were picking the all-time sports staff, he would be my NBA writer.

had shown up with warrants for the arrests of the referees and half the opposing team, when the actual case had been that the Celtics sucked.

When I had written the story, my job was only half done. We still had an evening paper to account for. That meant a separate story that would be read the following late afternoon or evening, presumably by people who were up to speed on the game account. The evening story was more feature oriented. But how could I get that story? Since I wasn't there, I had to ask Tom Heinsohn to call me after every road game. I would interview him and write my story. He never missed a call.

I told you it was a different NBA then. No coach would do that today.

That first year was a complete learning experience, on and off the court. I needed to understand what made the NBA tick, which meant building a relationship with Heinsohn and the players. Believe me, these were two very separate things.

Tommy Heinsohn was great to me that year. I don't know if he really liked me and thought I was worth his time, or if he recognized that it was wise to cultivate the representative of the single most important media outlet in New England, which we were, by far. Local TV was not yet a big factor, so whoever was covering for the *Globe* was, by definition, the most important person on the beat.

He had to recognize how much I loved the game, and perhaps even that I knew a little bit about it, and not just the history. Tommy had been a great player, albeit one whose career was cut short by terrible knee issues, and thus had deep knowledge and insights. He was a pretty good storyteller, to boot.

While I was getting to know him and vice versa, I was doing the same thing with the players. I could not have been any luckier than to have John Havlicek, Satch Sanders, and Don Nelson as guides, patiently teaching me the ins and outs of how the NBA worked. In addition I was just about the same age as young players Steve Kuberski, Don Chaney, and Jo Jo White. It was all very intoxicating.

About a month into the season, when I was just starting to feel accepted, Frank Deford of *Sports Illustrated* came to spend a few days. He was therefore the first national writing star I ever met. More than that, he was a true idol, someone I had been looking up to for years.

One day at a Boston Garden practice I looked into the trainer's room and there was Frank sitting on a stool and chatting with Larry Siegfried as he reclined in the hot tub. They were laughing and joking as if they were old friends, and in a sense they were because Frank had spent lots of time with the team during the 1969 playoffs, which had ended with the great Celtics' Game Seven triumph over the Lakers in the Los Angeles Forum, the so-called Balloon Game.* Frank really did know all these guys, and I remember wondering if I could ever reach that stage in my career, where I'd be welcomed to sit and joke while someone was soaking in the hot tub.

But I had to earn some credibility before that would ever happen, and I was just a twenty-three-year-old kid who loved basketball and who had everything to learn about what the NBA was all about, not to mention how to cover a professional sports team.

---

* Lakers owner Jack Kent Cooke had placed balloons in the ceiling of the Forum, to be dropped when the Lakers won; they were never released.

CHAPTER 7

Joining the Club

The 1969–70 Boston Celtics were an organization suffering through severe withdrawal. Bill Russell was gone after thirteen years, and Sam Jones, perhaps the most underrated great player ever, had also retired. No team could survive that one-two punch. The cupboard wasn't bare. John Havlicek, at age twenty-nine, was at the peak of his formidable powers. He was no longer the best sixth man the game had ever known. Now he was the league's resident iron man, ready to go the full forty-eight minutes whenever needed. And very often it *was* needed. He was clearly the best all-around player in the league, and a strong case could be made that, given the things his team did not have, no man was more valuable to his team. He led the team in scoring, rebounds, assists, and floor burns.

Don Nelson was also at his peak. He wasn't fast and he didn't jump high, but he had dozens of tricks and was a deadly midrange jump shooter. Given more playing time than ever that season, he averaged a career-high 15.4 points per game. Satch Sanders, Bailey Howell, and Larry Siegfried were still around in varying stages of athletic decay. Jo Jo White, Steve Kuberski, and Don Chaney had the young legs and enthusiasm, but they had not yet mastered the fine points, frequently exasperating their elders.

The center situation was the big problem. Henry Finkel, a lumbering, hardworking seven footer, had come from San Diego. Jim ("Bad News") Barnes, whom player-coach Russell had practically exiled to Siberia in the 1969 playoffs, was there to flex a few muscles. Rich Johnson, a cadaverous six-nine kid from Grambling, was there to run rival centers into the ground. Tom Heinsohn mixed and matched this trio as best he could. The joke was that the starting Celtics center was named Bad News Finkelbarnes.

The team went 34-48, finishing sixth in the Eastern Division. But the one consolation for their fans was winning the season's series from the Knicks, 4–3. I'm still not sure how they did it.

That was the year Knicks fans had been waiting for. They got the nation's attention by winning eighteen straight en route to a 23–1 start. Willis Reed was the MVP of the All-Star Game, the regular season, and the playoffs. Walt Frazier made his alter ego "Clyde" into a folk hero. Coach Red Holzman, a basketball lifer who for many years was an out-of-sight scout, was suddenly "discovered." Madison Avenue stood up to take notice. The Knicks generated more attention in one year than the Celtics had in winning eleven titles in the previous thirteen, and don't think that didn't frost Red Auerbach in Boston, who wasn't fond of the Redhead in New York (and vice versa).

My first encounter with Holzman was enlightening and educational. He was unflappable to the tenth power. After his team had beaten the Celtics in a game at Boston Garden, in large measure due to some strong bench performances, I brought up the play of the subs. "So?" he said. "They all get in line at salary time, don't they?"

A year or two later, I heard him sum up his philosophy of coaching life in the NBA. "We win," he explained. "I go get a steak and a scotch. We lose, I go get a steak and a scotch." The man was obviously not an ulcer candidate.

As a matter of policy, the *Globe* had never covered neutral playoff series. But when the Knicks and Lakers came back to New York for Game 5 of the finals, tied up at 2–2, I was dispatched to New York to cover my first playoff game. That was the night Willis Reed went down in the first quarter with Los Angeles already up by a 25–15 score and a Knicks team with no player on the floor over six seven in the entire second half outhustled and outfoxed the Lakers and Wilt Chamberlain.

With Reed sidelined, the Lakers won Game 6 at home, and I was back in New York for Game 7, seated in the upstairs press box, a mile and a half from the action. The Knicks took the floor with ten men. Then a tall black man came out—Cazzie Russell. Only then did a second tall black man come out—Willis Reed. What basketball fan doesn't know the rest? A limping Reed, his ailing hip shot up with God knows what, started the game and hit jumpers on New York's first two possessions. Frazier took over from there, leading the Knicks to a 113–99 triumph with thirty-six points and nineteen assists. But Reed was the story.

Here's how different the times were then: the relatively few of us there to cover the game were allowed into the Knicks' locker room to await their arrival by NBA PR director Nick Curran and Knicks PR man Jim Wergeles. You read that correctly—we were inside waiting for the Knicks! They burst in and Frazier yelled out, "Man, I need a beer!" That made my copy, of course. No one will ever again have a chance to report a line like that. Such was NBA life in 1970.

At the end of that year I felt I belonged in that world. I realized later all kinds of things must have gone on with the Celtics that went unreported. The growing friction between Heinsohn and Siegfried alone would probably have been good for a few stories. But that's what happens when you don't travel. I have long maintained that if I were given a choice between covering all the home games or all the road games I would take the road games because that's when you learn what a team is really like on and off the court or field.

However, my rivals didn't travel, either. There were three Boston newspapers then, each with separate morning and evening editions. My chief competitors were very different men. Joe Looney of the *Boston Herald Traveler* was an old-school gentleman who lived in tweed on Pinckney Street on Beacon Hill. He had been around since the early days of the Celtics and was a straightforward, no-frills writer who referred to basketball quarters as "chapters" or "stanzas." Dry-witted, he loved to joke that the foolproof lede for any basketball writer, in any game, at any level, was "Scoring in every period, the So-and-Sos beat the So-and-Sos, etc." He loved the Celtics, and, if I remember correctly, his vanity license plate was "13909," the celebrated capacity of the Boston Garden.

Ed Gillooly was the beat man for the tabloid *Record-American*, a fun-loving guy and impossible to dislike. He would eventually join me on the road, and we were the epitome of friendly competitors. But, unlike me, he never would have the luxury of covering the Celtics as an exclusive job assignment. For a couple of years he had three tasks for his paper. He covered the Celtics, home and away. He was "Mr. Z," a football prognosticator, during the football season. And he worked the copy desk. No wonder he was often frazzled.

The 1969–70 season was a launching pad for what would turn out to be, for me, thirteen and a half years of NBA beat coverage, during which time the league would go from fourteen to eighteen teams, culminating in the merger with the ABA that would make it a twenty-two-team league the year after I got off the beat for the first time in 1976. I began as a huge college fan with casual interest in the NBA, and I wound up riding a wave of unprecedented basketball interest in Boston.

When I started, a crowd of ten thousand was considered pretty good. After Dave Cowens arrived for the 1970–71 season, fans quickly became enraptured by his spirited style of play. The team went from thirty-four wins in my first year, to forty-four, to fifty-six, and then to sixty-eight in year four. Fan interest grew. The Celtics beat became a prized job. Year five brought championship number twelve. Year seven brought championship number thirteen. Sellouts had become commonplace. I could never have imagined any of this. I was a kid from New Jersey who had come to Boston as, if anything, a 76ers fan. In truth, I was more anti-Celtics than pro-anything. That I would wind up covering them on a day-to-day basis for the most important media outlet in New England had not been even remotely conceivable when in college I was sitting in the second balcony of Boston Garden rooting against the team in green and white. Indeed, I had been ecstatic when Philadelphia beat them in the 1967 playoffs.

The 1970–71 season was a breaking-the-ice transition year between the "Old Celtics" of Bill Russell & Co. and the "New Celtics" of Dave Cowens and Jo Jo White, anchored, of course, by the great John Havlicek.

Cowens, who had been the fourth pick of the 1970 draft, was a revelation. At six eight and a half he was a bit undersized to be a quality NBA center, but he made up for his lack of height with an uncommon aggressiveness bordering on recklessness and his sheer enthusiasm. In today's parlance, he had a "great motor." He was a natural-born rebounder who could run the floor better than any rival center. He had a reasonably reliable faceup jumper and he had a powerful jump hook. He was able to overpower less physical players inside and he could take larger foes outside. He also loved playing defense, and his quickness enabled him to switch off to smaller players as well as guard big people.

The team got the NBA's attention with a ten-game winning streak in November and December, and although their final record of 44-38 was not good enough to get them into the playoffs under the existing format, it was regarded as a season of great progress and hope, with Havlicek being a first-team All-Star and Cowens sharing the Rookie of the Year honors with Portland guard Geoff Petrie.

The Celtics established themselves as a major NBA force the following season, winning the Atlantic Division title with a 56-26 record and then defeating Atlanta in the first round of the playoffs. But the wily Knicks proved to be far more playoff-savvy, knocking off the Celtics in five games.

For a long period of time I was the only person covering daily Celtics practices. I would arrive about an hour before practice began and shoot the breeze with players, no notebook in sight. I got to know them on a one-to-one basis; I knew their wives' names, their kids' names, what car they drove, and all kinds of personal stuff. I would stop in Heinsohn's office, then watch practice. When it was over, I'd head back to the locker room and pull out the notebook to get my daily story. After that, I might even go to lunch with them. The players knew I could be trusted, that I knew what items were quotable and which weren't. This trust would come in very handy when my once-comfortable relationship with Tom Heinsohn began to deteriorate.

The problems started because of Jo Jo White. The talented guard became a flash-point figure. Simply put, the veterans thought Heinsohn coddled him and didn't hold him accountable for such transgressions as taking too many shots, not playing good enough defense, and even not being willing to block out larger people after making a defensive switch. Heinsohn's view was that Jo Jo was a needed scorer on the team and he was taking unnecessary flak from his teammates. When my writing reflected the players' view more than Heinsohn's, he took offense.

As time went on, there would be more situations in which I sided with the players' view, as opposed to Heinsohn's. He would occasionally pull me aside for a heart-to-heart, one such session taking place during a flight delay. I remember Paul Silas, the man's man who quickly became the conscience of the team after his arrival in 1972, kidding me before we boarded the plane by saying, "We saw that; we're watching you."

On at least two occasions Heinsohn told the team not to talk to me, that I was not their friend and I couldn't be trusted. On each occasion I was essentially delivered the minutes of a team meeting by a friend on the team within half an hour. The situation sometimes bordered on farce. When Paul Westphal joined the team in 1972 we quickly became friends. But being a known friend of Bob Ryan's for someone struggling to earn playing time was not a wise career move. Thus, in Portland, Oregon, we took separate cabs to the movies, and in Landover, Maryland, we staggered our departure times to a nearby restaurant so he would not be seen with me.

Havlicek and Cowens are in the Hall of Fame. Westphal was a first-team All-NBA selection three times and a second-team choice once. Had injury not stymied him, he might very well have been a Hall of Famer, as well. Paul Silas is not in the Hall of Fame and he never made an All-NBA team. But he was as absolutely indispensable to the Celtics in the four years he was with the team as anyone.

The cause-and-effect of his presence is clear. The 1971–72 Celtics were quite good but were a cut below the Knicks, mainly because the Celtics had no answer to Dave DeBusschere, the league's dominant power forward. Silas came the following year, and everything changed. During his four years in Boston, the team was 238-90, winning two championships and losing twice in the Eastern Conference Finals. He was, by acclamation, the best offensive rebounder in the league, was twice a first-team All-Defensive selection and once a second-team member. However, none of this fully explains Paul Silas and his impact on the team.

At six seven and, in his Celtics incarnation, two hundred twenty-five pounds or so, he was no leaper. But he was smart and aggressive. He had come into the NBA weighing thirty pounds more. He had averaged twenty points and twenty rebounds a game at Creighton, and in his years with the Saint Louis Hawks he had been content to bang people. He was traded to Phoenix in a deal that everyone understood was racially motivated; the Hawks had moved to Atlanta, they wanted a white player, and they got one in Gary Gregor.

Silas decided he was tired of being good, that he'd rather be great, so he lost the weight. Now he could move quicker, play better defense, and, as a bonus, get up and down the floor. He wound up in Boston because Red Auerbach had the NBA rights to Charlie Scott, whom he'd drafted in 1970. Scott had jumped instead to the ABA, but now that he wanted to join the NBA Phoenix Suns, the Redhead wasn't giving Scott over unless he got Silas in return.

He was the perfect complement to Dave Cowens. They immediately became the NBA's best one-two rebound duo. Though not an offensive virtuoso, Silas fit well into the Celtics' running game, both as a rebounder/outlet man and a lane filler. He once showed me his own fast-break implementation. He would angle himself to take a defensive rebound while moving toward the other basket. He would take one or two quick dribbles to the foul line and then hit either Havlicek or White with the ball before filling a lane himself. Send up a flare the next time you see an NBA forward initiate a fast break in this manner. Or *any* manner.

By the time Silas arrived, I had been fully indoctrinated in the Celtics fast-break philosophy. This was a team fully committed to the idea that the best way to go through a forty-eight-minute NBA game was to get as many easy-opportunity baskets as possible. They had set plays, and good ones. But the Auerbach/Heinsohn version of basketball put a heavy emphasis on an orchestrated fast break that included a rebound, an outlet pass, a middle man, wing men, and a trailer. Every practice included fast-break drills.

The word "indoctrinated" is apt, because when anyone became connected to the Celtics, he was taught to think "fast break" on every change of possession. Other teams talked about running, but no one was as committed to it as the Celtics. And now, in the space of three years, once via the draft and once via a trade, Auerbach had given Heinsohn an ideal center and an ideal forward to initiate the fast break.

One important thing I learned was that a team doesn't have to be ultra-quick to have an efficient fast break. What's needed is a complete commitment to the cause. I also realized there was a place in a fast-break attack for someone who wasn't fast at all but who could shoot. Don Nelson was just such a man. He was taught to follow the break and be open for a pull-up jumper as a "trailer." Cowens also made a great living as a trailer.

The Saint Louis Silas could never have taken part in all this. He would have been forced to sit and watch. But with his new body he became an important cog in the Celtics' fast break. And what a powerful personal presence. He was a street-smart guy from Oakland's McClymonds High, the same school that had given the world Bill Russell, Frank Robinson, and Vada Pinson, among others. He was great at sizing up people, and he was a born leader. I always thought that if he had not become a professional athlete he would have been a great local politician.

He was confident always, bordering on cocky. One night prior to a game with the Buffalo Braves, who had become a big rival, he asked me, "How many are out there?" I told him it was a sellout and they were saying it was going to be the biggest crowd ever at the Buffalo Aud. "Good," he said. "We're going to send them all home unhappy."

He wasn't much of an outside shooter, but he did have a little tippy-toe set shot/jumper that could keep people honest. He was good for a basket or two on follow-ups and the occasional layup after filling the lane on the break, and averaged thirteen points per game in that sixty-eight-win year, but his contribution was so much greater. On a team with Havlicek, Cowens, White, and Nelson, Silas emerged as the conscience of the team.

We had many talks about family, race, many things. He had it all together. Getting to know him, not to mention watching him play, was one of the great pleasures of my first go-round covering the Celtics.

That 1972–73 Celtics team might have run the fast break more consistently well than any team I've ever seen. Cowens had a big year and was an easy MVP. Guard Don Chaney, 6-5 with a pterodactyl wing span but limited outside shot, managed to match Silas's thirteen-point average, something no one would ever have predicted when he came into the league. But Chaney represented Heinsohn's great individual coaching triumph. Tommy worked tirelessly with him after practice trying to get him to go up straight and not flail around with a different release every time.

But they did not win the 1973 championship. The Knicks did,

though the Celtics will always believe they would have won it all had Havlicek not injured his right shoulder while being caught in a third-game crunch between DeBusschere and Bradley. He missed Game 4 in New York, an affair that will forever be viewed in New York as a great double-overtime triumph and one that will forever be regarded in Boston as the day the referees put on Knicks uniforms and stole a victory from the Celtics. Led by Cowens, Silas, and White, Boston led by sixteen going into the fourth quarter, at which point Jack Madden and Jake O'Donnell created a monumental shift in momentum by calling everything in New York's favor. I believe they inadvertently succumbed to a phenomenon I call "subconscious crowd orchestration," and in 1973 there was no better NBA crowd than the one in Madison Square Garden.

During one stretch the Celtics committed seven consecutive turnovers, at least half of which, if you accept the Boston version, were the result of New York muggings. The one play I'll never forget was a Walt Frazier steal that resulted in a three-point play after he was allegedly fouled by Nelson. However, a photograph showed Don Nelson running alongside Frazier with both his arms pulled down to avoid any contact, obviously willing to concede the basket to Frazier. Yet in the background Madden had his right arm in the air, ready to signal the basket and foul before Frazier even shot the ball. The Knicks won the game 117–110 in double overtime to take a 3–1 series lead. After the game we were all talking about the refereeing: Jack Kiser of the *Philadelphia Daily News* went so far as to call what happened in that fourth quarter "the Rape of Madison Square."

Havlicek returned in Game 5, scoring eighteen points while basically playing with just his left, or off, hand. They won again in New York to tie the series up, but the Knicks were not going to lose to a one-armed, wrong-armed man in Game 7, swarming Havlicek and forcing turnovers. New York won handily, 94–78. It was the first time Boston had ever lost a Game 7 at home. With Russell, they had never lost a Game 7, period.

New York blew by the Lakers in five to win their second championship in four years. The Celtics felt they would have done the same thing, since they had swept the Lakers in the regular season and Cowens had laid a thirty-one-point, nineteen-rebound-per-game hurting on the creaky Wilt Chamberlain. But for the Celtics, all that would remain conversation.

Life was pretty easy for the 1973–74 Celtics, at least in the first half of the season. Cowens was now settled in as the reigning league MVP, Silas was a marauder, Nelson had fun embarrassing young whippersnappers who could jump to Neptune but didn't really know how to play, White was now a perennial All-Star, Chaney may have been the best defensive guard in the league, and John Havlicek was merely the Best All-Around Player in the World. They got off to a 31–8 start and had the Atlantic Division wrapped up by New Year's. Then they lost focus and were only 25–18 from that point on, raising concerns among their fans that the playoffs would be a problem.

The first series with Buffalo was sticky. Dr. Jack Ramsay was an excellent coach, and he had a potent offensive team at his disposal. Bob McAdoo had become a serious threat to Cowens's supremacy in the middle, while the backcourt of Ernie DiGregorio and Randy Smith was a great merger of creative playmaker and efficient scorer. Smith, a renegade soccer player, may have had the best straightaway speed of any guard in the league. Boston needed six tough games to subdue the Braves.

The next foe was New York, but Father Time had made a house call. Willis Reed was hobbling and DeBusschere had to watch the series finale with a torn abdominal muscle. The Celtics dispatched them in five, leading to one of the more intriguing series in NBA Finals history between Boston and the Milwaukee Bucks.

Milwaukee was always a most convivial stop on the NBA circuit, what with its great restaurants, its brats, its basic gemütlichkeit, and the compact nature of the city. We always stayed at the Hyatt Regency Hotel, with the Milwaukee Arena diagonally across the street. Major Goolsby's, arguably the best bar in the league, was directly across the street. Everybody gathered at Goolsby's, so much so that before the series was over the off-day press conferences were being held there, rather than at the arena or hotel.

The Bucks had the home-court advantage, though the road team would win five of the seven games, including the final four. The Celtics could easily have won in four, and the fact that Milwaukee was in it at all was a tribute to Kareem Abdul-Jabbar, who had thirty-five, thirty-six, twenty-six, thirty-four, thirty-seven, and thirty-six in Games 1 through 6, all while being single-covered. The Bucks had lost two key guards, Lucius Allen and Jon McGlocklin, putting more pressure than ever on Kareem to score. He won Game 6 with a seventeen-foot right-corner hook in the waning seconds in response to a nine-point second overtime period submitted by Havlicek. What I remember most about that moment is grabbing my typewriter and clutching it to my chest because the crowd would have come right over the press table if the Celtics had won the game.

After the game a brainstorming session ensued in the Celtics offices and a decision was made: in Game 7 they would double-team Kareem. While most teams did so, Heinsohn had entrusted the job of guarding Kareem to Cowens or his sub, Hank Finkel. However, in Game 7, in Milwaukee, the Celtics sent legions at Kareem in support of Cowens. The Celtics' center was in a redemptive mood himself, having shot a dismal five-for-nineteen in Game 6. "You never saw a man madder at himself than Dave after Game Six," Havlicek noted. "He felt he had really let us down." This time he was eight-for-thirteen in the first half as the Celtics moved to a 53–40 halftime lead. The gap grew to seventeen before Milwaukee made a run. Kareem was held scoreless for a seventeen-minute stretch in the middle portion of the game, finishing with a manageable twenty-six, and the Celtics won, 102–87.

It was their twelfth championship. On a self-centered note, it was my first. Covering a championship *should* mean something to a writer. I had invested many a night drinking many a beer with the players and watched this team take shape. Basketball was a business, but this had also been fun—the daily practices during which I learned all the plays, watching the city take to the team. I had myself grown as a writer and relished the chance of describing a championship. I'll admit it: their success was my success, too.

The Celtics had to play the first seventeen games of the 1974–75 season without Dave Cowens, who had broken his foot chasing Fatty Taylor of the ABA Carolina Cougars in an exhibition game. Taylor was on a sneak-away, and Cowens, exhibition game or no, decided to contest the shot, crashing to the floor in the process. Only Cowens had such intensity. When he returned, the Celtics surged to tie the Washington Bullets for the best record in the conference. During the season Cowens was never better, but the Bullets beat the Celtics in six close games in the Eastern Conference Finals.

Less than two hours before what would turn out to be the concluding game, Tom Heinsohn sat in the Capitol Centre stands and told me I was being "schnookered" by the players. I was of the opinion he might have had more pressing issues on his mind, like, for example, how he was going to stop Elvin Hayes.

Watching the Celtics lose to the Bullets was galling to me because Hayes was my least-favorite NBA player (although Wes Unseld was one of my favorites). But the truth is, the series was there for the Celtics and they couldn't get it done. Washington came from fourteen down at the half to win Game 1 in Boston and the Celtics couldn't recover. The better—or, at least, the most deserving—team won. It was a small personal consolation when they lost to the underdog Warriors in the finals. Better than that, they were swept. Even better than that, rookie Jamaal Wilkes spotted Hayes three inches and forty pounds and kicked his ass. I've never been above a little schadenfreude.

The fan in me has no obligation to be rational, and I admit that in those days I had an irrational antipathy toward Elvin Hayes. Looking back, I guess it began on January 20, 1968, on the fateful night in the Astrodome when Houston defeated UCLA 70–68. Hayes had thirty-nine and he outplayed Lew Alcindor. That didn't sit well with me because I was a UCLA fan, and when it was revealed that Alcindor had played the game with double vision resulting from a poke in the eye during a game against Cal, I was resentful that anyone would think that Hayes was Alcindor's equal.

After Hayes had been in the league for a while, things started to be said about him. Supposedly Rockets coach Jack McMahon, whom everyone loved, had called Hayes "the worst human being in the world," or something to that effect. He was not supposed to be a good teammate. Eyebrows were raised when the Rockets traded him to the Bullets for Jack Marin, a nice small forward, but if Hayes was as great as he was supposed to be, how could the Rockets make that trade?

I remember one night when the Rockets were in town, Cowens was badly outplaying Elvin, and Elvin raised his hand to come out. I was all over him, calling him in print "Elvin the Lion-Hearted." Then I heard he had discovered the Lord at a swimming pool. I think that sent me over the top.

Hayes really was a limited player, completely mechanical with no Plan B: It was turnaround jumper, turnaround jumper, turnaround jumper, and maybe an occasional dunk. He was very unfulfilling artistically. But the fact is, what really bothered me was that during his Washington days he played Cowens quite well. He matched up physically as few did, and Dave did not have his way with the Big E as often as either of us would have wished.

On the other hand, I was enamored of Wes Unseld's game from the first time I saw him. Boston College played Louisville in the 1966 NIT when Unseld was a sophomore. He was six six, plus Afro, and a sturdy two forty or so, and he had thirty-five points and twenty-six rebounds against us. We prevailed in the third overtime, most likely because he had finally fouled out. In contrast to his final NBA days, when he must have been pushing three hundred pounds, he actually had lift when I first saw him.

Unseld was always about team and winning. Along with Bill Russell and Bill Walton, he was one of the three greatest fast-break outlet passers in history. In his early Bullets days, he would amuse teammates in practice by throwing court-length two-hand overhead passes that would hit the backboard ninety feet away. Later, after his girth had grown, one wag observed, "He sets a pick, and it takes you twenty-four seconds to run around him." He was a totally majestic figure on the court, and he was also a nice guy. The anti-Elvin to me.

The 1975–76 season was a reminder that you just never know. Or why you should never bet. Golden State was the best team in the league during the regular season, without question, at 59-23. The Celtics were next at 54-28, but they sleepwalked into the playoffs, losing seven of their last eleven. They had to huff and puff mightily to subdue both Buffalo and Cleveland in six games amid growing tension between the team (the key veterans, anyway) and Coach Heinsohn.

They were growing tired of Tommy's voice, thought his practices were too talky and that he frequently violated the "if it ain't broke, don't fix it" dictum by tinkering with their tactics. Tommy did fancy himself a clever coach. Cowens, ever the iconoclast, had reached the point where he didn't even pay attention to what was being said in the huddle during time-outs. He would then ask someone what they were supposed to be running as he walked back onto the court.

They lurched into the finals against Phoenix, not Golden State. The Suns, 42-40 in the regular season, had upset the Warriors and stars Rick Barry, Keith Wilkes, and Phil Smith in the Western Conference Finals. Barry seemed to stop playing in the second half of Game 7.

Boston was thus the prohibitive favorite over Phoenix and won Games 1 and 2, as expected. Everyone assumed they would win at least one in Phoenix and come home to wrap things up. But the Suns took both Games 3 and 4, led by Paul Westphal, who had been traded at the conclusion of the previous season for the same Charlie Scott whose ABA defection had led to the Celtics getting Paul Silas.

Things were not going well between the coach and me even before the finals started. After Game 1 I wrote an innocuous column quoting some Celtics players about strategies they were employing. Heinsohn stormed into practice at the Boston Garden the next day, upset that, according to him, Celtics secrets were being dispensed in the newspaper. He even lit into Howie McHugh, the beloved septuagenarian public relations man who had been with the team since day one in 1946. That was absolutely ludicrous. So I wrote another column in which I described Heinsohn's behavior as that of "a spoiled brat whose father took away the car keys."

We were officially not speaking.

I had no problem writing a tough column because I had spent enough time around the team to know how tired they were by then of Tommy Heinsohn. I knew he wouldn't like it, but the team would silently applaud, the only possible exception being Jo Jo White. By today's standards, the fact that I was simultaneously writing game stories and a column would be unthinkable.

In Phoenix for Games 3 and 4, and for Game 6, I stayed at Westphal's house. I'm reasonably certain this was the only time during any professional sports championships where the main writer covering a local team for his newspaper was sleeping in the house of a prominent member of the opposing team.

It was the place to be. Practice would be over by two or so. I'd write and go back to Westphal's house, where we'd congregate at the pool, "we" being Westphal, his neighbor and Phoenix star center Alvan Adams, and the team's thirteenth man on the twelve-man roster, the guy who had been left off when the playoffs began—some guy named Pat Riley.

When people think of that series they focus on one thing—Boston's 128–126 Game 5, triple-overtime win at the Garden. I can't blame them. For years it was fashionable to say that it was the best game ever played. Now I just say, I don't know for sure, but I know it's among them. The Celtics played their best ball of the entire playoffs in the first fourteen minutes, getting up by twenty-two. Phoenix wouldn't quit. The Celtics led by sixteen at the half. Phoenix kept coming. The Celtics led by nine with just over three minutes left. Phoenix rallied to tie.

The game featured so much athletic splendor, so much craziness, and so many timely plays made by so many different people. It would have been a very good NBA Finals game had it ended with the Celtics winning in regulation. But the events of the final second of the fourth quarter and the ensuing three overtimes transformed this very good game into a true NBA epic.

With the score tied at 95 and one second left in regulation, Paul Silas tried to call time, not realizing the Celtics were out of time-outs. Referee Richie Powers shook his head, ignoring the request. Had he granted the time-out, the Suns would have had a chance to win via a technical foul shot. Richie would later admit, "I did not want Boston to lose like that."

With nineteen seconds left in the second overtime the Celtics led, 109–106. Then Dick Van Arsdale hit a jumper and Westphal stole the ball on the next possession and threw it to forward Curtis Perry. He missed a left-side jumper, but the long rebound came back to him and he reloaded—swish. Suns up, 110–109, with five seconds left.

Havlicek took Nelson's inbounds pass, dribbled hard three times, and somehow made an amazing leaning banker from the left. It could only be described as a Nolan Ryan fastball of a shot. Celtics timer Tony Nota did what any self-respecting home-team timer would do and let the clock run out, although clearly a second or two remained. The Celtics rushed off the court. Jo Jo White took off his ankle tape. Silas later joked that he probably already had a cigarette dangling from his lips.

While this was going on, a fan came out of the stands and attacked referee Richie Powers, jumping on him and rolling with him on the floor. Honestly, who could make this stuff up?

Play resumed with one second on the clock. Down by a point, the Suns needed to go ninety-four feet to score. They, too, were out of time-outs. During the lengthy break Westphal cleverly inquired at the scorer's table what would happen if the Suns called time. He was told that the Celtics would get a technical foul shot but the Suns would then get the ball at midcourt. You can clearly see Westphal talking and gesticulating to Suns coach John MacLeod on the videotape. The Suns called time. Jo Jo White made the technical, and Boston led, 112–110.

The Suns inbounded at midcourt to forward Garfield Heard, who spun and swished an altitudinous and utterly improbable jumper about three feet right of the foul line. Do not listen to anyone who tells you it would have been a three-pointer had the rule existed then.* It was foul-line extended, but under the circumstances it was incredible. Game tied at 112. What everyone does remember with great clarity is the spectacular arc of Heard's shot. Teammate Ricky Sobers called it a "moon rock." Perry settled for "Heard's aurora borealis shot."

At 1:37 into the third overtime, Silas fouled out, taking his seventeen points and fourteen rebounds with him. Boston's bench was depleted. Heinsohn inserted Glenn McDonald, the 1974 first-round draft choice who had made little impact in his then-two-year NBA career. "I was sitting next to Steve Kuberski, who would ordinarily replace Silas," McDonald would later say. "I said, 'You're in there.' Instead, Tommy Heinsohn said, 'Mac, go in.' I was in initial shock."

But McDonald was somehow sent over from central casting to be the game's—there is no other way to put it—closer. He scored six points in one sixty-three-second burst, his second field goal a baseline turnaround at the end of a fast break that Sobers later labeled "Jordanesque."

The Celtics went up, 126–120. At 126–122 backup center Jim Ard had two free throws, and Sobers, a brash rookie, began trash-talking. "He said, 'You really think you're gonna make 'em?'" Ard recalled. "And I said, 'If I didn't think I could, I wouldn't be out here.'" He made them both.

---

* The three-point rule was added before the 1979–80 season.

Back came the Suns. Westphal made an almost preposterous spinning 360-degree banker. McDonald, his magic carpet crashing to earth, missed a weak shot, actually hitting the underside of the rim. Sobers rebounded and threw an eighty-foot touchdown pass to Westphal, who laid it in to cut the lead to 128–126 with twelve seconds left. Westphal actually got his fingertips on a pass Nelson threw to Ard, who finally got it to White, and Jo Jo dribbled out the clock, throwing a hook shot to the ceiling as time ran out.

The craziness continued after the game. Havlicek, who had played fifty-eight minutes despite dealing with plantar fasciitis, was lying on a trainer's table when Heinsohn plopped down next to him. "I was a sick puppy," Heinsohn would explain. "Somebody was asking me a question and the next thing I knew I was waking up in the trainer's room. I had colitis. I was dehydrated. I had a blood pressure problem. I wound up going to the hospital. I wasn't sure I could even go to Phoenix for the next game."

Go ahead. Try to find another game in the history of the league to match. It was significant enough to warrant an extensive twenty-fifth-anniversary tribute in the pages of the *Boston Globe*, the story running on June 3, 2001. Peter May and I tracked down every living principal—players, coaches, team chief executives, trainers, radio announcers—and they all gave the game unanimous rave reviews.

Paul Silas and Don Nelson, with, at that point, 2,620 regular-season and playoff games between them (and then tack on their coaching days), each said it was their most memorable game.

Red Auerbach said, "[It was] the best game I ever saw. People talk about the Scott-Westphal trade. They got the best of it, and we got the best of it, if you know what I mean." Even Westphal exulted: "What a privilege to play in a game people can't forget. There really is a bond we all share."

Later, Suns assistant coach Al Bianchi, who truly hated the Celtics from way back, had a guy in Philadelphia make up a mock 1976 championship ring with the following inscription on the inside: FUCK YOU, RICHIE POWERS.

Bianchi wore that ring for years before leaving it in a men's room. "I don't mind losing that ring," he told me in 2001. "I'm at peace with it. Richie is dead [he died in 1998], and he really was a good referee. The funny thing is, some guy probably thinks he got an expensive ring. It cost sixty dollars."

Not surprisingly, Game 6 was an anticlimax. The teams resumed play in Phoenix thirty-nine and a half hours later. The players were flat and the Suns crowd even flatter. There was no life in Veterans Memorial Coliseum, the erstwhile "Madhouse on McDowell Road." "It was almost like it took more out of the fans than it did the players," surmised Suns trainer Joe Proski.

All the Celtics principals were predictably exhausted, save one—Charlie Scott. He had fouled out of Game 5 in just thirty-three minutes of play—his fifth consecutive disqualification—and he really did owe them one. Scott had come to Boston in exchange for Westphal as Red thought Jo Jo White would pair better with Scott, whom he saw as a better player than Westphal. He was—and this is putting it mildly—a character. He was a champion know-it-all: There was no topic on which he would not venture an opinion. If you asked Charlie Scott what time it was he would give you the political history of Switzerland.

Charlie was a flamboyant player. When he was on, he was a big-time scorer, and he had delivered clutch performances in series-clinching Game 6 triumphs over both Buffalo and Cleveland. He came up big again when his team most needed a pick-me-up, posting an impressive twenty-five-point, eleven-rebound stat line, augmented by five steals.

Following Game 5, Red had come into the locker room and told Scott, "Don't get upset with the referees. Get dressed and go home. You're going to be important on Sunday." As usual, Red had his finger on the pulse of events. The final score was 87–80. But everything will always revert to Game 5.

During the course of the locker room celebration I walked up to Tom Heinsohn. "Congratulations," I said. "Thank you," he replied. We would not have another conversation for almost two years.

For people like Havlicek, Nelson, Silas, and Cowens it was more of a glad-this-thing-is-over feeling than a wow-we-won sensation. The second half of the season had been a struggle. Nelson, whose playing time had been dramatically reduced, would retire. Silas wound up in a major contract dispute and was traded to Denver. Cowens would respond to that by leaving the team for a two-month sabbatical. Havlicek continued being himself for two more years, but the 1976 championship was the end of this chapter of Celtics history.

It was also the end of my first stint covering the team. By 1976 I feared that my writing was getting repetitive. I still loved the NBA and would defend it fiercely against critics who mistakenly thought that the players didn't play hard, that coaches didn't matter, that nobody played defense, and that only the last two minutes, and not the first forty-six, mattered. But I did not want to face a year of being at odds with the coach, and he wasn't going anywhere. That would not have done me, the paper, or the readers any good.

I also had to admit that I really *had* gotten too close to the players. I cared too much, and it was starting to wear me out. This had actually manifested itself a year earlier. When the 1975 playoffs were over, I came home and said to Elaine, "I can't believe I'm saying this, but I really need a vacation." And we put together a quickie trip to Puerto Rico.

At the end of the 1976 season I was thirty. I had put together a pretty intense seven years of Celtics and NBA coverage, and since January that year I had also picked up the two weekly columns of legendary columnist Bud Collins, who had given up his full-time job at the *Globe* to devote more time to his life as a tennis commentator.

But I had one more task before I said good-bye to the beat. The 1976 NBA league meetings were in Hyannis, Massachusetts. There was a lot on the owners' plate, starting with the proposed merger with the ABA. But what I most remember was a conversation with Dr. Jack Ramsay, who was leaving the Buffalo Braves to coach the Portland Trail Blazers. I always liked Dr. Jack.

"Jack," I said, "how are you going to deal with all that rain in Portland?"

"Bob," he replied, "during the season, I don't have time for weather." I think I knew right then and there that someday I'd be rejoining those people.

The postmortem on me and Tom Heinsohn is that he absolutely killed me in a book he wrote with *New York Post* writer Leonard Lewin, calling me, among other things, a "cancer." That was fine. He got it off his chest.

It's all in my Wikipedia entry. But what Wikipedia does not relate is that sometime in the next few years Heinsohn, whom Red Auerbach fired early in the 1977–78 season, became interested in the Knicks job and asked me to write a recommendation. (He didn't get the Knicks post.) And it doesn't mention that when he subsequently expressed interest in the Houston job I wrote a glowing column on his behalf.

Wikipedia also fails to account for the night in 1978 when we were both at a testimonial dinner for his old buddy "Jungle Jim" Loscutoff and I walked up to him at the bar. "Would it spoil your night if I said hello?" I inquired. "Not at all." he said. And we have been completely simpatico ever since.

Tom Heinsohn can lay claim to being Mr. Celtic as much as anyone, and that includes Auerbach, Russell, Cousy, or Bird. He has been a loyal Celtic since 1956—a Hall of Fame player, a two-time championship coach, and in the last three decades a TV color man with an enormous following. If anyone bleeds green, he does. Things did not end well back in 1976, but I have never forgotten how accommodating he was in my early years. The man never missed making that phone call!

Did you know that Tom Heinsohn is an accomplished artist? He does portraits and landscapes, and for many years a Heinsohn has hung in our living room. Life seldom follows a straight-line path. It took us a while to get where we should have gone, but we got there. I'm glad Tom Heinsohn came into my life.

CHAPTER 8

Take Me Out to the Ball Game

This may seem strange coming from someone best known for his basketball background, but baseball is the greatest game ever to spring from the mind of mortal man. I believe that with my heart. Most every man and woman knows more about one thing than they do about any other. Think about it. If you were asked to filibuster on just one topic until you ran out of something to say, what would it be? In my case the answer would be baseball.

That doesn't mean I know more about it than statistician Bill James, Peter Gammons, or other historically knowledgeable baseball writers such as Bill Madden of the New York *Daily News* and John Lowe of the *Detroit Free Press*. I can't compete with the New Age stat freaks with their hair-hurting statistical knowledge. I sometimes wonder if they ever bother to watch a game for sheer enjoyment. Any number of people know more about baseball than I do, but I know more about baseball than most people. And I know more about baseball than I do about anything else.

I suppose I'm largely talking about its history. The 1906 Cubs with their 116 wins, and the Hitless Wonder White Sox with their great pitching staff that was able to offset the .228 team batting average, seem very real to me. I can close my eyes and place myself in Shibe Park when the 1929 Athletics were running off that ten-run inning against the Cubs in the 1929 World Series. I can see myself in Yankee Stadium when Hugh Casey's spitball eluded Mickey Owen and led to that dramatic Yankees comeback over the Dodgers in the 1941 World Series.

Bobby Thomson's home run? Wasn't I in a third-base box? Larsen's Perfect Game? Well, I actually did see the end of that one, flipping on the TV as soon as I got home from school. You get the point.

I think I have a pretty good feel for what makes the game tick. One of the great experiences of my life was working on my first book, a treatise on minor-league baseball entitled *Wait Till I Make the Show*. It grew out of a two-part Sunday series in the *Globe* about the Red Sox Eastern League AA affiliate in Pawtucket, and ultimately, over the summers of 1971 and 1972, led to my traveling from Trois-Rivières, Quebec, to Honolulu, touching on every classification in as wide a geographic range as possible to learn about the training ground for major leaguers from the viewpoint of players, managers, coaches, executives, owners, and, of course, fans. It was a master's program and Ph.D. in diamondology combined.

I saw and heard things that filled in a lot of gaps. One of the biggest revelations was this: what ultimately separates big leaguers from so many who never make it is being able to repeat their success, day after day, night after night. Raw skill can manifest itself at the lowest level of play just as easily as it can in a World Series game. On any given day or night during the baseball season the best single play and the single best-played game might be in an A league and not in the bigs. In the course of my travels for the book I saw pitchers break off breathtaking curveballs. I saw batters hit 425-foot homers. I saw fielding gems. I even saw a perfectly executed two-strike bunt, something seldom seen in the majors. But had I returned the following evening—as I usually did—I would see many instances of sloppy, almost unprofessional baseball, reminding me where I was and why these players were where they were.

Hanging around the minors broadened my baseball appreciation beyond measure. If I were a sports editor of a newspaper or Internet outlet, I would reassign my chief baseball writer periodically to one of the major-league teams' minor-league outlets, just to observe and ask questions. I guarantee he or she would return better prepared to cover major-league baseball. I would also insist, for obvious reasons, that my baseball writers have a reasonable knowledge of Spanish.

Having written that book gave me a leg up in my dealings with major-league players, managers, and coaches for many years, if only because I could initiate conversations by saying things like "How close *did* those stands feel in Visalia?" or "Did you ever hit your head on the dugout in Kinston?" or "Can you believe they say Boog Powell hit one into the Piggly Wiggly parking lot in Appleton?" Every once in a while, a player would tell me he had actually read the book, usually because a relative had recommended it.

That my first book was about baseball was important to me because I had been covering the Celtics for four years when it was published and people were logically assuming the only sport I knew anything about was basketball.

I'm not like most baseball fans. I have no idea when I saw my first big-league game, or even my first minor-league game. The fact is I cannot remember a time in my life when I wasn't going to games. So I have no great story to tell about my memorable first trip to the ballpark. But I did have a Ballpark Moment in 1972.

Both the Celtics and Bruins were opening their respective seasons on the same night in Detroit. The Tigers were playing the Oakland A's in the American League Championship Series, and sports editor Ernie Roberts dispatched me and hockey writer Fran Rosa to the ballpark to augment our ALCS coverage of Game 4. I distinctly recall walking up the Tiger Stadium ramp for the first time and feeling like a seven-year-old kid marveling at the green-on-green-on-green of that wonderful old park. It appeared to me to be the greenest place on earth. The park was painted green. All the fifty-thousand-plus seats were green. The only things not green were the infield and the bases.

Tiger Stadium immediately became my new favorite ballpark, and that feeling never changed. I liked it better than Yankee Stadium, better than Wrigley Field, and even better than Fenway Park. The seating capacity was about 50 percent more than Fenway's at the time, but it was even more intimate. The seats were sooooo close. The upper-deck seats were beyond-belief good. They weren't all that high, and you could hear voices when the first-base coach talked to the runner or the runner talked to the first baseman.

Dead center field was 440 feet, but somehow even the view from those bleachers felt chummy. I cannot exaggerate how much I loved Tiger

Stadium, enough so my wife Elaine and I said good-bye in 1999 by attending a three-game farewell series. I requested the lowest possible upper-deck seats and we were thus stationed at first base, listening to those voices for the last time. Fenway and Wrigley are great, but for me they get the silver and bronze. The gold for the best ballpark I ever knew was Tiger Stadium.

A few weeks after I left the Celtics beat, I was on vacation with my family when Peter Gammons accepted an offer from *Sports Illustrated*, and the legendary Clif Keane retired. The *Globe* was suddenly in need of a baseball writer. I did something that is unimaginable today: I wrote sports editor Dave Smith a letter, asking him not to do anything permanent with the baseball beat until he talked with me. Yes, a letter—paper, envelope, stamp, the whole bit. Pretty quaint!

Happily for me, I got the job. We decided I would split the remaining road trips with Larry Whiteside, who had been the main guy with the evening *Globe*, but that in 1977 I would become the Red Sox primary beat man for the morning paper.

During my years covering the Celtics I had had occasional baseball opportunities and I cherished them all. The *Globe* policy of the day was to allow staffers to write columns when regular columnists Ray Fitzgerald, Bud Collins, and Harold Kaese were on vacation or having off days, and I got to Fenway Park on business every now and then. One of those columns turned out to be a little more than routine.

In June 1975 the Red Sox were playing decently, but not as well as had been expected. They were about to embark on a whopper thirteen-day road trip to Chicago, Kansas City, Detroit, and Baltimore with a 28-22 record. I had a column to write on the day the trip started in Chicago and I offered a detailed analysis of the team. Let's just say I didn't exactly pull a Johnny Mercer and accentuate the positive. Sometimes the headline on a column or story is misleading, but not this time—FRANKLY, SOX ARE IN TROUBLE, it read.

Among my observations was that Captain Carl Yastrzemski should be batting no higher than sixth against lefties, that the Sox should consider trading Dwight Evans, that "as far as Diego Segui and Reggie Cleveland are concerned, there's a charter plane leaving tomorrow with

Amelia Earhart at the controls," and that "Doug Griffin is a totally unacceptable major league second baseman." Among other things.

Red Sox TV color man Ken Harrelson tore me apart that night on his pregame report. That was to be expected. But the most interesting reaction came the next morning when the phone rang at the *Globe* sports department, and on the other end was a woman identifying herself as Amelia Earhart's sister. She lived in Squantum, Massachusetts, and she was not pleased with my reference. I had reasoned that some sort of statute of limitations existed on Amelia Earhart references since the famed aviatrix had disappeared thirty-eight years earlier. I must admit I had not considered the possibility of offending her sister.

Two or three days later the Red Sox made a deal for a second baseman to replace Doug Griffin. Denny Doyle hit .310 the rest of the season and played a big role in their drive to the American League East pennant and trip to the World Series. So I had gotten that one right.

The Sox had a good 9-4 road trip, ripping off six straight in one stretch. They came home for three against the Indians—all losses—and then the Yankees came to town. I had not attended any of the Cleveland games, but I made sure I got to the New York series. I had to go back to the locker room sooner or later. Them's the rules.

On Saturday afternoon, June 27, the Red Sox rolled, 9–1. I entered the locker room when it was opened to the media and was heading over to say hello to Johnny Pesky, Mr. Red Sox himself and someone I considered a friend, when I had the sensation someone was behind me. I turned, and there was Doug Griffin. He started shoving me, yelling something like "You don't belong in here!" The clubhouse man came over and suggested I exit before something regrettable happened. I took his advice. As soon as I got outside the door Dwight Evans made his move. He spat on the floor and told me never to write anything about him again—good *or* bad. I thought that was pretty creative.

I wouldn't go so far as to say that such a thing is an unofficial rite of passage, but I do think most any writer who has ever taken a stand or offered a harsh opinion has had some kind of boisterous encounter with a player, manager, coach, or administrator, even an owner, and sometimes they get physical, as this one did. It is an unsettling experience but something you must be prepared for. If you go negative, you must give the target a chance to respond in person.

It was a pretty big deal in the tight little journalistic community. The Associated Press ran a small story and I heard from people by phone around the country in pre-Internet days, among them Paul Westphal, the ex-Celtic who had just been traded a few days before to Phoenix and had read about the altercation in Los Angeles.

The tension blew over, as it had to, but I needed some kind of assurance things were okay. I got it a short time later when I placed an interview request for a chat in the dugout before a game to rookie sensation Jim Rice. He was a bit late, and I feared he was going to stiff me, but he showed up and I got my story. The long and the short of it was that both Griffin and Evans were on the team two years later when I took over the Red Sox beat and we got along fine. Evans played for the Red Sox until 1990 and he never once objected if I happened to lavish him with praise.

Was I excited about going to my first spring training in 1977? The short answer is yes, and the long answer is that I was so fired up about finally becoming a baseball writer that I kept score for all nine innings of each exhibition game I covered. *Nobody* does that.

I recall one spring training incident in 1977 above all. The Red Sox had a rookie right-hander named Bob Stanley. He hadn't pitched higher than A ball, but he impressed one and all that spring with his hard sinker, which the catchers said was like a bowling ball. Manager Don Zimmer took an immediate liking to him.

On March 27 the Sox went to Tinker Field in Orlando to play the Minnesota Twins. Stanley worked the first five innings, allowing two runs. The custom was that Zimmer would have his postgame press briefing after returning to the Sox' base in Winter Haven. He told us that Stanley was going to make the big club, but that he'd appreciate it if we didn't speak with him until he had told him the good news himself.

That night I was having a few beers with my friend George Kimball of the weekly *Boston Phoenix* when we saw Stanley across the bar. We said we should buy him a beer and went over to say hello. Stanley was somewhat dazed by the day's events.

"What am I going to do with twenty thousand dollars a year?" he said.

Stanley remained Everyman in his demeanor for his entire thirteen-year career, all with the Red Sox, but let me assure you George and I referenced *that* one many times over the years.

Once I became a full-time baseball writer, keeping score became a daily necessity. The difference for me was that even after I ceased becoming a full-time baseball writer I felt some kind of inner need to keep score, whether I was in the press box or in the stands, at a major-league or a minor-league game or perhaps even a college or Olympics game. Scorecards can, years later, recall individual plays or oddities and historical occurrences, which a rabid fan like me will appreciate.

I have kept score at every baseball game I have attended since that first spring training game in Winter Haven, Florida, between the Red Sox and White Sox on March 14, 1977. The Red Sox won, 8–7. Eric Soderholm, Jim Spencer, and Wayne Nordhagen homered for the White Sox; Jim Rice, George Scott, and Butch Hobson went deep for Boston. Andy Merchant won it with a sacrifice fly in the ninth, driving in Carl Yastrzemski, who had walked to lead off the inning, advanced to third on an error by Soderholm (why he advanced two bases will forever remain a mystery), and then was brought home on that fly to right fielder Royle Stillman. The winning pitcher was Tom House. The loser was Jim York. Bill Campbell, recipient of an unheard-of four-year, $1 million contract as a newfangled free agent, was roughed up, allowing two runs on four hits and two walks in two and two-thirds innings of work. Carlton Fisk had a passed ball. The time of game was 2:25. Anything else you want to know?

Once baseball season comes, I never travel without my score book because you never know when a baseball game is going to break out. Exhibit A: While I was in Phoenix covering the 1984 NBA Western Conference Finals between the Suns and Lakers, North Carolina had come to town for a series with mighty Arizona State. I had a free afternoon and was able to attend the game, score book in hand.

It turned out to be a very interesting day. Batting third and playing left field for Arizona State was Barry Bonds, who went two-for-three with both a regular and—what a surprise!—an intentional walk. Several other players in that game would make the big leagues, among them Bonds's teammates Oddibe McDowell and Luis Medina. Leading off and catching for Carolina was B. J. Surhoff. Batting second and playing shortstop was Walt Weiss. There were even two future major-league managers, Arizona State catcher Don Wakamatsu and Weiss. Arizona State won, 6–4. That score sheet is quite a baseball artifact.

I can't tell you how many times over the years I've been sitting in my seat at a ballpark other than Fenway, score book in hand, and someone will say, "Are you a scout or something?" Very few people keep score anymore, and it's sad. My wife does. Unlike me, Elaine does not add up the totals at the game's conclusion and she never looks at her notations again. But she has her own book and it wouldn't be right for her to be at a game and not keep score. She always checks to see if the caught stealing went 2-4 or 2-6, whether the rundown went 1-6-5-6-5 or 1-6-4-6-5, or if the putout on that shift was 6-3 or 4-3. That's us, Mr. and Mrs. Score Book.

The 1977 season was a good year to cover the Boston Red Sox. They were a lopsided, ball-bashing team trying to win a pennant with a spotty pitching staff. They hit 213 home runs. Eight players hit 14 or more. Jim Rice was the league leader in both home runs (39) and slugging percentage (.593).

Sixteen of those home runs came in one scintillating three-game sweep of the Yankees starting with six on Friday, June 17. The noble Catfish Hunter was chased from the game in two-thirds of an inning as Rick Burleson, Fred Lynn, Carlton Fisk (the first of two), and George Scott hit first-inning solo home runs. The Sox hit five more homers the next day in the famous game when the ever-combative Yankee manager Billy Martin embarrassed Reggie Jackson by removing him for a defensive replacement after Reggie had already taken the field, and the two got into it, not just verbally, in the Yankee dugout.

The bombardment continued on Sunday when the Red Sox hit five more home runs in an 11–1 rout, the last of which was an eighth-inning Yaz bomb off Dick Tidrow that missed becoming the only ball ever hit over Fenway Park's right-field roof by a foot or so. That was the first time anyone had ever hit the facade and it has never happened again.

The Red Sox went to Baltimore, where they swept a four-game series highlighted by a five-homer bombardment off Jim Palmer in the third game. When they got on the bus to the airport after winning the final game they were in a joyful mood, having just won seven in a row, thirteen of fourteen and sixteen of eighteen.

Their next stop was Yankee Stadium, and things were looking good as Bill Campbell, working since the sixth, took the ball in the bottom of the ninth to protect a 5–3 lead. He quickly retired Mickey Rivers and Bucky Dent. The Red Sox were one out away from a big road win.

I was standing next to my friend Charlie Scoggins of the Lowell *Sun* at the top of the press box, ready for the usual sprint to the elevator that would take us down to the locker room level. Willie Randolph hit a ball to left-center and Yastrzemski moved to get it. I don't know which one of us said, "Captain's got it," and which one of us replied, "Not this one," as the best defensive left fielder of his generation mysteriously overran the ball, which went over his right shoulder for a triple. Roy White promptly launched one into the third deck, tying the game.

The teams played into the eleventh. Veteran left-hander Ramón Hernandez was brought in for the Red Sox. As long as I live, I will never forget the sequence: Walk to Graig Nettles. Balk to second. Intentional first-base-open walk to Mickey Rivers. Single by the pinch-hitting Reggie Jackson. Game over. Yes, indeed—walk, balk, walk, single.

The Yankees won easily the next day. Sunday was a killer. The Red Sox scored three in the top of the ninth to tie the game at 4–4, but Campbell was unable to hold the lead in the bottom half, Paul Blair winning the game with a bases-loaded single to left.

The season had been turned upside down. The Sox went to Detroit and lost all three. They came home and lost three more to Baltimore. That made nine straight losses after they had won sixteen out of eighteen to take over first place. They reversed course to win nine of their next eleven but would spend the rest of the season trying to catch up, eventually finishing tied with Baltimore in second place, two and a half games behind the Yankees.

Pitcher Reggie Cleveland did throw a game late in the year that I am certain will never be duplicated. On September 25, a sunny Sunday afternoon, he beat the Tigers 12–5 with an eighteen-hit complete game. I'll let that one sink in for a moment. The Tigers had a hit in every inning, with three hits in the first, third, and eighth. But Reggie walked nobody and only had two three-ball counts. Sadly, his pitch count was lost to the ages. Zimmer paid him a visit in the ninth after Detroit scored twice and had men on first and second, but Reggie was able to talk his way into staying in the game. Phil Mankowski lined to Rick Burleson at short and that was that. It was the last road game of the season and it was also Reggie Cleveland's last victory in a Red Sox uniform. And it remains one of my all-time favorite games. I have shown that score sheet to baseball aficionados many times. That's why I still score every game. You never know.

I got along well with just about everyone, I thought, but there was one memorable moment of discord. As part of my baseball duties, I had to produce the popular Sunday notes column, and I led off one Sunday late in the year by mentioning that one of the big problems with the season was that pitcher Luis Tiant, who had been a beloved figure among both fans and his mates since 1972, had not gotten in proper shape, and this partially explained his so-so performance thus far that year.

I was in the clubhouse early that day, and so was he. The man had a right to have his say, and he exploded angrily, ending up his tirade by saying something pretty foul and pretty dumb. We have gotten along nicely these many years since, and he doesn't need to be reminded of that one slipup.

There was a buzz at the batting cage about our set-to, I'm told. When the game was over, I made my rounds. Carlton Fisk, who had caught Tiant all year, told me he wished I had written this sooner. Shortstop Rick Burleson, for whom "Good morning" was a lengthy soliloquy, told me I had done a good thing and said, "You've got a lot of friends in here." That was nice to know.

Immersing yourself in a full baseball season is a test of fidelity. Covering basketball full-time is taxing: there are eighty-two games and possible playoff games, but you still have a little time for a life. Covering baseball from spring training to season's end is a lifestyle, and that's a very different thing. You are at the ballpark virtually every day, and interacting with many of the same people for upwards of nine months. You get home from a road trip and get out to the ballpark hours later. I recall once getting home at five A.M. from the road and seeing my neighbor, who worked in Boston's flower district, going to work as I was coming in.

Manager Don Zimmer was great to work with. He was a treasure chest of baseball lore, having broken into Organized Baseball at age seventeen in 1949. He was well-known to baseball fans for having been twice hit in the head as a member of the Dodgers organization, thus short-circuiting a promising career and turning him into a journeyman, rather than the star shortstop he was projected to be. On one of those occasions, he spent two weeks in a coma. As a result, he had a cork placed in his head. People assumed it was a plate, but he would always patiently explain it was a cork.

Even by 1977, with more than thirty years of baseball service ahead of him, "Popeye," as he was known throughout baseball for his forearms, was regarded as the quintessential baseball Lifer. He had been married at home plate in between games of a doubleheader at Dunn Field in Elmira, New York, in 1951, and his wife, Soot, once told me she'd have gladly done it all over again.

He did not, however, get along very well with his pitching staff. The armchair psychologist in me reasoned that his two beanings gave him an innate antipathy toward pitchers. He was not very solicitous of a pitcher's feelings and this came to a head the following year when there was practically an open revolt led by Bill Lee and Ferguson Jenkins.

Lee was well-known for his rather iconoclastic ways. Zim was a high school–educated baseball lifer with a somewhat limited worldview. He was, thus, an easy target for someone of Lee's erudition and wit, and Lee, a.k.a. "the Spaceman," couldn't resist making fun of his skipper. This, to me, was regrettable because, whatever their personal differences, the thing that should have bonded these two very different men was a mutual love of the game. I'm surprised no one tried to broker a truce between them on that basis. Perhaps I should have tried.

Zim would sit in the dugout and tell stories about the Boys of Summer Dodgers any time you wanted. He was still spry enough, despite his growing girth, to jump into the batter's box at the tail end of an occasional batting practice and pepper the left-field wall, or even hit one over it. As far as I was concerned, he was a joy to be around.

On a late-season road trip to Chicago, he invited the traveling writers to his suite for food and drinks. That was not the baseball norm. A year later, when he found out I was heading to do a story on his son, Tom, then managing an independent-league team in Butte, Montana, he called me over, pressed a $50 bill in my hands, and told me to take Tom and his wife Marian out to dinner ($50 was perfectly adequate to cover three steak dinners in 1978).

That first season behind me, I was feeling pretty good about things. Luckily I didn't get too comfortable. Sometime in the winter of 1977 Peter Gammons did a U-turn. He had spent most of the previous seventeen months at *Sports Illustrated* covering just about anything but baseball and now he was ready to come back to the *Globe*. If you're the sports editor and can get someone who had a chance to be the Best Baseball Writer Ever, you grab him first and ask questions later. That's exactly what Dave Smith did. And so, like Sparky Anderson, who had one full year in the bigs, I was going to be a one-year wonder as a baseball writer.

CHAPTER 9

"You'd Eat That?"

A few months after my baseball reporting career ended, one of the greatest players in the history of basketball retired—John Havlicek.

The man hung his knee-length socks on a hanger in his locker. He arranged his assortment of accessories in order, smallest to the left, tallest to the right. If a general had ever chosen to spring a surprise locker inspection, John Havlicek would have been ready for each of the 1,270 regular season and 172 playoff games in which he participated for the Boston Celtics, and only the Boston Celtics.

But he was more than a meticulous, well-organized, 100 percent orderly human being. He was the very best basketball player of his time, period. I'll repeat that. John Havlicek played in the NBA from 1962 through 1978 and during that time no non-center was better. Better than the vaunted Big O? Better than Mr. Clutch, Jerry West? Better than Dr. J? That's exactly what I'm saying. I'm taking John Havlicek over all of them. Furthermore, given his off-the-charts athleticism, intelligence, and adaptability, there is no doubt whatsoever in my mind that if he played in today's game, he would flourish to the exact same degree.

Time has done a nasty job on the memory and legacy of John Havlicek. Since he played his final game in 1978, non-center luminaries such as Michael Jordan, Magic Johnson, Larry Bird, Charles Barkley, Kobe Bryant, Isiah Thomas, and LeBron James have won over NBA audiences with dazzling demonstrations of skill and competitiveness. When the discussion of the all-time greats is convened, the names of Elgin Baylor, Julius Erving, Oscar Robertson, and West are automatically included.

John Havlicek has become something of an afterthought. People need to be reminded of his greatness.

As Bruce Springsteen might say, John Havlicek was born to run. He had grown up in Lansing, Ohio, a small community across the river from Wheeling, West Virginia, and his house happened to be on U.S. 40, a prominent highway.

"The house was smack on a curve," he explained in the autobiography, *Hondo: Celtic Man in Motion*, I wrote with him, "and our front door was no more than 10 or 12 feet from the highway. When a big truck would go by at night, the house would vibrate. Consequently, they never wanted me to have a bicycle, because they thought it was too dangerous." So he ran. The other kids pedaled and Johnny ran. "They'd get there first," he said, "but I'd be pulling in right after."

When we were working on the book, John took me to see where he grew up. It was a small and restricted world. The school was close by. The church was close by. Cocky Pyle's gas station, the local gathering spot, was close by. And towering above were the hills, which were a dominant part of local life.

"Maybe that's where I began to develop my stamina," he observed. "I do have a theory about how I developed my ability to change direction. I used to play a game with myself. I would go up into the woods—they were only about a hundred yards from my house—just looking for animals, or just looking to be alone. I'd take a path to get to the top of the hill, but on the way down I'd run without taking the path. In doing so I would dodge trees, using all kinds of different fakes and maneuvers. I fell down many times, but maybe I developed the instincts for the shuffle step in basketball, using all these various things I did running down that hill."

Like many great players, Havlicek was a physical freak. I'm not talking about the body you could see, but what was inside it. At six five and two hundred ten pounds, it was surely a body built for basketball, then and now. But there have been countless guys who are six five and two ten. Havlicek happened to have such abnormally large lungs that his X-rays needed an extra plate. This allowed him to be in constant motion, especially without the ball, a facet of the game at which he has had few peers. No opponent ever looked forward to an evening spent chasing Havlicek around the basketball floor. Former Philadelphia guard Matt Guokas, who played on the great Sixer teams of the late 1960s, once famously said, "I'd give my left arm for his stamina."

I first encountered John Havlicek at an interesting juncture of his career. He was twenty-nine in the fall of 1969, a veteran of seven NBA seasons. With one exception (1967), all he had known as a Boston Celtic was championship success. The 1968-69 team—the season before I began covering the Celtics—had fooled everyone in the basketball world by winning a championship that had been practically bequeathed to the Los Angeles Lakers. Old by any standard, they had taken a cue from player-coach Bill Russell, negotiating the regular season wisely and carefully, qualifying for postseason play by finishing fourth in the Eastern Division with a solid 48-34 record. The new hot outfit that season was the Baltimore Bullets, who had been transformed from a harmless run-and-gun curiosity to a viable force by the addition of Westley Unseld. The Bullets went 57-25 with Unseld being named both Rookie of the Year and MVP.

The core group Russell put on the floor during the 1969 playoff run that culminated in the seven-game victory over the Lakers consisted of thirty-five-year old Sam Jones, thirty-year-old Emmette Bryant, thirty-year old Satch Sanders, twenty-eight-year-old Don Nelson, thirty-two-year-old Bailey Howell, twenty-nine-year old Larry Siegfried, twenty-nine-year-old John Havlicek, and Russell's thirty-five-year-old self. Jones had already announced his retirement, and no one was certain what was in Russell's mind, so there was a clear understanding that as far as the great Boston Celtics' run was concerned, the 1969 playoffs were going to be a last hurrah.

By the time the Celtics convened for the 1969–70 season, Russell had indeed bade his farewell, and thus the idea that there would have to be life without the greatest winner in the history of American sport had become reality. Suddenly, the Boston Celtics were John Havlicek and Friends.

By then, Havlicek had an established identity and was acknowledged to be the greatest sixth man the game had yet seen. Some say Knicks coach Joe Lapchick pioneered the sixth-man concept in the 1950s with his use of Ernie Vandeweghe, who was six three and able to slide back and forth between the frontcourt and backcourt as needed. But Red Auerbach glamorized the position with Frank Ramsey, also about six three. Auerbach wasn't afraid to spot him against much taller players, figuring that the other guy was going to have a lot of trouble keeping up with Ramsey at the offensive end. Ramsey had been a part of great teams at Kentucky, and Auerbach easily convinced his sixth man that he would be serving a strategic purpose coming off the bench—not to maintain anything, but to improve the team with his first substitution. His best five players were not necessarily his five starting players. "It's not who starts, it's who finishes," Red frequently explained.

Playing the sixth-man role as it had never been played before, Ramsey became a vital part of Celtics championship teams in 1957, 1959, 1960, 1961, 1962, 1963, and 1964, and found himself elected to the Hall of Fame in 1981. Before he retired, he performed an additional valuable service for his team: he passed the by-now-sacred sixth-man torch to Havlicek, who had joined the team in 1962. He discovered that this kid from Ohio State was an apt pupil.

Havlicek said in his autobiography,

> My big influence was Frank Ramsey. I learned a lot simply through experience, but I also learned a lot of specific things by watching Frank. Frank taught me to sit on the bench with my warm-up jacket hanging loosely on my shoulders, so when Red called on me I wouldn't have to waste time fiddling around. I see so many kids today blow opportunities to get into a game because they've got to unzip or unsnap their pants, and then their jacket. Then they saunter over to the scorer's table and sit down. When I was the Celtics' sixth man, I would run on the floor and get the referee's attention before I got the official scorer's eye. I didn't want to miss one second if I could help it, and Frank was the same way.

Havlicek went on to say that Ramsey also taught him what he called "little defensive tricks," and he learned those lessons well. He could be very annoying on defense, but not once during his illustrious career did anyone even hint that he was remotely dirty.

He had come into the league under ideal circumstances. So often a young player is plopped onto the wrong team, with the wrong coach in the wrong city, and he never manages to right the ship. An entire career can get sabotaged before it begins. Havlicek had the opposite experience. He was drafted onto a team that had won the previous four championships and five of the previous six. He wasn't asked to play a primary role at first, which was a good thing because he was somewhat limited offensively as a rookie. Nonetheless, he averaged 14.3 points while playing twenty-seven minutes a game as part of a basic eight-man rotation. "All I did that year," he would tell me many times, "was run around and make layups on passes from Cousy."

It was, in fact, the last year for the celebrated Bob Cousy, and if Havlicek was happy to have him on his side, the feeling was quite mutual. For as every teammate over the next sixteen years would discover, throwing a pass John Havlicek could *not* catch was an achievement. He had been gifted with large, strong, and yet soft hands. He had arrived at his first Celtics rookie camp directly from an exhibition-season tryout with the Cleveland Browns. Let the record show he was cut in favor of a guy named Gary Collins, who became an All-Pro end. That Havlicek had gotten so far was amazing, given that he had not played football since high school and when last seen on the gridiron had been a quarterback, not a wide receiver. But Havlicek was an athlete, with a capital A.

The Celtics had drafted him because of that sheer athleticism and the assumption that, if nothing else, he could play defense. He had not been the star of his college team. The big cheese at Ohio State had been Jerry Lucas, who will go down in history as one of the more intriguing characters in NBA history. The six-eight Lucas was a three-time All-American and an Olympic gold medalist. At Ohio State Havlicek had been his wing man.

Auerbach knew he had something special after watching Havlicek athleticize himself to those fourteen points a game his first year, and the way he fit into his defensive concept. Havlicek, of course, knew there was much work to do before he could become a truly significant NBA player, so he went home the next summer to work on his jump shot. His playing time was bumped up to thirty-two minutes a night and he responded by scoring 19.9 points a game, the entire package being impressive enough for him to earn a berth on the NBA's second-team all-league squad, the first of eleven appearances on either the first or second team.

When Ramsey retired, Havlicek was ready to assume the role of sixth man. The concept was strategic since by 1965 he was clearly the second-most important Celtic, behind only the great Bill Russell. Then a play in Boston on April 15, 1965, at the end of the seventh game of the Eastern Conference Finals against Philadelphia, elevated him into something more than just another excellent basketball player—it made him a certified local folk hero, something he will always remain.

Boston was leading 110–109 with four seconds left. Wilt Chamberlain had just dunked the ball, but Russell had done the unthinkable as he inbounded underneath the Philadelphia basket. At that time, the baskets in the Garden were held up by guide wires that ran from the left and right corners of the backboard to the first balcony. Russell's inbounds pass hit a wire, causing a turnover. Philadelphia got the ball back under its own basket needing one point to tie or two to win. During a time-out, Russell pleaded for somebody to bail him out.

It was a treacherous situation for the Celtics, for Philadelphia's options were many. Hal Greer, a great shooter, would put the ball in play. He could get it to Chamberlain, who could maneuver for something inside; set up Chet Walker, another great shooter and a master of drawing fouls with the world's greatest up-fake; or throw it in and get a return pass. Regardless of the shooter, Philadelphia's giant front line of seven-one Chamberlain, six-ten Johnny Kerr, and six-nine (and beefy) Luke Jackson would be crashing the boards for a put-back basket.

Greer took the ball and the five-second count began. Here is Havlicek's explanation of what happened next, given to me on the occasion of the game's twentieth anniversary in 1985:

"As the ball was handed to Greer, I started to count, 'One thousand one, one thousand two,' etc. By now, nothing was happening. Now I'm thinking it's coming to Walker, who was a pretty good shooter. Out of the corner of my eye I saw this lob pass, and I just deflected it, tipping it over to Sam Jones. I went up, but I couldn't get control of it. I saw Sam going the other way, and, fortunately, nobody was in position to foul him."

Thus was born a phrase that everyone of a certain age in Greater Boston remembers: "Havlicek stole the ball!" He really didn't steal it, but "Havlicek deflected the ball!" lacks a certain je ne sais quoi.

A couple of unique personalities made the play live on. Celtics radio play-by-play announcer Johnny Most, a true Boston institution, was at the mike for forty years until his death in 1993, but the pinnacle of his career came that night with a call that could never be duplicated. It took him one minute and four seconds to immortalize both himself and John Havlicek:

"All right, Greer's putting the ball into play . . . He gets it out deep and HAVLICEK STEALS IT! OVER TO SAM JONES! IT'S ALL OVER! JOHNNY HAVLICEK IS MOBBED BY THE FANS. IT'S ALL OVER! JOHNNY HAVLICEK STOLE THE BALL! OH BOY, WHAT A PLAY BY HAVLICEK AT THE END OF THIS BALL GAME! JOHNNY HAVLICEK STOLE THE BALL ON THE PASS-IN. OH, MY, WHAT A PLAY BY HAVLICEK! A SPECTACULAR SERIES COMES TO AN END IN SPECTACULAR FASHION! JOHNNY HAVLICEK BEING HOISTED ALOFT . . . HE YELLS AND WAVES HIS HANDS. BILL RUSSELL WANTS TO GRAB HAVLICEK . . . HE HUGS HIM. HE SQUEEZES JOHN HAVLICEK. HAVLICEK SAVED THIS BALL GAME. THE CELTICS WIN IT, ONE TEN TO ONE OH NINE. WE'LL BE BACK WITH OUR WRAP-UP IN JUST ONE MINUTE!"

But that wasn't the end of it. WHDH radio broadcast the Celtics locally, and its morning show was in the hands of Jess Cain, Boston's number one radio personality for a good two decades. He seized upon the call, running it over and over the following morning. Later, an outfit called Fleetwood Records in Revere, Massachusetts, put out a compilation of Johnny Most radio highlights from the championship decade and you don't have to guess what the album's title was.

Even if John Havlicek had done nothing else the rest of his career, he was now fixed in Boston sports history, and nationally, too. The careers of both men were strongly affected by the play and the call. "I was starting to make inroads," Havlicek said at the time of the anniversary, "but, after that play, people realized I might be around for a while. And the record album definitely influenced the way people thought of me."

"It gave me some of the healthiest publicity I ever got in my life," said Most. "It was something to be remembered for, something to hang my hat on. It gave me and John a sense of 'foreverness' I could never have had otherwise. And it sold about fifty thousand records."

True confession: I was married at two thirty on the afternoon of May 17, 1969. In the morning I played three-on-three with some friends and then I put on "Havlicek Stole the Ball." You can supply your own punch line. Hey, Elaine can't say she didn't know what she was getting into.

Bringing Havlicek off the bench was fine as long as it made sense, but when Russell became the coach following Auerbach's 1966 retirement he changed things up, especially at playoff time. Russell had him out there for thirty-six minutes a game during the 1967 playoffs, and by 1968 the gloves were officially off. Havlicek averaged forty-six minutes in the 1968 playoffs, and that included playing all but two of the two hundred eighty-eight minutes in Boston's six-game conquest of the Lakers in the finals. He had forty points in Game 6, and by that time people had come to the realization that it hardly made sense to take him out since he never seemed to get tired.

Tom Heinsohn had hopes of resurrecting the sixth man when he took over in 1969, but the idea was quickly shelved because this post-Russell Celtics team needed Havlicek on the floor every conceivable second. The 1969–70 season was the dividing line in his career. And the NBA was about to discover what an astonishing force John Havlicek Unleashed was going to be.

By then Oscar Robertson and Jerry West, the dominant guards of the 1960s, had reached the point where their peak years were behind them. There is no question in my mind that Havlicek was clearly the best all-around player in the league that season, and would remain so for another three years.

The 1969–70 Celtics—the team I debuted with as a reporter—were bad. I'm sure Havlicek knew from the first day of practice that it was going to be a long, hard, and ultimately unfulfilling season. And while young guards Jo Jo White and Don Chaney had promise, and young forward Steve Kuberski likewise offered some hope, Havlicek had to be worrying that this dismal state of affairs might continue well into the future. But he was the ultimate professional and made the most of the situation, leading the team in scoring, assists, and rebounds. The team won thirty-four games and might have won half that many without him.

His time in basketball purgatory was mercifully brief. He received some valuable help the following year when Red Auerbach drafted Dave Cowens out of Florida State to be the center. The team won forty-four games, and though they did not make the playoffs, anyone could see it now had a bright future. Havlicek actually elevated his play in 1970–71, leading the team in scoring with 28.9 points a game and placing fourth among the assists leaders with 7.5, a pretty nice total for someone who was only a part-time guard.

The John Havlicek of 1971 was only partly recognizable as the Havlicek of 1962. A born move-without-the-ball forward—this would always be his calling card—he had made himself into someone who could run offenses and lead textbook fast breaks. He was routinely putting up double-figure games in points, rebounds, and assists long before Laker public relations chief Bruce Jolesch coined the phrase "triple double" when Magic Johnson arrived in 1979. There were no holes whatsoever in his game.

But he was still human and occasionally dropped his guard as he struggled to acclimate himself to a new basketball circumstance. Once he had been the young guy taking it all in while keeping his mouth shut. Now he was the older guy and things that seemed logical to him did not always resonate with his younger teammates, and one day during the 1970–71 season he vented, saying, "This is the dumbest team I've ever played on."

Basketball was never complicated to John Havlicek. If an opponent called out a play, a number, or a phrase, he watched how it unfolded and filed that away in his memory bank. The next time it happened, he would instinctively know how to disrupt the play. Not all his teammates could absorb information that quickly, however, and their confusion really annoyed Havlicek. The same was true on the offensive end. John expected all newcomers to learn the plays yesterday.

Things always worked out when he was paired with like-minded people. In the 1974 finals against the Milwaukee Bucks Paul Silas was in a medium post-up when he suddenly slipped a blind overhead pass that Havlicek caught for an unmolested layup. When I asked Silas what prompted him to do that, he smiled and said, "That's easy. I saw John's man out of the corner of my eye where he wasn't supposed to be and I knew that John would be cutting to the hoop."

There seemed to be no end to Havlicek's analytical powers. He once was sent hard to the floor in a playoff game by Atlanta's Herman Gilliam. After the game, he was asked about the spill, and the fact that he didn't appear to have been hurt. Much to the astonishment, not to mention amusement, of the inquisitors, Havlicek delivered a five-minute dissertation on the art of falling. I'm sure what he said would have been seconded by champion bronco busters or bull riders, but it wasn't something on offer in any other NBA locker room.

I would get to know a dichotomy involving John Havlicek. The meticulous, obsessively neat guy whose locker was always ready for the general's inspection, the guy who needed six napkins for a hamburger with or without ketchup, the guy who once looked at me as I was shoving a bit of fat on the end of my steak in my mouth and said, "You'd eat that?" was his dominant persona. But there was another John Havlicek, a mirthful, fun-loving guy who grew more and more uninhibited the longer he played.

One example occurred in 1976. He had torn the plantar fascia in the arch of his left foot during Game 1 of an opening-round series against the Buffalo Braves, and for the rest of the postseason nursed himself back to health. He was told by doctors to ice his foot three hours daily, and so purchased a turquoise dishpan and carried it around on the road. He figured that if three hours was good, six would be better.

During the second round in Cleveland, I and a young reporter for the *New York Post* covering his first playoff series, Mike Lupica, were watching TV with John as he soaked his foot. At one point Havlicek needed more ice; he left and came back with a refilled dishpan.

"Two Hondo handfuls!" he beamed, gesturing toward the ice. I'm telling you, at this point in his career he was almost borderline goofy.

Havlicek was an extremely useful player until the end. He averaged 17.7 and 16.1 points a game in his two final seasons, and his defensive job on a much younger and friskier Julius Erving in the 1977 Eastern Conference Finals against Philadelphia was nothing short of spellbinding.

The 1977–78 season was not a pleasant one for anyone connected with the Celtics. Heinsohn was let go after thirty-four games, not that the team's 11–23 record at the time was even remotely his fault. Satch

Sanders, John's old teammate, and even his onetime roommate, was put in charge. Satch was, and is, a fabulous person, but he was not a good coach. He was just too cerebral and unemotional, in my opinion. And the team itself just wasn't very good.

But it still had John Havlicek. Due to a weather postponement, Boston was forced to play four February games in sixty-six hours. Havlicek played forty minutes a game, scoring twenty, thirty-two, twenty-seven, and twenty-five. He was seven weeks shy of his thirty-eighth birthday.

He was the first megastar I covered, and he set a standard of behavior against which most everyone I would encounter would fall short. He was as gracious and polite in his pre- and postgame dealings with some guy from a weekly, or even a high school, paper as he was with the stars of our profession. Win or lose, good game or bad, exhibition, regular season, or playoff game, he was always accommodating.

He was the first person who asked me to collaborate on a book. I remember exactly where he asked if I was interested: we were crossing the street in Houston during a road trip. I'm not sure whether I needed two or three seconds to say yes.

The challenge of writing with someone is to make sure the subject's voice shines through, not the collaborator's. I spent a week at John's house in Columbus, Ohio, with John; his wife, Beth; and their children, Chris and Jill. John and I would sit on the banks of the Olentangy River and I'd tape him talking. I was somewhat in awe of my subject. By the time I worked with Larry Bird, twelve years later, I was a little more sure of my professional self. *Hondo: Celtic Man in Motion* is not a great book, but it's a good one. In retrospect, I could have pushed John a little harder, but during the entire week I felt more like a guest than a collaborator. The truth is, John was never going to be controversial. He wasn't out to drill anybody. He had a positive, upward-mobility story to tell. The one interesting revelation was how angry he was about not being chosen for the 1960 Olympic basketball team. He was disappointed in the outcomes of both the 1961 and 1962 NCAA championship games—Ohio State had lost each to in-state rival Cincinnati—but that was competition and he could deal with it. However, he felt an injustice had been perpetrated on him by the 1960 selection committee; that was his one chance to be an Olympian and he felt cheated.

"John Havlicek Day" was the salvation of the otherwise dreary 1977–78 season. John had announced his retirement during the season, and thus the final game against the Buffalo Braves was a final chance to honor a living-legend Celtic. John Powers, who had succeeded me on the daily Celtics beat two years earlier and had developed great respect and admiration for the "Captain," as he liked to call him, and I took John to lunch and grilled him for every bit of Havlicek and NBA trivia for a special farewell section. John himself contributed a nice piece, in which he joked about what it was like for a shy kid from the Midwest to encounter the madness that is Boston driving when he arrived in town sixteen years earlier.

"Being a Midwesterner," he said, "my first year in Boston was a trial. I loved the team, but adjusting to city life was most difficult. The pace seemed to be about one hundred times faster than I was used to, and, although I was a good driver in Ohio, I was terrified in Boston. My first decision was to send my car back home, feeling I was much safer on the MBTA [Boston's subway] than behind a wheel." I'm willing to bet that all Celtics rookies, no matter where they come from, can identify with that sentiment today.

The final game itself was strangely wonderful, meaningless as it was in the standings (the Braves and Celtics would finish a combined fifty-one games behind the division-champion Bullets). Havlicek got the first Celtics basket, and he would also get the last one with just under a minute to play.

He scored the final nine points, and eleven of the final thirteen, finishing with twenty-nine. He always said that he had begun his career in 1962 by running the floor and taking passes from Bob Cousy, and now he had ended it sixteen years later by running the floor and taking bullet passes from Ernie DiGregorio, who, more than any player in NBA history, evoked memories of Cousy with his vision and passing wizardry. A day after his thirty-eighth birthday, John Havlicek had ended his career running and running and running.

I can't say this is a fact, because it's an opinion, but it is an honest and a reasoned one: at the moment of his retirement, John Havlicek had established himself as the best all-around player in NBA history. Yes, better than Oscar Robertson, better than Jerry West, better than Elgin Baylor, better than Dr. J, and thus better than anyone in the pre-Jordan, pre-Magic, pre-Larry, and pre-LeBron eras. If you're picking a twelve-man All-Time NBA squad today, he *has* to be on it. There has never been a better two-position player. He was the greatest sixth man in NBA history, and when he outgrew that job and became the team's focal point, he was first-team All-NBA in 1971, 1972, 1973, and 1974, and second-team the next two years, when he was thirty-five and thirty-six years old respectively. He was first-team All-Defense in 1973, 1974, 1975, and 1976. Before the triple double was invented, he played too many games to count in which he had double figures in points, rebounds, and assists. This is my story and I can assure you I will always stick with it.

CHAPTER 10

It Was Still in My Blood

I'm somewhat ashamed to say I pulled a bigfoot move in order to get myself back on the NBA beat in 1978. John Powers, then, as now, the best purveyor of prose on the entire newspaper, had done a fabulous job. For reasons I don't recall, he was getting off the beat after the 1977–78 season. Steve Marantz would cover the team, and the Celtics job was going to be in good hands.

But a huge upheaval happened at the league meetings in 1978 that got my attention, as the Buffalo Braves and Celtics were playing musical franchises. The Braves, owned by John Y. Brown, moved to San Diego, where they would be known as the Clippers. Irv Levin owned the Celtics then, and in effect he and Brown traded their teams, Levin taking control of the Clippers, while Brown took over the Celtics.

To further complicate matters, the Celtics and Clippers announced a trade. The Clippers sent Tiny Archibald, Marvin Barnes, Billy Knight, and future draft choices to Boston for Kermit Washington, Kevin Kunnert, Sidney Wicks, and the rights to Freeman Williams, who had been the Celtics' second first-round draft pick that year at number eight, the same draft in which they took Larry Bird at number six.

Tiny Archibald? Billy Knight? *Marvin Barnes?* I was intrigued. The Celtics may or may not be all that good next year, I thought, but they sure will be interesting. I went to sports editor Dave Smith and said I wanted back in. Putting me back on the Celtics beat had to be one of his final acts before he left us for the *Washington Star*.

My second NBA tour would last four years. That first year, 1978–79, was educational for me. The team flat-out stunk, and covering a bad team presents challenges. Their record was 29-53, and they weren't even that good. Coach Satch Sanders was fired with a 2-12 record. Dave Cowens succeeded him as player-coach, but unlike with Russell, the player-coach idea simply didn't work with him.

Compounding the challenge, this was the first time I had covered a team with racial issues. It wasn't horrible, but it wasn't always comfortable, either. I told people the team had three factions: the blacks, the whites, and Don Chaney, the only guy who got along with everybody.

Archibald was still recuperating from a torn Achilles tendon injury he had sustained in 1977. In those days a torn Achilles was often a death sentence, and many people were surprised he was playing at all. He was a little pudgy, and on a small body like his even five additional pounds were a huge detriment. Knight was a finesse player on offense and a nonfactor in every other facet of his game. He didn't defend, he didn't pass, and he didn't appear to work up a sweat—ever. One letter writer told me his personal theme song should be Jackson Browne's "Running on Empty." The Boston Garden crowd loathed him, and he shrank at home. He would be traded to Indiana in mid-January of 1979 for center Rick Robey.

And then there was Marvin.

On any short list of extremely talented NBA screwups the name of Marvin Barnes would be quite prominent. His Celtics stint was classic Marvin. There were occasional flashes of talent, but only occasional. I wasn't well versed in substance abuse, but even I learned to detect in advance games in which Marvin might not be of much use by observing him in the locker room prior to the game. As always, when the mood struck, Marvin demonstrated great game savvy and instinct. But he was hopelessly incorrigible and he was released before the end of the season.

The one saving grace of the season was the fact that Red Auerbach had secured the draft rights to Indiana State forward Larry Bird at the 1978 draft. During the season, Red had traded Charlie Scott to the Lakers and gotten Don Chaney back along with one of the Lakers' two number one picks, from New Orleans in compensation for their signing Gail Goodrich. That gave the Celtics a second first-round pick. It's likely Red would not have gambled on Bird if he had only had one pick, and irony of ironies, the second pick came via the Lakers.

The drafting of Bird led to a curious happening in late February 1978. The Celtics were on a five-game road trip out west. We were in San Diego watching Indiana State make its only national TV appearance of the regular season during its run to the NCAA championship game. And by "we" I mean just about everyone on the team was gathered in that room, with most of them knowing there was little chance Bird would ever be a teammate. A team as bad as they were would be making lots of changes. My recollection is that Bird didn't take a shot for the first five or six minutes and still finished with forty-nine.

Larry Bird arrived the following season and the Celtics would average fifty-seven wins a season over the next fourteen years. We would all become very, very spoiled.

The NBA I reentered was in something of a lull. Back-to-back finals between Washington and Seattle had not created any national sparks, and the specter of drugs, cocaine in particular, was hovering over the league. Kareem Abdul-Jabbar should have been the game's biggest star, but he was bored, famously telling Ted Green of the *Los Angeles Times* something like, "They pay me to show up and shoot a few hook shots." The great "Dr. J," Julius Erving, was a regal figure, but he alone could not carry the league.

So you can see why Bird and Earvin "Magic" Johnson created a little excitement when they showed up in the same year, strategically placed, as luck would have it, in cities with a heated bicoastal rivalry and a true shared history. Larry was named Rookie of the Year, but Magic had the last laugh, leading the Lakers to a championship with one of the most memorable performances in league history in Game 6.

If you've only read about Game 6 of the 1980 finals between the Lakers and 76ers in Philadelphia, please find some way to see it. Kareem had been destroying the Sixers. His point-rebound numbers in Games 1 through 4 were 33-14, 38-14, 33-14, and 23-11. Then he put up 40-15 numbers in Game 5 before spraining his left ankle late in the game. Magic had been excellent, but after five games Kareem was the clear MVP of the finals.

Nobody thought the Lakers could win Game 6 on the road without him. The main thing most of us had on our minds was where we were going to have dinner in Los Angeles before Game 7, and I'm not being remotely hyperbolic when I say that. And yet, the Lakers did win, 123–107. Words, including those from my game story the next morning, do not do justice to the show Magic put on.

> There didn't appear to be much left for the Magic Man to do in order to convince basketball people that he is one of the greatest winners who has ever laced up a pair of sneakers. But Magic submitted his absolute Renoir last night as he scored a career-high 42 points, hauled in 15 rebounds, accounted for seven assists and simply dominated the ballgame while seemingly playing every normal position and some that haven't been invented yet. From that first period, when he scored 13 points on five baskets that were not even distantly related, to the last period, when he brought out his hammer and bucket of nails to do the coffin-closing honors, this was Magic's Extended Moment.

And I was trying hard not to overstate it.

I can't recall whether or not I had a finals MVP vote that year. I know I would have voted for Kareem. He got them to the Red Zone of the Promised Land, but Magic sure took them into the End Zone, with a performance that may never be surpassed. One and all should be reminded that, on the night in question, Magic Johnson was twenty years old.

Thus began a decade that transformed the NBA, making it into a global colossus. Magic, Bird, Michael Jordan, Commissioner David Stern—all of them were integral parts of the transformation. And those of us print people who were fortunate enough to be in the forefront of NBA coverage while print still mattered pretty much unanimously agree that life for us was never better than in the 1980s.

The league had not yet gotten away from us. Things would begin to change when the Chicago Bulls assumed the identity of a traveling rock band, complete with airtight security, as the next decade began and the Bulls were on their way to becoming six-time champs. Back in the 1980s the NBA was still remarkably accessible, and if I could live my *Boston Globe* life over, changing nothing, from January 1, 1980, till Sunday, June

14, 1990, when the Detroit Pistons knocked off the Portland Trail Blazers in five games to win their second title in succession, I would do so.

Four teams dominated the league. The Lakers challenged throughout the decade. The 76ers did so in the beginning. The Celtics were contenders for the most part, while the Pistons came on strong at the end. Houston sneaked in with a pair of odd trips to the finals, with two entirely different teams (Robert Reid was the only connective tissue), but they weren't going to win either series, and everybody outside Houston knew it. They were strictly character actors in this production. Los Angeles, Philadelphia, Boston, and Detroit were the leading men.

The basketball was exquisite. In Boston's case it was astonishing how quickly the team was transformed from a fractured mess into a league power in 1979–80. Bird's arrival was only part of it. Tiny Archibald got healthy—finally—and made himself into a pass-first, shoot-second point guard who could hurt you if you left him alone. M. L. Carr was signed as a free agent and he provided athleticism and aggression (sometimes too much of that) and effervescent spirit off the court. Cowens, now shed of the coaching burden, had another All-Star season. And they had a real coach.

His name was Bill Fitch and some people initially weren't sure why Red Auerbach wanted him at all. He had been Cleveland's only coach since their inception in 1970, and though that team had improved enough by 1976 to beat Washington and throw a real playoff scare into the eventual champion Celtics, he was known more for his wisecracks than his coaching. He really was funny, although a portion of his humor was a bit too sarcastic for some people. Coupled with that sharp wit was an ex-marine's toughness. He was incredibly organized. I will long remember the first time there was a twenty-four-second shot malfunction at Boston Garden during his coaching tenure, and he immediately ran to the scorer's table waving a stopwatch. He said he always carried one in his pocket in case of just such a happening.

Not everyone took to him right away, but Larry Bird did. We were all learning about Larry and one of the things we quickly discovered was that he loved authority. Police, military, coaches with rules . . . Larry loved them all. That fidelity never wavered. When things went sour for the Celtics and Fitch in the 1983 playoffs, just about everyone who mattered essentially quit on the coach. His one staunch ally was Larry Bird.

The 1979–80 Celtics set a league record by improving from twenty-nine wins to sixty-one in one season. Bill Fitch had a great deal to do with it. If nothing else he prevailed on Cedric Maxwell to use his formidable athletic talents on defense. Max, a consummate inside scorer, had never taken much pride on defense. In just one year he became a defensive stopper capable of shutting down a Dr. J. Max couldn't believe it himself. But even though the Celtics were a very good regular-season team, they weren't good enough to go all the way for a reason that is as old as basketball itself: they just weren't big enough.

The starting front line was Cowens at six eight, Bird at six nine, and Maxwell at six eight. Carr came off the bench at six five. And while Rick Robey was a rugged six ten, his primary asset was getting up and down the floor. He was not a rim protector. This size deficiency was exposed in the playoff series against the 76ers. Philadelphia won in a relatively easy five games, and both the six-eleven Darryl Dawkins and the seven-foot Caldwell Jones had their way, though they then lost to the Lakers in the finals. Auerbach and Fitch knew something had to be done.

The Celtics were in the fortunate position of being a sixty-one-win team in possession of the first pick in the 1980 draft, the result of fortuitous Auerbach maneuverings. In signing M. L. Carr in 1979, by the rules of free agency the Celtics owed compensation to the Pistons. While negotiating that compensation, Red found a loophole in Carr's Pistons contract, which would have eliminated the need for compensation. Nonetheless, Red offered the Pistons the high-scoring Bob McAdoo in return for two Pistons number one picks. One of them, again via New Orleans, became the first pick in 1980, and there was a seven-foot prize available that year. The only problem was that his name was Joe Barry Carroll.

A Purdue senior, Carroll had all the makings of a future NBA coach killer. He had a nice scoring touch and he got his share of the rebounds any seven-footer should get just rolling out of bed. But he played with an air of utter indifference. I saw him up close at the 1980 Final Four in Indianapolis and was horrified at the thought he might become the Celtics' pick. Make no mistake: I was not some detached observer whose job happened to be covering the Boston Celtics. I was also a fan and season ticket holder who was emotionally invested in the team. I had a lot at stake with this number one draft pick selection and I did not want Joe Barry Carroll.

Auerbach gave no signals about his interest in Carroll, one way or the other. So when we gathered in the Celtics' office for the draft on the morning of June 9, 1980, no one was quite prepared for the momentous happening that would take place shortly after noon, when the drafting would start.

The move to get the One and Only Bill Russell while holding the third pick in the 1956 NBA draft will always remain Auerbach's number one draft-day coup. But what he did on this day in 1980 is a close number two. He traded the first pick (from Detroit) and Boston's own thirteenth pick in the draft to Golden State in exchange for the third pick and seven-foot center Robert Parish. Golden State took Carroll with the first pick, Utah chose Darrell Griffith at number two, and with the third pick Red selected a gangly six-eleven kid from Minnesota named Kevin McHale.

McHale was no secret—no Big Ten star could ever be a secret. But he did have a funny body. Minnesota teammate Mychal Thompson said when he first laid eyes on McHale all he could think of was Herman Munster, and people weren't sure how well he would hold up in the NBA. Everyone knew he had good inside moves, but no one knew he would establish a standard of post-up excellence that, two decades after his retirement, has yet to be equaled.

Parish was an intriguing puzzle. I've always wondered how much Red knew about Parish, who had been in the league for four years, putting up decent numbers without earning any widespread respect. But I do know that Bill Fitch most definitely had his eye on Parish, because he rhapsodized about him more than once in my presence. Fitch and I frequently had morning coffee at the airport when on the road, and he would say, "Man, I'd like to get my hands on that Robert Parish." Fitch believed he was underutilized in the Bay Area because Fitch knew the big guy could run and he was not being asked to do that by Warriors coach Al Attles. This resonated with me because I had seen Parish in 1976 when he was a member of a United States team getting ready for some international competition and Providence coach Dave Gavitt was gushing about how well this big kid from Centenary could get up and down the floor.

With that trade the Celtics won sixty-two games—only one more than the year before, and the same as Philadelphia—but when the playoffs began they were not going to be out-bigged by anyone. We all had a feeling the 1981 Eastern Conference Finals would be an epic confrontation. And so it was.

The 76ers had also improved, in their case the big addition being a rather frightening rookie guard named Andrew Toney. Sadly, Andrew Toney has fallen through the cracks of NBA history. His career consisted of eight seasons and five hundred forty combined regular-season and playoff games. But only his first five years were viable. Recurrent problems in both feet reduced his effectiveness after the 1984–85 season. He labored on, but he was basically through at age twenty-eight, though he would play for parts of three additional seasons.

He stood six feet three inches and weighed about 185 pounds—a sturdy NBA body—and he had the requisite NBA quickness. A very good jump shooter with modern three-point range, he had absolutely no technical weakness on offense. He could take anyone off the dribble, either right or left. He was an 80-percent foul shooter. But what really distinguished Andrew Toney was a fierceness and an arrogance bordering on contemptuousness that permeated his game every second he was on the floor. He laughed at double-teams. He *invited* double-teams. And just when you thought the guy was forever determined to embarrass you by scoring on your double-team he would make the perfect pass to an unguarded teammate for a layup. He always kept you on the defensive.

I'm not surprised to learn he was a handful for 76ers coach Billy Cunningham. He didn't always follow orders when he was on the court. I can still hear Billy yelling, "Andrew! Andrew!" in a tone of sheer exasperation. But Toney was a particular problem for the Celtics. Finding an Andrew Toney repellent became an obsession. One year they traded for Quinn Buckner, hoping he would be the answer. He wasn't. Finally, in year four of the Andrew Toney Era, the Celtics found their man—the only guard in the league with a defensive mentality strong enough to cope with Toney's attitude. I am speaking of Dennis Johnson.

The 1981 and 1982 Celtics-76ers battles for the Eastern Conference championship ought to be repackaged and distributed to any NBA fan under forty so they can understand why their father, uncle, or grandfather gets a glow on while talking about the Good Old Days of the NBA. These were teams good and deep enough to bring greats such as McHale and the 76ers' Bobby Jones off the bench. A young Larry Bird matched up with a cagey Dr. J. Hall of Famers battled Hall of Famers and Absolutely-Should-Be Hall of Famers such as Maurice Cheeks and Jones, an eminently dignified and worthy six-nine force who I fear, like Toney, has fallen through a significant crack in NBA history.

The 76ers coulda/shoulda won both series. They were leading the home-team Celtics three games to one and in possession of the ball, up six, with 1:40 to play in Game 5 of the 1981 series, but they could not close. The Celtics wormed their way back, winning 111–109. The 76ers had a ten-point lead in the second half of Game 6 in Philadelphia, when Cedric Maxwell ignited his team by going into the stands after a taunting fan, an act that today would result in ejection, suspension, perhaps incarceration, but which on that evening was regarded as an extracurricular activity. McHale made a big block on Toney, Bird hit a key jumper, and the Celtics sneaked out of town with that one, 100–98.

Game 7 was one of my three favorite games of the entire Bird Era. Of all the wonderful Celtics-Lakers, Celtics-Knicks, Celtics-Pistons, and Celtics-76ers games I was privileged to see and cover, this one was special in its sheer emotionalism. The totality of events, with the Celtics back in prominence, the drama of having been so close to extinction in Game 5—76er general manager Pat Williams says he was being congratulated by some Celtics fans when his team was up six with 1:40 remaining—and just the fact that it was ancient rival Philadelphia sent the Garden crowd into a frenzy. The 76ers were up by nine with just under six minutes to play, at which point referees Jake O'Donnell and Darrell Garretson put their whistles in their pockets and basically said, "Okay, boys, you're on your own"—much as O'Donnell and Jack Madden had done in New York eight years earlier. The Celtics ramped up their defense, the crowd seemingly roaring louder with each possession. The 76ers scored just one point in their final ten possessions. With a minute left and the scored tied at 89, Darryl Dawkins attempted a shot from the low left post. He was hammered by every Celtic, alive or dead, but got no call. Bird grabbed the rebound, dribbled up-court, and drained a jump shot off the glass. Bird never used the backboard, preferring straight-on shots, so why did he do it this time? "I don't know," he said when asked.

"I just know I wanted the ball in my hands. That's the only place I wanted it."

The Celtics held on, winning the game and the Eastern Conference championship, 91–90, Maurice Cheeks having missed one of two free throws at the end. After coming within a minute and forty seconds of losing in five, they had won Games 5, 6, and 7 by margins of two, two, and one.

The aftermath became a Sunday afternoon of personal panic. After doing all my postgame interviewing I went to the *Globe* office, about four miles away, to write my stories. When I got there I was missing my notebook, my running sheets, everything! I realized I must have left them in the Celtics' locker room. I drove back to Boston Garden, not even sure I could gain entrance. Happily, when I got to the Celtics' locker room there was my stuff. A writer could have no scarier moment in the execution of his job.

No one outside of Houston expected them to give the Celtics much of a battle in the 1981 finals, but the Rockets proved to be surprisingly resilient before losing a six-game series that brought the championship back to Boston. The Rockets were a 40-42 team during the regular season, but they knocked off the Lakers, San Antonio, and Kansas City to reach the finals. They were led by feisty center Moses Malone, who added some spice by declaring that he and "four guys from Petersburg" (his hometown of Petersburg, Virginia) could defeat the Celtics. Among those who took note of that remark was Larry Bird.

Moses and friends got Boston's attention by winning Game 2 in Boston. The teams split Games 3 and 4 in Houston, with Rockets coach Del Harris making some sort of NBA playoff history by employing just six men in Houston's 91–86 triumph in Game 4. Back in Boston for Game 5, which is always crucial in any best-of-seven series, Cedric Maxwell took charge, spinning and whirling his way to twenty-nine points, a performance that led to his eventual series MVP award, and the Celtics put the Rockets away in Game 6, 102–91.

Revenge for the 76ers was sweet in 1982. Again they went up, three games to one. This time the Celtics blew them out in Game 5, 114–85, and won a defensive battle in Game 6, 88–75. The NBA had not yet entered its offensive Ice Age: the Philadelphia squad was mocked, even at home, by people calling them the "75ers."

Game 7, in Boston that year, was the ultimate foregone conclusion. The Sixers had looked horrible in both Games 5 and 6. The Celtics were in gear and they were playing at home. The only question was whether or not they could cover the spread. And yet, led by Julius Erving, the 76ers took control of the game by the end of the third quarter and won big, 120–106. They, not the Celtics, were going to the finals. Boston fans struck a blow for righteousness and sportsmanship late in the fourth quarter; with the outcome no longer in doubt, a fan began chanting, "Beat L.A.! Beat L.A.!" Thousands picked up on it. As much as the people hated losing to the 76ers, they hated the Lakers even more.

Unlike the Celtics, the 76ers did not win the championship, losing to the Lakers in six games. But these great rivals had given the basketball world a pair of series to remember.

CHAPTER 11

"Now That's *a Foul!"*

"Who's your favorite player?" You can imagine how many times I've been asked that over the years.

The "best" player, the one I'd most like to go back and watch forever? That would be Larry Bird. But my "favorite" player, the most inimitable and unforgettable combination of athletic skill and personality? That would be Dave Cowens, in a landslide. He overlapped only one season with Bird and retired just before the 1980–81 season began. I can only imagine what a front line of Bird, Parish, McHale, *and* Cowens might have accomplished.

Dave Cowens was a man of deep principle, and one major violation of his personal code was the act of falling down upon minimal, or even nonexistent, contact in the hopes of fooling an official into calling an offensive foul. Celtics radio announcer Johnny Most called it "pulling a Stanislavsky," after the noted Russian method acting teacher. Latter-day folk know it as "flopping." By any name, Dave Cowens regarded it as a despicable act.

In a game against the Houston Rockets on February 25, 1976, Cowens was victimized by just such a maneuver in the first half. He took a pass at the foul line. Houston's Mike Newlin, a rugged six-four guard, slipped in behind Cowens, felt some contact, fell down, and got the call. The same thing happened again in the third period.

On the change of possession, Newlin ran down the right side of the court. As he crossed midcourt, he was met by a rampaging, six-foot-eight, two-hundred-twenty-five-pound mass of fury. Cowens had run diagonally across the court and delivered what could only be described as a double forearm shiver, knocking the well-constructed Newlin to the floor. (Frank O'Brien, the great *Boston Globe* photographer, captured it beautifully for the morning paper.) Cowens then ran over to referee Bill Jones and screamed, "Now *that's* a foul!"

The Celtics, trailing by fifteen at that moment, launched a comeback, abetted by timely non-calls by Jones and his referee partner, Jake O'Donnell. The Celtics won, 103–102, but all anyone could talk about was the vigilante justice carried out by Cowens.

I had a Sunday basketball notes column, and in my lead the following Sunday I chastised Cowens for his out-of-control temper and the Celtics for being enablers. Auerbach had congratulated Cowens after the game, bellowing, "It's about time!" At this point in his career Cowens was at the top of his game, so much so that I had no hesitation declaring him "the single best basketball player in the world." But his behavior had become troubling.

"What is going on here?" I wrote. "Do the Celtics really believe that getting away with falling down to draw an offensive foul can be equated with smashing into a smaller player from the blind side after running the length of the court to get up steam? Are the Celtics telling us that, no matter what they preach about class and pride, the end, in fact, justifies the means? . . . I am truly afraid that some day he [Cowens] will seriously hurt somebody unless he is made to realize that his famous temper tantrums will simply not be tolerated by management, if only because he is needed to play in the game (the foul on Newlin was his fifth, for example)."

A few days later a letter arrived at the *Globe*, addressed to me. It was on David W. Cowens Basketball School stationery. Copies had been sent to John Nucatola, the NBA's officiating supervisor; Larry Fleisher, the executive director of the Players Association; and Mike Newlin. Cowens also requested that the letter be printed in a forthcoming Sunday *Globe*.

Dave Cowens was explaining himself, as only Dave Cowens could. After agreeing that "violence has no place in sports or in any other realm of society," and after conceding that "it is dangerous when a person's temper becomes uncontrollable and they are unable to channel their adrenalin supplied energy to result in scoring points, grabbing rebounds and playing defense," he vehemently disputed the notion that he had acted in an uncontrolled manner when he knocked Mike Newlin to the floor.

"What you described as an outrageous, indefensible, brutal, raging, blind-sided attack on poor, helpless, Mike Newlin was actually a pre-meditated, calculated risk (fifth foul), which was not done to deliberately hurt anyone, which it did not. I ran from one side of the court to the other when Newlin got the inside step on Kevin Stacom and was dribbling toward the basket. He was not hit from behind but was easily able to see me coming at him just as if I was able to double-team the ball which of course was not my intention."

I thought that was a wee bit of revisionist history, but the really good stuff was coming, as Dave Cowens laid out his philosophy on the act we now know as "flopping," and why he felt perfectly justified to respond to the Newlin shenanigans as he did.

> THE PURPOSE—To once and for all impress upon the referees, coaches, players and fans that fraudulent, deceiving and flagrant acts of pretending to be fouled when little or no contact is made, is just as outrageously unsportsmanlike as knocking a player to the floor. I would not and never have taught youngsters to play other than by the rules, morals, ethics and character of the game.
>
> The following list are the reasons why I disagree with the acting that is going on in high school, college and professional basketball.
>
> 1. Pretending makes players think they can achieve their goal without putting in the work or effort that it takes to develop any skill or talent.
>
> 2. Hostilities arise among the players who are obviously being victimized by the *actor's* ability to make officials react instinctively to any flagrant, out-of-place action.
>
> 3. It distracts anyone who attends the game to study fundamental basketball skills and traits of the game, i.e. scouts, coaches, players, etc.
>
> 4. It arouses the ignorant fans who react vehemently to violent gestures or seemingly unsportsmanlike conduct (almost

always on the home court of the actor) and can lead to minor uprisings, thrown articles on the court, etc.

5. If this practice continues unrestrained or the actor is allowed to utilize this fraudulent exercise successfully, it will gradually become an accepted strategy and will be taught to kids more enthusiastically by their coaches. After all, everyone wants to win and will take advantage of any ploy to do so. This way, a weak defensive player will have another method of getting by without having to learn how to play defense properly.

You may think I am exaggerating this point and I am sure the public is tired of hearing about this technicality, but I have noticed that the number of pretenders has risen over the past three or four years resulting in numerous invisible contact fouls being assessed. This happens especially when the fundamentally sound strategy of creating mismatches close to the basket, with the smaller player taking a dive because of the high percentage that the big man will score. Nowadays, some average defensive big men are taking to falling down unnecessarily to get the more skilled big men in foul trouble, leaving the better player at a disadvantage. This, in plain words, is "cheating."

As an articulate, knowledgeable and enthusiastic sports journalist, your comments on my being a terrific basketball player reinforced your expertise on the game (just kidding), but your observation that I must learn to *act* better is not in my repertoire.

I would appreciate receiving equal time on this matter and request that this letter be printed unedited in the *Boston Globe*. As I once told you, I believe it is your responsibility to report the facts and your opinions are note-worthy, but this is an issue of principle and whether or not you agree with me has little to do with the respect that I have for you and the contributions you have made to the Boston sports scene.

Sincerely,
David W. Cowens

His request was granted on Sunday, March 14, 1976.

Every aspect of this was in keeping with the unique Dave Cowens behavior pattern that had manifested itself from the moment he had arrived in Boston six years earlier. Cowens had never read the manual. He was more than just the most uninhibited and spontaneous athlete. He was the most fascinating person I had ever encountered.

He chose to live not in a spiffy apartment, but in a rented poolside cabana house owned by a Weston, Massachusetts, lawyer named Richard Gold. Feeling he had oodles of spare time on his hands once the daily practice was finished, he enrolled in an auto engine repair course.

He had a "My turn, your turn"/Russian-lumberjacks-swigging-vodka fight with Buffalo's Bob Kauffman in which, after slugging Kauffman in the face, he stood there, inviting a return swing. Which he got. Cowens wound up with a black eye. Kauffman had a dislocated jaw. And they became friends.

He asked me if writers ever have slumps and if I ever knew beforehand what I was going to write. He gave me a line for the ages. After the Celtics had won the 1974 NBA championship by defeating the Milwaukee Bucks, I caught up to him as we were changing planes in Chicago on our way back to Boston. I asked him how it felt to have accomplished this career milestone. "The fun for me is in the doing," he said. "This is just something for my portfolio of basketball experiences."

He spent the following night sleeping on a park bench in Boston Common. When he awoke he went to the apartment of an American Airlines flight attendant he knew and asked her to make breakfast.

He sought a "leave of absence" from the team in November of 1977, saying he didn't understand the public fuss that ensued and, "I don't feel like a superstar; I just feel like a normal person who quit his job." He then became player-coach of the team almost two years to the day after walking away from it with the season in progress.

Between quitting and coming back to the Celtics, he briefly drove a Boston cab and was surprised and disappointed when he picked up a reporter who had heard about what he was doing and had gone out in the streets hoping to find him.

He retired in my hotel room and unretired two years later in a Milwaukee uniform. It didn't go very well.

He attended the funeral of Red Sox great Tony Conigliaro in 1990 wearing an overcoat and a Red Sox hat. I asked him if he had actually known Tony C. He said no, they had never met. "I'm here out of respect for the family," he said. "The love and support and care they gave Tony impressed me very much. I would have to say that Tony C. was a very special sports story in Boston."

To best understand Dave Cowens it is important to know that he may have come into the NBA as uninformed as to what it was all about as anyone in league history. I suspect the international players who are now such a vital part of the NBA all have a better idea of what the NBA is than Dave Cowens did when he entered in 1970 as the fourth man chosen overall, out of a juicy NBA draft that included such luminaries as Bob Lanier, Pete Maravich, Rudy Tomjanovich, Geoff Petrie, John Johnson, and Jim McMillian in the first round, and Calvin Murphy and Nate Archibald in the second. Dan Issel and Charlie Scott would also have been high picks, but they had already signed with the ABA. Some think it was the greatest draft ever.

Many an NBA player has grown up having posters of their favorite players on their bedroom walls. Dave Cowens was not one of those kids. Raised in Newport, Kentucky, across the river from Cincinnati, he was oblivious to the existence there of Oscar Robertson and Jerry Lucas, or, for that matter, Bill Russell, Wilt Chamberlain, or any other NBA marquee player. The same was true of football and baseball players. He was never a fan of anything.

What he liked to do was play. "I never dreamed of being a pro basketball player when I was a kid," he once told me. "Being a pro player wasn't a dream come true. I wasn't a card collector. I was always open to suggestion. I was just out there grasping for straws, wondering what to do. I just migrated toward basketball. I liked it."

He went to Florida State. The school was on probation for his three varsity years and thus was not allowed to play in the NCAA tournament. It doesn't seem to have bothered him. One thing we know for sure: he didn't watch any of it on TV.

For him the NBA was a blank canvas. He didn't know or care who the other players were. Lew Alcindor? Wes Unseld? Willis Reed? Nate Thurmond? Even Wilt Chamberlain? The first time he ever saw any of them play was when he first competed against them in the NBA. He thought this was an advantage. "Instead of me wondering what these people were all about," he told me, "I decided I was going to show them what I was all about. I figured, Hey, what can I lose?"

Even in 1970 he was an undersized center. There was much initial debate as to whether a six-foot-eight-inch white center—this was an important issue—could hope to compete on a level with the larger and often better-skilled black stars of the day. Let's make it clear: Cowens never made his race an issue. Others did. The NBA is that rare American institution where a black man is automatically assumed to be the better candidate for any job position.

In his mind, he was about effort, unrelenting effort. "My attitude was, 'Let's see what these players are all about.' I knew a Wilt Chamberlain could overwhelm me on offense, but I said, 'Let's just see how hard these guys want to work.' I think they got pissed at me because I wanted to work hard. They weren't used to somebody who played the way I did. I'd be running them and after a while they'd think, The hell with this. That's intimidation, when you're in condition and you can run somebody all the time. That, to me, is true intimidation. If every time you're down-court you're right in a guy's face, if every time you're screening him out—I mean *every* time—it gets to a lot of people."

As a six-eight center he could never just show up and be effective. He had to work as hard against a Steve Patterson or Dorie Murrey as he did against Kareem Abdul-Jabbar or Bob Lanier. And that was fine with him. That type of effort, combined with a surprisingly nice jump shot, got him off to a good career start. He shared Rookie of the Year honors with Portland's Geoff Petrie as the Celtics went from thirty-four wins to forty-four in his rookie season, escalated to fifty-six, and then, in his fourth year, to sixty-eight as he was named the league's Most Valuable Player. He was averaging twenty points and fifteen rebounds a game, but he was never about the statistics. He was about making the unmakeable play or doing things no one else would even think of doing.

One night in Portland, typical Cowens hustle resulted in his jumping over the Celtics bench out of bounds. Rather than reentering the court where he had left it, he ran behind the press table before getting back into play at the other end of court by jumping over the Portland bench. Only Dave.

But the greatest Cowens play has been seen and re-seen. Every year at playoff time someone will take us back to Boston on the night of May 19, 1974, Game 6 of the finals between the Celtics and Milwaukee Bucks. In the final minute of regulation, Cowens switched out onto Oscar Robertson. This very act separated him from the pack, but he had the mobility to guard smaller players as well as the strength and spring to take on the likes of Chamberlain or Abdul-Jabbar. And how he loved these mini-challenges.

Cowens poked the ball away from the great Big O. He then began pursuit of the bouncing ball, stumbling as he approached before corralling it into his chest to complete a sensational effort that would have been beyond the capability of any other center in the league, none of whom would have found themselves ever guarding Oscar Robertson in the first place. His effort had caused an important twenty-four-second clock violation. I'm going to guess that if Dave Cowens were asked how he'd like to be remembered, he would cite this play.

There was no NBA force like him, for in addition to the box score numbers he also led the league in BODs (back on defense), GSOs (great switch-outs) and RLBs (recovering loose balls). At draft time coaches and player personnel directors would instruct their scouts to find them a "Cowens type." They never have, and they never will.

One Sunday afternoon in College Park, Maryland, he grabbed twenty-eight rebounds against the renowned Washington Bullets frontline duo of Wes Unseld and Elvin Hayes. After the game I posed a hypothetical question to Bullets coach Gene Shue. "What would happen," I inquired, "if big guys like Kareem and Bob Lanier played as hard all the time as Dave Cowens? What could they accomplish?"

"Can't happen," Shue replied. "Hustle is part of ability."

Red Auerbach had no hesitation making him a player-coach in 1978 despite the fact that he had walked away from the team two years earlier. He had returned saying that it was easier to play than not to play and no one questioned his uniquely Cowensian logic. He never considered himself a coach and was happy to relinquish the chore in favor of Bill Fitch in 1979. Larry Bird held him in such high regard that number 33 publicly declared he was not up to taking the last shot in a game as long as Dave Cowens was around.

The years of pounding took a toll on his feet and ankles, leading him to my hotel door with a retirement statement in 1980. I've never had a bigger honor than being asked to help shape that historic item.

When he made it to the Hall of Fame in 1991 he was predictably humble and emphatic about what had mattered most to him as a player. "The real turn-on for me was being able to *help*," he said. "I liked being in situations where you weren't supposed to be successful. Being back on defense with Dr. J and Bobby Jones coming at you on a two-on-one and then somehow stopping the basket from being scored. Actually *doing* it; that was my rush."

Did Dave Cowens feel he belonged in the Hall of Fame? It certainly had never been a goal. "When I started playing in high school," he said, "I never even thought of a college scholarship. In college, I never even thought about the pros. So it stands to reason that when I was playing in the NBA I never dwelled on the Hall of Fame."

But now that he really was in the Hall of Fame, how did he feel? "I feel I represent the working class of the NBA," he replied. "I'm honored they selected me, because I could name a whole lot of guys who were better than Dave Cowens."

Maybe so, but in terms of great people for a writer to cover, I'll take Dave Cowens. You can have the field.

CHAPTER 12

Time to Powder Up

You want to know the power of television? I could be in Bellingham, Washington, or Coral Gables, Florida; in Caribou, Maine, or Chula Vista, California; Cody, Wyoming, or Valdosta, Georgia, and I will probably be recognized on the street. It's certainly not because people know me as someone who has spent forty-six years writing for the *Boston Globe*. The reason I am recognized approximately 350 out of 365 days in any given year is because I've been fortunate enough to have been on national television for the better part of the last twenty-five years.

Even before I began doing shows on ESPN, though, I learned about the impact of television. It doesn't matter if the show in question is in prime time or not; somebody is watching, even if it's two in the morning.

For a brief period in my life, from September 1982 until April 1984, my primary paycheck was drawn from television as I was a full-time employee of WCVB, the Boston ABC affiliate. I covered stories and then put together, with the able assistance of a producer and a tape editor, what is known in TV as a "package"—a video backed by voice-over and interviews, or "sound bites." They lasted anywhere from a minute and half to, on rare occasions, four or five minutes if the story was special. I also did live shots from game locations.

The job had belonged to Clark Booth, an enormously talented man who had drifted into television from the world of print and then distinguished himself as a brilliant observer of everything, especially sports and politics. He had a sharp wit and was a magnetic broadcast presence with a voice and delivery I would gladly have written a large check to obtain, were that possible.

We were friends. And he was very persuasive. When he decided in the summer of 1982 that he wanted out of sports, he asked me if I'd be interested in succeeding him in the WCVB sports department. I had never once considered leaving the *Globe*, or the print world in general. I had been an occasional local TV guest starting in the midseventies, and I had even done color for the local Catholic school basketball tournament on the public station, but I had zero interest in making TV my life.

But Clark Booth hit me at the right time. I was vulnerable. We had just lost a great columnist and a truly wonderful man in Ray Fitzgerald. Cancer. Nuff said. He was in his early fifties. It was a huge loss to anyone who treasured fine writing and gentlemanly behavior.

For many years I had assumed I was in line to be a columnist when a vacancy occurred, having been one temporarily in 1976 and on other occasions. Having a column has always been the highest calling for a newspaper writer. A column is personal; it requires one to take stands and create a special connection with readers. So when Ray Fitzgerald died I naturally assumed I would get his column. But as my wife Elaine always says, "Assume nothing." The column was given to Mike Madden, a fine writer but not someone I had regarded as a rival for this job. I was not happy. In fact, I was feeling pretty sorry for myself. And that's when Clark Booth began lobbying me to take over his position, which he called "the best job in town."

It didn't take long for me to say yes. It also helped that I'd be getting a decent raise. Relatively quickly, though, I realized that while I could do it, it wasn't me. The essential problem was that, as opposed to print, television news is a highly collaborative medium. If a writer has an assignment, he or she just picks up a notebook (and/or recording device) and goes to work. TV, on the other hand, involves a team.

The process started with an idea for that day's story. The reporter was assigned a cameraperson, and there were only so many to go around, so one had to coordinate the availability of the interview subject with that of the cameraperson, who may have been concerned about the battery life of his camera at the interview site. Taking in a backup battery was a pain because they were heavy, so he gambled he wouldn't need a new one. If he lost the gamble, he had to return to the car for a battery. The interview subject, possibly a coach who had already let you know he had a busy schedule and was going out of his way to make time for you, got fidgety. The vibes, which may have been good at the start, weren't so good anymore.

Once the interview was done, you screened your tape back at the station, stopwatch in hand to identify the spots on the tape where you wanted to use sound. You wrote your script, inserting the letters "SOT" (sound on tape) where you proposed to insert a sound bite.

Somewhere in here you would have made a request for an edit room. All editors were not created equal. In fact, usually one or two stood out and were generally available only to the talent highest on the station's food chain. Anyway, you were assigned to a certain editor for a certain time. The time came. As in a doctor's office, people could run late. But there was a finite amount of time before the telecast, so you may have had significantly less time to put together your piece than you expected. What you once envisioned as a nicely crafted piece became the TV equivalent of meatball surgery.

I would say this was the situation at least half the time. In the course of an average week's work I was pleased with my product perhaps once or twice, seldom more.

Live shots are tricky and require intense concentration. I remember one time I was live at Boston Garden prior to a hockey game. As the countdown was being made and they were preparing to throw it to me, my mind went blank somewhere around the ten-second mark. I remember thinking, Where am I? What's going on here? But somewhere around the two-second mark things mysteriously kicked back in. It was a very scary feeling.

The people I worked with were great. The anchorman when I started was Don Gillis, properly nicknamed "the Dean." He had practically invented the TV sportscast. When he introduced my packages you would have thought the Emmy was going to be delivered to me before I left the building. My issues were never with the people. They were with the nature of the job itself.

And there was something else. I was used to being viewed as an authority, especially on basketball. That feeling was pretty intoxicating. But the longer I remained in local TV, getting a brief ten seconds or so of face time while delivering the end-of-the-package stand-up, the less I thought I was being regarded as a sports authority. Not everyone watching the telecast was a sports fan and not all sports fans were watching channel 5. I was becoming just a generic TV face. This really hit me when a woman walked up to me while I was out shopping with my wife and said, "Shouldn't I know you?"

The entire mentality of television was different from anything I had ever known in the newspaper world. I was paid for working five *days* a week. If I covered a Celtics, Bruins, or Red Sox game at night, I could put in for overtime. That was very nice, but it always struck me as more than slightly ridiculous.

But the one thing I really did enjoy about working in television was the team feeling involved in working on an hour newscast. I found myself rooting hard for everyone to do well. You don't get that feeling on a newspaper because television is immediate. If I wrote a story for the *Globe*, it wouldn't be seen in those pre-website days until the following morning. But many's the time someone in TV finishes his or her piece minutes, or even seconds, before it is aired. It's a daily high-wire act, and people at home have no idea what has gone into the piece they're watching. Live shots are especially harrowing. So much can go wrong, and everyone has a feeling of immense relief and satisfaction when the newscast is done and everything has gone off perfectly.

After I was gone from the *Globe* for a few weeks, I got an interesting phone call from my old sports editor Vince Doria, asking if I would be able to write two columns a week for him on the side. I said one was feasible, so for the last seventeen of the nineteen months I worked at WCVB, I went to the *Globe* office most Monday mornings and pounded out a column before heading to the studio. I would frequently stop by the office of the paper's editor, Tom Winship, to say hello. Winship had been out of town when I made my decision to leave and had chastised me for not waiting until he had come back. He said he would never have let me go.

On the Monday before Thanksgiving 1983, approximately fourteen months into my TV career, I paid Tom Winship my weekly visit. He pounded his fist on his desk and shouted, "Goddamn it! Why don't you come back?"

"You know," I said, "I really have been thinking about that. But I can't come marching back in here, just like that."

"Don't you worry about that," he said. "I'll take care of it."

The night before Thanksgiving I received a phone call from Vince Doria. "I talked to Winship," he said. "Can you come in to see me on Friday?"

We met, and I said, "Okay, you sure this is okay?" And he said, "Hey, you can never have too many all-stars."

Aw, shucks.

Now I had to tell the people at WCVB what was going on. I was in the second year of a two-year contract, and while they didn't raise any serious objections to my departure, they couldn't let me go until they found a replacement. They found their man in fairly short order. However, he, too, was bound to a contract, and, unlike me, he was not enjoying good relations with his employer. In fact, they despised him as an employee more than they appreciated his unquestioned genius as a TV talent. So they were not about to let him go so much as a split second before his contract had expired.

The name of the company: CNN. The name of the TV talent in question: Keith Olbermann.

I was a lame duck for five months, not an ideal situation. I did my best, but I was always looking ahead, aching to get back where I belonged—in the newspaper. On April 15, 1984, I cohosted the pre–Boston Marathon live show, interviewing, among others, Boston mayor Ray Flynn, a noted running enthusiast. The show was over at twelve noon and that was the end of my Boston TV career. The next day I walked into the *Globe*; picked up a machine called a Portabubble, by which we transmitted copy then; and went to Detroit for Game 1 of the Knicks-Pistons best-of-five first-round series. I wasn't the beat man. I was a Big Picture guy, covering the NBA at large and writing features while doing occasional columns. The beat was in great shape with Dan Shaughnessy, the man I had lobbied for to take over the job when I left for television. During the NBA finals in the next two years, I would witness perhaps the most intense incarnation of the long-running bicoastal rivalry between the Celtics and Lakers.

CHAPTER 13

The Glorious NBA

Magic Johnson's arrival in the fall of 1979 had a similar impact on the Lakers as Bird's had on the Celtics, though the Lakers had been a better team pre-Magic than the Celtics had pre-Bird. Magic pumped life back into Kareem Abdul-Jabbar, and they (and Magic's amazing Game 6) led the Lakers to the championship in 1980. Injuries derailed them in 1981, they won the title back in 1982, and then they lost it to the 76ers in 1983 when injuries prevented them from mounting a fair finals challenge to one of the great one-season NBA teams ever, the Moses Malone–led 76ers.

The Lakers were loaded with stars, but they were defined by three people: Abdul-Jabbar, Magic, and coach Pat Riley. The basketball world was not prepared for the tour de force that was Pat Riley. The son of a baseball lifer and minor-league manager, the Schenectady, New York–bred Riley had become an all-time Kentucky Wildcat icon before carving out a nine-year NBA career as a scrappy backup, neither a true point guard nor a shooting guard. His career concluded after he was left off the playoff roster by the 1976 Suns.

He was out of basketball for a while, working as a carpenter, before he joined the legendary Chick Hearn in the Laker broadcast booth. From there he went to the bench when Paul Westhead succeeded Jack McKinney after the latter sustained a serious bike-riding injury. And he was the right man in the right place at the right time when Magic Johnson led a palace coup against Westhead twelve games into the 1981–82 season. A lot has been said and written about Magic's role in this affair, but it was absolutely the right thing to do. Magic performed a public service for the Lakers and their fans. Westhead was no longer tenable and he gave them Pat Riley, who turned out to be a Hall of Fame coach.

Riley had obviously done a lot of reading and thinking, and he shaped the template for modern NBA coaching. He had a new mode of expression. He introduced the word "focus" into the NBA dialogue. He made us realize that the way to achieve success was to go far beyond the X's and O's. He talked about how "hidden agendas" could get in the way of a team achieving success. And he broke down the game in a new way.

Most games, Riley claimed, were decided by the outcome of what he called "skirmishes." The game wasn't an all-out war. It was a matter of gaining the upper hand in the small segments that would determine the game's outcome. A first-quarter "skirmish" when one team went on a 10–2 run might prove crucial. The game might then be played evenly until the fourth quarter, when another "skirmish" created a 7–0 run that either put the game away or drew a team level. Winning the majority of these key moments, night after night, would lead to success. This all made perfect sense, but no one had ever heard the game of basketball analyzed in this manner.

Riley had a distinct personal style. His wardrobe was scrutinized. His swept-back hair became the model for the Michael Douglas character in the movie *Wall Street*. He captured the pulse and pace of Los Angeles and presided over an enterprise nicknamed "Showtime." A man whose time and place had come, he was ready to capitalize on his opportunity.

He could also coach. He may have been exquisitely dressed and well coiffed, but there was nothing soft about Pat Riley. Larry Bird would say that no team made life more difficult for him than the Lakers, and not just because Michael Cooper was the best individual defender he had ever encountered. It was because Riley's defensive schemes were by far the best.

"He was a great game coach," Bird maintains today. "When he'd call a time-out, you knew he was coming with something different. He might steer you to the baseline one time or the middle the next. You always had to be on your toes."

The 76ers were never the same after their spectacular 1982–83 season.

They remained a fifty-win team for a few more seasons, but they were not serious championship threats. Beginning with the 1983–84 season the Lakers and Celtics would dominate the next four years, meeting for the championship in 1984, 1985, and 1987, the Celtics winning the first (and in 1986 over Houston), the Lakers winning the last two.

David Stern succeeded Larry O'Brien as commissioner in January of 1984 and he was presented with the greatest housewarming gift imaginable when the Larry Bird–led Celtics and Magic Johnson–led Lakers met for the 1984 championship. This was year five in their careers. The individual rivalry that had begun with the 1979 Indiana State–Michigan State NCAA championship game had taken root, and the teams had once again established themselves as the premier franchises in the league, L.A. with titles in 1980 and 1982, intersected by the Celtics' win in 1981.

The big addition to the Celtics prior to the 1983–84 season was guard Dennis Johnson, whom Auerbach had obtained from Phoenix for center Rick Robey with draft picks going back and forth. A fearless physical guard able to masquerade as point guard on a team whose offense revolved around Bird, he was also obtained in the hopes he could deter Philadelphia guard Andrew Toney, who had terrorized Boston guards since entering the league in 1980.

Los Angeles countered with an excellent rookie guard, Byron Scott, who replaced veteran Norm Nixon. The Lakers cruised into the finals, encountering no more than mild resistance from Kansas City, Dallas, and Phoenix. The New York Knicks, coached by Hubie Brown and led by Bernard King, then the league's reigning scoring machine, made the Celtics work for it, down to a classic Bird-showcase Game 7 in Boston. Larry's thirty-nine-point, twelve-rebound, ten-assist masterpiece settled the matter.

The Celtics hosted the Lakers to start the finals, but Los Angeles rolled to a stunning road victory in Game 1 and came within an errant James Worthy pass of taking a 2–0 lead. But Gerald Henderson's steal and layup forced an overtime and the Celtics escaped to L.A. with the series tied.

After the Lakers' big victory in Game 3, Bird declared that what his team needed more than anything else were "twelve heart transplants."

Game 4 was a mini-epic, with Magic committing a big turnover and Bird, who finished with twenty-nine points and twenty-one rebounds, hitting the game-winning turnaround. But the really big news was the third-quarter takedown on a sneak-away of L.A.'s Kurt Rambis by Boston's Kevin McHale, someone not noted for overt aggression. The tone of the entire series seemed to shift right there, and I wouldn't be surprised if that was the moment when Pat Riley vowed never to have a team of his out-toughed again.

Game 5 may have been the weirdest night ever in Celtics history. A June heat wave meant the game-time temperature in the unair-conditioned Boston Garden was 97 degrees. The Lakers did not take very well to the conditions, but Bird was unfazed, scoring thirty-four points on fifteen-for-twenty shooting while grabbing seventeen rebounds. He then said it was no big deal, that it was hotter in the summer back home in French Lick.

The Lakers won easily in Game 6, so it came down to a Game 7 in Boston and a hostile takeover enforced by Cedric Maxwell, who, after telling the team to "jump on [his] back," scored twenty-four points while abusing Worthy. Danny Ainge came off the bench to hit some big second-quarter jumpers and the Celtics won, 111–102.

They might as well have fast-forwarded themselves to the 1985 finals, because the Celtics won sixty-three and the Lakers won sixty-two the following year and they were indeed back for a rematch. In one significant difference, though, Bird had struggled with elbow and back issues throughout the season, and the Lakers had definitely gotten tougher by adding burly swingman Mitch Kupchak.

The Celtics annihilated L.A. in Game 1, 148–114, the infamous "Memorial Day Massacre," in which veteran Scott Wedman went eleven-for-eleven. After the game, thirty-eight-year-old Kareem Abdul-Jabbar, who had only twelve points and three rebounds, apologized to his teammates for his bad performance. He stewed in his hotel room from Monday night until Game 2 game time on Thursday evening, and when they threw the ball up he was ready, scoring thirty points and fighting for seventeen rebounds, the most he had pulled down in ten years.

For the rest of the series he brought his A-game out of the Way-Back Machine, and the Lakers put the series away by winning Game 6 in

Boston, the first time the Celtics had ever been forced to watch someone else celebrate a championship on their hallowed parquet floor. It was also the first time a Lakers team had ever beaten the Celtics in the finals, after eight prior losses.

Kareem, a New York–bred baseball fan, said, "I feel like Johnny Podres," referring to the Dodger pitcher who had brought Brooklyn its first and only World Series title with a Game 7 victory in Yankee Stadium back in 1955. Kareem was named both the series MVP and the *Sports Illustrated* Sportsman of the Year.

In January 1986, Peter Gammons, who had left the *Globe* for *Sports Illustrated* once before, answered the call a second time. He would be leaving the Red Sox beat. Dan Shaughnessy, whose first love has always been baseball, saw his big chance. He wanted to succeed Gammons, and I could certainly empathize: I had been there myself, nine years before. It was a no-brainer for sports editor Vince Doria. Shaughnessy was the obvious choice.

This left the Celtics beat empty in midseason, and it was a highly attractive assignment. These were the 1985–86 Celtics, a team of marauders. It was starting to look like the very best Celtics team of all, which was really saying something.

I didn't raise my hand at first as I was very comfortable in my big-picture/feature role. Vince Doria actually interviewed a couple of people, but he didn't offer anyone the job. All I remember now is that I told him, "Okay, I'll take it. But just 'til the end of the season. Then you can get someone else." The plan was that Dan would finish out a West Coast trip and I would pick up the coverage when the team returned home to play one of their three regular-season games scheduled that year in Hartford. In the end, I was on the beat for the next two and a half seasons.

That first game back from the road, the Celtics easily defeated the Indiana Pacers, with Larry Bird putting up a routine 30-11 12 triple-double, and it was all very entertaining. Two nights later they went to New York, again winning easily, and this time the man putting on the show was Bill Walton, who had fifteen points and fourteen rebounds in twenty-seven minutes. It was veeeery entertaining. I was thinking, Hey, this team really is fun.

If I didn't send Peter Gammons a thank-you note for triggering this chain of events, I should have. I had loved covering my beer-drinking companions in the 1970s. I very much enjoyed those first three Bird years. But I had *never* enjoyed covering basketball as much as I would reporting on this truly spectacular team. For the 1985–86 Celtics rendered meaningless the concept of the meaningless game.

Writing is about two things, in my view: confidence and rhythm. When I came back to the Celtics beat I had just turned forty and had been exposed to NBA coverage for seventeen years. I cared deeply about both writing and basketball, and now I was being given the best vehicle to marry those two interests that anyone would ever have. If I couldn't get excited about this opportunity I really should have said good-bye and gone off to do something else.

No one can say with any certainty which was the very best team of all-time. I'm sure the 1951–52 Minneapolis Lakers were pretty good, but I'm guessing that only Jim Pollard, a way-ahead-of-his-time player, could have competed athletically with modern counterparts. George Mikan, I'm sorry to say, would not make a team today. I know what the 1961–62 Celtics, the 1964–65 Celtics, the 1966–67 76ers, the 1969–70 Knicks, the 1971–72 Lakers, the 1977–78 Trail Blazers (of Walton and Maurice Lucas, who started off 50-10 before injury set in), the 1982–83 76ers, the 1986–87 Lakers, the 1989–90 Pistons, and the 1995–96 Bulls were all about. They are all historically significant teams, and three of them won more regular-season games than the 1985–86 Celtics, who were 67–15. But I would happily take the chances of that Celtics team against any of them. I think their best was the best of all time, and the single biggest reason was the simple fact that only that Celtics team was able to bring a healthy Bill Walton off the bench.

The front line of Bird, Robert Parish, and Kevin McHale was historic, and the backcourt of Dennis Johnson, Danny Ainge, and Jerry Sichting was superb. Augmenting that with a Bill Walton healthy enough to play eighty-two regular-season and eighteen playoff games, and with Scott Wedman, another former All-Star, made this truly a dream team.

Watching Walton bound off the bench that year to team up with Larry Bird was an orgasmic experience for Boston fans—the greatest (and smartest) forward of all time matching basketball wits with the man whose game demonstrated more mastery of the center position than anyone ever. I have said and written the following many times, always, as is the case now, when I am cold sober: If planet Earth were playing a winner-take-all game of basketball, the loser going into servitude for all eternity, my first pick of any player who has ever laced up a sneaker would be a (key word) *healthy* Bill Walton. I say that full-well knowing that Bill Russell is the most decorated winner in the history of North American sport.

No center has ever brought better depth and balance to the most important position on the court. Bill Walton was a control tower through which you could run both your team offense and your defense. The better offensive centers were not as good on defense. The better defensive centers (and there haven't been many) were not as good on offense. He was also one of the handful of best passing centers of all time.

What I didn't fully realize until I had the pleasure of watching him every night was his extraordinary rebounding technique. I had never seen anyone with his sense of timing. He had an amazing knack of whisking the ball off the rim at the exact instant when it may actually have constituted goaltending. Picture someone sweeping the crumbs off the table into a cupped hand. I've never seen anything quite like it. And his ability to maneuver himself while in the air in order to get off an outlet pass was remarkable. He thought fast break first, last, and always. That's how he played at Helix High in San Diego, then at UCLA, and that's how he performed in the NBA, whenever he was healthy enough to play.

Red Auerbach had picked Walton up in exchange for Cedric Maxwell, a great player who had fallen out of favor in Boston not long after his Game 7 performance against the Lakers had delivered Boston a championship in 1984. He injured his knee in the 1984–85 season and some questioned his recuperation diligence. I knew it was not going to end well for him in Boston after Bird himself told me something interesting in a phone conversation while I happened to be standing in the living room of his French Lick house talking to his mother.

"Bob," he said, "Max doesn't want to play for us anymore."

Maxwell has always disputed the idea that he wasn't working hard enough to come back, and Bird has never said a bad public word about his old teammate, but I know what he told me and I was not surprised when Auerbach exiled him to the Clippers following the 1985 finals loss to the Lakers. For their part, the Clippers were exasperated with Walton, who was always hurt. When Walton arrived in Boston he had never played a full NBA season, not even while being named the league MVP in 1978, when he suited up for only sixty-five games. He had played in just 52 percent (169 of 328) of available games during his four years with the Clippers. The idea of his making a meaningful contribution was an abstract.

But the Hoop God was smiling down on both Walton and the Celtics. He participated in every preseason practice, even the second of early camp two-a-days, and the only two regular-season games he missed (one with a broken nose and the other with the flu) had nothing to do with his famously fragile lower limbs. When Walton entered a home game, the Boston press corps began smirking. We all knew that at some point he and Bird were going to victimize someone with a classic give-and-go. They could endlessly vary the angle of entry and the timing of the pass so as to be close to unstoppable.

No man on earth was happier than Bill Walton during the first four and a half months of the 1985–86 season. He was as healthy as he'd been since high school. He was playing with Larry Bird and for the team of his idol, Bill Russell, and in front of nightly sellout crowds that were completely hip to what he was doing. The revelry subsided on the night of March 14, 1986. He was driving the left baseline when Atlanta's massive, and aptly named, Tree Rollins blocked his shot. Walton's right wrist was hyperextended.

Though he never missed a game, and continued to make significant contributions to the Celtics' cause right through the clinching finals game against Houston, he was never quite the same again. Aware of his balance because he was afraid of falling, he did not play with quite the same degree of aggression.

Another key element in 1985–86 sat on the bench: that team had the perfect coach. The last thing the club needed was a taskmaster; what they did need was someone who would let them play and add a suggestion here or there that would make a difference, someone who wasn't going to require public credit. They needed K. C. Jones. And they had him.

K. C. Jones was the antithesis of a detail man. I can testify that he knew less about league personnel or league minutiae than any of his peers. I believe that if you had sat all the coaches down, handed them a yellow legal pad, and simply asked them to name as many players in the league as they could, K. C. Jones would have had the fewest names listed. I used to sit with Bill Fitch on the bus or in the coffee shop and talk NBA. He always knew what had happened the night before. He used to get on the phone in the wee small hours, chatting with some like-minded coaching buddies. He knew where every player in the league had gone to college. If K. C. Jones went to bed late, he hadn't been on the phone chewing up NBA gossip. He might, however, have been singing in a piano bar. He had a terrific voice. If he sang "You're Nobody 'Til Somebody Loves You" once, he sang it hundreds of times, coast-to-coast.

A beloved Celtic, a defensive specialist on the great 1960s teams, he had a capacity for making veterans want to play for him. Walton, the biggest John Wooden fan who has ever lived, was also a K. C. fan, and the two coaches couldn't have been farther apart in their approach to the game.

I always felt K. C. made three very important decisions that year. The first was to call off practice at the right time during the playoffs. The second was to reinsert Bill Walton into Game 4 of the finals against Houston, allowing him, and not Robert Parish, to finish the close game. Walton made a key block and converted a vital offensive rebound. The Celtics won in six games, Bird was the finals MVP, but Walton made the season truly special.

I can't remember the third.

The time would come when the Celtics would need a different approach and K. C. would not be the right man for the job. But the Celtics should be very grateful that K. C. Jones was available to them for the 1985–86 season.

I will always believe that the only reason the 1985–86 Celtics did not become the first NBA squad to win seventy games is that it never occurred to them to make a push for it. The Walton Era, alas, lasted one year. In classic Bill Walton fashion he injured himself riding an exercise bike the following fall and was able to play in only ten regular-season and twelve playoff games. That was the end of his career. The Lakers had picked up their own Triple A version of Bill Walton in Mychal Thompson that year, and it probably represented the difference between the two teams as Los Angeles defeated the Celtics in six games for the championship. I think a confrontation between the 1985–86 Celtics and the 1986–87 Lakers is the Greatest Series That Never Was.

Ten days after the Celtics' victory over Houston, on June 18, 1986, I was backing out of my driveway when my sixteen-year-old son, Keith, came running out of the house.

"Dad! Dad! Len Bias is dead!" he cried out.

He had just heard on the radio that Len Bias, only hours into being the first-round pick of the world-champion Celtics and the second pick in the entire 1986 draft, was gone. Instead of the *Globe* office, I was now heading to Boston Garden.

Incredible. Impossible. Who could believe such a thing? Fifteen hours earlier I had been one of his inquisitors on radio. He was wearing a nice gray suit, newly purchased for the occasion, I'm sure, and there was a green Celtics baseball hat perched on his head. His father stood there beaming, as you would expect.

And now he was dead?

It turned out to be a sad, ugly story. He had flown back to Washington and done some partying with friends. Cocaine was involved. We would learn that Len Bias had died of a cocaine overdose. Fingers would be pointed in every direction. It was his first and only time.

No, it wasn't.

Len Bias had been a too-good-to-be-true draft pick for the Boston Celtics to begin with. They had the number two pick in the 1986 draft because general manager Jan Volk, Red Auerbach's protégé and successor, had traded guard Gerald Henderson to Seattle in 1984 for Seattle's 1986 first-round pick and the Sonics had cooperated by going 31-51 before finishing second in the lottery, then in its second year of existence. The obvious top picks were North Carolina center Brad Daugherty and Maryland's star Bias. Cleveland had the first pick at the conclusion of some wild trading, and they chose Daugherty. The champion Celtics were very pleased to take Len Bias.

I know I was excited. In addition to the many times I had watched the six-eight forward play on television, I had also lucked out by being in Duke's Cameron Indoor Stadium on a night when Bias dropped forty powerful points on the Blue Devils. Indeed, on two separate occasions Mike Krzyzewski later told me that the two toughest opponents during his time as Duke head coach had been Michael Jordan and Len Bias.

Bias had a perfect NBA body. A power forward with a small forward's mobility, he had a reliable midrange jumper and excellent inside moves. He could put the ball on the floor and take it to the hole. On paper, he represented an almost sinful addition to a team that was boasting of having the best frontcourt ever assembled, and his death would haunt the Celtics for years.

How good was Len Bias, really? I believe he would have been at least a James Worthy–level All-Star performer, and a key transition figure as the Big Three aged. He wouldn't have had the impact of a Bird, Magic, or Jordan, but he would have been a regular All-Star Game participant and a major component of a championship team. If Bias had lived, it's very reasonable to think the Celtics would have won it all again in 1987. They were a man or two short and they still went to the finals. They might also have won it all in 1988, when they were eliminated by the surging Pistons while again a man or two shy. *Might have.* Who knows?

Sooner or later a deal or lineup adjustment would have had to be made. Like McHale before him, Bias would have had to play more. McHale had been accommodated by trading Cedric Maxwell to the Clippers; would McHale himself have been traded? Hard to imagine. Would Robert Parish? Equally hard to imagine. Would Bias himself have been traded? Regardless, in the short term he would have had a major impact, and in the 1988–89 season, when Bird only played six games after wrecking his ankles, he would have been essential.

Len Bias's death devastated Red Auerbach. Red had been a Washington, D.C., resident since the early 1940s and he was partial to local basketball products. Bias was born and raised in nearby Landover, Maryland. He played at Maryland for Lefty Driesell, and Red was fond of Driesell. The idea of a local kid, trained by Lefty, carrying his team into the next era of Celtics greatness appealed greatly to Red. He found it very hard to let go. He would talk about the effect Bias's death had on the Celtics for years.

There were also enormous ramifications for the University of Maryland. Bias's death wound up costing Lefty Driesell his job. He had told us in a radio interview, "Leonard's only vice is ice cream." I'm sure he believed it.

Four months later, I was back in Houston, where the Celtics were playing an exhibition game with the Rockets. When the game was over I rushed to a bar I knew in order to see the conclusion of Game 6 of the Red Sox–New York Mets World Series. The Sox were up, three games to two, once more close to their first championship since 1918. I heard Dave Henderson's go-ahead homer on the car radio. When I arrived at the bar I struck up a conversation with a couple and said that when the game was over, and the Red Sox were the champs, I'd be buying.

The on-field happenings in the bottom of the tenth have been recounted uncountable times and are now legendary, though at the time they were just unbelievable. When the ball went through Bill Buckner's legs, I excused myself, saying, "I've got to go," and left. If that couple ever identifies itself, I'd be happy to honor my promise. But I trust they understand why I was no longer in a chatty mood that particular evening.

I continued covering the Celtics for two more years. The 1986–87 season was memorable because Kevin McHale elevated the art of pivot play as very few centers, and no forward, ever had. Kevin had been an acknowledged star for years, but at age twenty-nine everything came together.

Once he got the ball, the opponent was at the mercy of what Hubie Brown would call "his bank vault of moves." These included, but by no means were restricted to, a jump hook, turnaround jumpers in either direction, and an up-and-under "swinging gate" move.

No one ever snaked along the baseline to curl in layups from ridiculous angles the way Kevin McHale did, and in midcareer he also developed a reliable faceup jumper. And he could always make his free throws, making him ever more effective at game's end.

He had outplayed every rival forward, and many centers, that year when his career took a turn south on the night of March 11. Toward the end of a thirty-six-point game against the Suns, Phoenix forward Larry Nance accidentally stepped on McHale's foot, causing a stress fracture.

He played through it, but the injury became a huge playoff issue (with Bird telling the media at one point in the finals that if he were Kevin he'd go home) and he was never the same for the rest of a career that wouldn't end until the 1992–93 season.

McHale did something that year that has never been done again: he became the first person to shoot 60 percent from the floor (.604) and 80 percent from the line (.836). The following year he came within three hundredths of a point of doing it again when he replicated the .604 but only shot .797 from the line.

He was a perfect complement to Bird, enabling Larry to rack up assists, but also guarding many a difficult rival who might have been Bird's responsibility were Kevin not so incredibly versatile defensively. He was six eleven with an absurd wingspan, so he was able to effectively guard players who were both significantly smaller (the likes of six-three Adrian Dantley) or taller (the giant seven-four Ralph Sampson). I'd go so far as to say he saved Larry a lot of defensive embarrassment.

He had a loosey-goosey personality that often led people to the mistaken conclusion he was not sufficiently competitive. He would laugh and joke until the moment the referee threw the ball up, which some people, Bird included, never understood. He was one player Bill Fitch could not intimidate, which had become evident during his very first night in a Celtics uniform.

McHale had been a rookie holdout, so much so that he had actually gone to Italy during contract negotiations. When the agreement was finalized, he was flown back from Milan and taken directly to the Celtics' night practice at Hellenic College, in Brookline, Massachusetts. Among other things, Fitch had famously joked that if McHale didn't like the Boston offer, "he could go eat spaghetti," and wanted to teach the rookie some sort of lesson. As tired as he must have been, McHale was thrown into the scrimmage, and the Celtics found out immediately that he could block shots with both hands. They also learned that, unlike 99 percent of young big men, he did not automatically dribble once or twice after catching the ball in the low post. He kept his arms high and did not bring the ball down where smaller players could swipe at it—a skill some people in the Hall of Fame never mastered.

Fitch never could break him. No matter how much the coach blustered or tried to assert his authority, McHale would forever be the kid sitting in the back row of the class, throwing spitballs against the blackboard when the teacher turned his or her back. By comparison, he loved playing for K. C. Jones.

The third member of the great Boston Big Three was Robert Parish. If McHale was Gehrig to Bird's Ruth, what, then, was Parish? George Harrison to Bird's McCartney and McHale's Lennon?

Robert Parish played exceptionally well and kept his mouth exceptionally shut for a you-gotta-be-kidding-me twenty-two years, the best fourteen of which were spent with the Celtics, and wound up participating in more games—1,611—than anyone else. It would be interesting to know what his postgame words-per-game ratio was.

To say he was a consistent offensive force is to diminish the concept. In one thirteen-year stretch, his shooting percentage never dipped under .535, and when it did, at age forty, it "slumped" all the way to .491. He wasn't all about dunks and tips either, as is the case with the gaudy shooting percentages posted by many a big man. Parish combined a devastating turnaround jumper (taken with such uncommon force that often his follow-through momentum took him out of bounds in front of startled members of both teams), a jump hook, a nice little running hook, and, yes, some dunks, many of them at the end of fast breaks countless other centers would never have been involved with.

He and Bird were one of the great pick-and-roll duos of all time. He rebounded well, protected the rim effectively, did his job, and then went home. Much to the Celtics' benefit, he intuitively understood the team's star-power pecking order. On many a team he would have been the Man, and he might even have been the best player in the history of some clubs. As far as I'm concerned, he was an all-time top ten center.

My professional life would have been incomplete had I missed those two and a half years covering the Celtics. And I was prepared to keep going, perhaps as long as the Big Three stayed intact, when I was taken off the beat prior to the 1988–89 season.

I had a book coming out with Larry Bird and my boss, *Globe* sports editor Don Skwar, felt we needed to honor a "conflict of interest" spirit.

But I knew something *Globe* readers didn't: they weren't going to lose anything. I was going to be succeeded by Jackie MacMullan. A lot of them were shocked two or three years down the road when they found out her birth certificate name was Jacqueline, not John.

CHAPTER 14

"I'll Decide"

From 1950 until his death in 2006, Arnold "Red" Auerbach was the living embodiment of the Boston Celtics. On any list of twentieth-century larger-than-life public figures, he would have to be included. He was in charge in every situation, as I discovered on a certain day at the end of my first year on the beat.

The NBA draft was a different proposition in 1970. Television? Ha! It was a nationwide conference call, held the day after the 1969–70 regular season had ended. In the case of the Celtics, the affair was held in Red Auerbach's Boston Garden office. The small corps of local press—the term "media" had yet to attain its current stature—sat on folding chairs. Forget about elaborate draft camps or working out guys. You had done your scouting. You had talked to your basketball friends. And now you were ready for the draft. There was a small squawk box on Red's desk. There were no big boards, only what few papers Red and his assistant general manager Jeff Cohen had available with the names of potential draftees.

Red Auerbach was also ready for something else. No sooner did I, twenty-four-year-old Bob Ryan, fresh from my first season covering the team for the *Globe*, walk through the door than the Great Man bellowed, "Ryan! I ought to cut your balls off!"

It's easy to see why I remember my first NBA draft, isn't it?

My crime was a predraft piece I had written in which I suggested that the 1962 selection of John Havlicek had not necessarily been a pure Auerbach call, that he had been put onto the Ohio State star by Bill Mokray, then a renowned statistician who had been enshrined in the

Naismith Memorial Basketball Hall of Fame as a contributor. But if Red had been somewhat simpatico with Mokray then, he had soured on him in the ensuing years. While implying that Red had not made his own choice was insulting, writing that he had been advised by Mokray, of all people, was an even more serious crime.

I don't recall what I said to defend myself, but the little crisis passed. I don't know if Red remembered the interview I'd had with him four years earlier at Boston College. As I was to learn over the course of a relationship that lasted for the next thirty-six years, Red could be very charming. And one thing was always constant: he was absolutely, positively never, ever, ever dull.

Some people reach the point in their life when they have achieved what matters to them and are sufficiently comfortable in their own skin to say or do whatever they wish. I suspect Red Auerbach reached that stage when he was about eleven. The man I knew from 1970 until his death in 2006 was as self-confident and sure of his place in life as anyone I have ever known.

Red Auerbach grew up a Brooklyn gym rat. He always liked to point out that he was second-team All-Brooklyn in high school because that was better than being All-State somewhere else. But he never made a mark in New York after that. He went to George Washington University in the nation's capital and coached at the high school level before joining the navy during World War II. When the Basketball Association of America was formed in 1946, he became, at twenty-nine, the first coach of the Washington Capitols, talking his way into the job by assuring owner, Mike Uline, that he could get ballplayers thanks to his connections from three years in the navy.

Auerbach spent three years in Washington before taking over the Tri-Cities Blackhawks in 1949. He became infuriated with owner Ben Kerner after he traded six-eight center John Mahnken, an Auerbach favorite, to, of all teams, the Boston Celtics, informing Auerbach, who was on the road, by telegram. The day after the Hawks were eliminated in the playoffs, Red walked into Kerner's office and quit, and the next several months were the only time in a sixty-year span when he was not associated in some form with professional basketball.

When the Celtics were in need of a coach for the 1950–51 season, team owner Walter Brown consulted with more knowledgeable basketball people than he, and the name that he consistently heard was that of the thirty-two-year-old Auerbach. He hired him, and history would be made.

Red and I had our occasional problems, because as much as I admired and, I'm not afraid to admit, loved him, I was still a media guy and he was always the kosher godfather of the Boston Celtics. He was, first and foremost, an interview subject. So he was not pleased when I wrote a column concerning the 1975 preseason holdouts of John Havlicek and Paul Silas in which I included the following passage: "Auerbach's behavior through all this has been alternately childish and devious. He lied when he said neither man said he wouldn't be at camp unless he were signed. He was informed several times, including once within the two weeks that camp opened, that neither Havlicek nor Silas would report to camp without a new, signed contract. He lied when he said Havlicek had never held out before. In 1972 Havlicek reported to camp four days late under similar circumstances."

I had that one nailed. Havlicek and Silas were both friends of mine, and I had spoken to both of them directly on several occasions.

Red's response was precise. "Nobody has ever called me a liar before," he said. Note that he didn't say he hadn't been at odds with the truth. He just said that no one had ever before pointed out something like that about him in public.

Things were a bit frosty between us for a while. But the day came when I needed to elicit an off-season response on another matter, this one involving Jo Jo White. I placed a call to his Washington home. His wife, Dorothy, answered. I asked for Red. She said she'd go get him. After what seemed like a long wait, during which I convinced myself he would never speak to me again, he came to the phone. I posed my question, he answered, and that was that. Time had worked its charm. We never had another problem.

Red was, among other things, a great employee, although I doubt he viewed himself in that light. By this I mean he was completely devoted to the concept of the Boston Celtics. Owners would come and go, but he would remain, and his number one concern was always the general welfare of the team. So that, by definition, made him a sensational employee, especially when it came to the subject of money—it wasn't his, but he sure acted as if it was. And as the team's general manager all those years, he came right out of the George Halas school: he threw nickels around as if they were manhole covers.

When Ye Olde Celtics get together to tell their Auerbach stories, there are a few general categories. The first is the way he ran the team, of course. He was never a believer that all athletes were created equal. He regarded himself as a master psychologist, priding himself on knowing how to deal with different personalities. Thus, he did not yell at Bob Cousy, the possessor of a sensitive Gallic soul. By contrast, he never stopped yelling at Tom Heinsohn, who found himself blamed over the years for everything but the Great Chicago Fire, because Red knew Heinsohn could take it and understood the game Red was playing.

The second thing everyone remembers was Red's driving. To say it was legendarily bad would be no overstatement. For many years the Celtics barnstormed throughout New England, Maine in particular, during the exhibition season. Unlike today, when teams generally schedule eight exhibitions at prominent sites, teams in the 1950s and '60s played as many as eighteen or twenty preseason games, many in local high school gyms.

There was no team bus. The Celtics drove however many station wagons or reasonably large vehicles were needed, and the universal goal among veterans was to avoid being in the car being driven by the team president, general manager, and head coach. Rookies, of course, were stuck with him.

Finally, there are the money stories, contractual and otherwise. His ex-players derive great amusement from recalling the procedure on the road when arriving in a city. They would split up into cabs for the ride to the hotel, and one player would collect the fare money and then be reimbursed by Red. The only catch was that Red knew the fare from the airport to the hotel in every city, and if the amount sought was one penny more than the amount he had deemed to be correct, too bad for the player. Red did not give change.

Contracts were much more serious, and Red guarded the owner's money in pit bull fashion, no matter whether the owner was Walter Brown, John Y. Brown, or Bad Bad Leroy Brown. There was a quasi–good cop/bad cop juxtaposition during the Walter Brown era because everyone regarded the gregarious owner as a soft touch. "We'd sometime go behind Red's back," recalls Heinsohn. "We'd wait 'til he was out of town and then try to negotiate with Walter."

I quickly got a firsthand look at the wily Red Auerbach at work. Having taken a job as head coach of the Cincinnati Royals in 1969, at the last minute Bob Cousy decided to un-retire as a player at age forty-one, six years after he had last worn a uniform, in order to give his young Royals some backcourt stability.

Auerbach saw an opportunity to help his own team. According to league bylaws, Cousy was still the Celtics' property as a player. If he was going to play for someone else, Red wanted another player in return. Cousy couldn't believe it. He and Arnold, as he and he alone called Red, had been very close. It's no stretch to suggest that the Cooz was the surrogate son Red, father of two daughters, never had. But this was business, and Red was not going to budge. No player, no Cousy un-retirement. And that's how a six-seven forward named Bill Dinwiddie became a member of the Boston Celtics.

On the court, it all turned out to be much ado about very little. Cousy's Phase II consisted of seven regrettable games during which he shot one-for-three, handed out eleven assists, and made two famous bad passes that contributed to a huge comeback victory for the Knicks on the very night they won their eighteenth consecutive game to break a league record held by Auerbach's Celtics.

Dinwiddie, a player with a great deal of raw talent, continually frustrated Coach Tom Heinsohn, who lamented on just about a daily basis that he wanted the flashy Dinwiddie to tone down his game into what he termed a "three-piece suit" mode. But Dinwiddie was constitutionally incapable of such a transformation and was out of the league following the 1971–72 season, that one being spent in Milwaukee.

What mattered was that Red had made, and won, his point.

Red is celebrated, and rightly so, for the maneuvering that brought Bill Russell to Boston in 1956, which can be properly labeled a coup. It remains to this day the greatest trade in NBA history, Russell having been the anchor of eleven championship teams.

The story has been told time and time again, about how the Celtics, picking third in that draft, needed to find a way to get Russell, the college player Red coveted. The Rochester Royals, with the first pick, were placated when Red got Walter Brown, owner of not only the Boston Garden but also the Ice Capades, to deliver key Ice Capades dates to Royals owner Lester Harrison in exchange for the latter passing on Russell. That's the way the NBA, barely a decade old, did business in those days.

The Saint Louis Hawks, however, picking second, were a more complicated matter. Here Red lucked out. He had a slender six-eight center, Ed Macauley, who was a multiple All-Star and a very good player of the times. Macauley was a Saint Louis native and a graduate of Saint Louis University. He also had a sick son who would be better off back home. So Red asked Macauley if he would be willing to facilitate the deal for Russell's draft spot by agreeing to play for the hometown Hawks. Macauley, who was twenty-eight and had some good gas left in the tank, said yes.

"If Macauley didn't want to go?" Red once told me. "Forget it." The trade would never have happened.

It's easy to look at history and assume that all this manipulation was a no-brainer on Auerbach's part. After all, with eleven NBA championships in thirteen seasons, two prior NCAA championships at the University of San Francisco, and a 1956 Olympic gold medal, Russell proved himself to be the greatest winner in the history of American team sports. But not everyone believed in Russell, and not merely the Royals or Hawks, each of whom would be tormented countless times by the man they passed on.

Russell was a different type of center, one whose game was predicated on defense and rebounding, augmented by perhaps the greatest mind for the game the NBA has ever known. His offense was regarded as pedestrian, and that was all that mattered to some. Red, however, saw possibilities in Russell that eluded many of the great basketball sages of the time. "Everybody now thinks he [Russell] came out of school as the Second Coming, but it wasn't that way at all," Red said in a 1996 interview I conducted on the occasion of the NBA's fiftieth anniversary. "You take a guy like [Seton Hall star] Walter Dukes. He was bigger, stronger, and he could shoot much better than Russell. A lot of people couldn't figure out how a guy who couldn't shoot would be that good in the pros."

Red had been tipped off to this strange new West Coast phenomenon by Bill Reinhart, who had coached Red at George Washington. "I do have a recollection of Arnold coming to me in December of 1955, and saying, 'I think we're going to get a guy at center who's going to turn it around,'" Cousy told me. "And that was at a time when the jury was out as to whether or not Russell would make it in this league."

As to Cousy, whose name Walter Brown famously plucked out of a hat during a dispersal draft in 1950, Red had no choice but to admit that the basketball gods had smiled on him that day. When asked not long after he arrived in Boston about the idea of perhaps drafting the Holy Cross star, the new Celtics coach had sneered, "Am I supposed to win, or please the local yokels?" He had passed on Cousy, preferring Bowling Green six-eleven center Chuck Share. Upon the demise of the Chicago Stags, Cousy's name went into a fedora along with those of Max Zaslofsky and Andy Phillip. Red would have much preferred either of them, but Walter Brown agreed to pick last and Cousy thus became a Celtic.

No one, not even Red Auerbach, hits a home run on every draft day, and the cigar smoker had his share of clunkers, notably Bill Green, his 1963 choice. A six-six forward from Colorado State, Green might have been a nice NBA player, but his career never got started because he had a fear of flying. Other first-round picks who didn't fulfill their promise include Ollie Johnson (1965), Clarence Glover (1971), Norm Cook (1976), Charles Bradley (1981), Darren Tillis (1982), Michael Young (1984), and Michael Smith (1989). But Russell, Havlicek, Cowens, Bird, and McHale remain an amazing quintet.

Red had other draft and trade coups, and even a free agent coup. The tip he got from Bill Reinhart about Russell was no one-off. He drafted Sam Jones out of North Carolina College in 1957 solely on the recommendation of Bones McKinney, who had played for him on his first NBA team, the Washington Caps. Jones made it to the Hall of Fame and still may be the single most underrated guard of all time. There is also almost no way Red would have claimed Don Nelson off the waiver wire in 1965 had Heinsohn not said that Nelson was a guy he did not like to play against. That was enough of an endorsement for Red.

Dave Cowens was another coup. His Florida State teams did not play in the NCAA tournament during his four years there, and this being the pre-ESPN era, he therefore had no national profile. Auerbach went to see the six-eight redhead play in a game at Dayton, and recalled: "I only stayed five minutes, and I made a big scene when I left so people would think I was disgusted." He was disgusted enough to take Cowens as the fourth pick of the draft on the day he recommended removal of some key Bob Ryan body parts—and was rewarded with two more NBA championships.

I still don't know how he managed to spring Kansas guard Jo Jo White, who was his number one pick in 1969. This was the height of the Vietnam War and service duties were very much a part of American pro sports life. Red had many friends of prominence, among them Red Sox general manager Dick O'Connell, who had connections to the military. So we all got to say hello to marine reservist Private Jo Jo White, whose first press conference in Boston was conducted in full uniform.

Red's drafting of Larry Bird was memorable. The NBA had a long-standing rule in 1978 that college players were eligible for the draft four years after they first entered college. Since Bird had had spent a partial year at Indiana University, and had to sit out his freshman year at Indiana State, he was thus eligible for the draft at the end of his junior year. Red had exactly one year to the day after drafting him to sign him, or he would have gone back in the pool.

The beat goes on. A remarkable athlete, Danny Ainge was playing baseball for the Toronto Blue Jays at the time of the 1981 NBA draft. NBA teams needed to know his career intentions. General Manager Pat Williams of the Philadelphia 76ers caught up with Ainge in Cleveland, who assured Williams he was remaining in baseball. Williams took him at his word. On the night of the draft the Celtics took Ainge in the second round. He then decided to play basketball. It took what I would call a custody trial in New York later in the fall to free him from a very unhappy Blue Jays organization, but he became a Celtic, ultimately a two-time champion, and a future Boston general manager. Pat Williams's personal consolation prize was sticking around Cleveland long enough that night to see Len Barker throw a perfect game.

* * *

The acquisition of Robert Parish and drafting of Kevin McHale in 1980 proved to be almost in the same league as acquiring Russell, and the trade of Cedric Maxwell for Bill Walton was inspired. But my personal favorite of his coups involved Charlie Scott. Red had drafted Scott with the seventh pick in the 1970 draft, even though he had already signed with the ABA's Virginia Squires, just to establish his NBA rights. (He also drafted Mike Maloy of Davidson and Bobby Croft of Tennessee for the same reason.) In 1972, I attended a Squires–New York Nets game at Nassau Coliseum and after the game was in the Squires locker room conducting interviews. Charlie Scott has no reason to remember this, but he asked to borrow my pen. I gave it to him and for all I know he still has it.

Not long afterward, he made some big news: He was jumping to the NBA Phoenix Suns. Red immediately stepped in, and I knew the man who had squeezed Bob Cousy until he yielded Bill Dinwiddie wasn't going to sit by and watch the Suns scoop up Charlie Scott when he, Red, held his NBA rights.

On a Sunday afternoon soon after, who was sitting with Red at a Celtics game but Suns general manager (and future owner) Jerry Colangelo. I was no math major, but I did have the capacity to add two and two. That 1971–72 Celtics team won fifty-six games, but they lost to the New York Knicks in the playoffs primarily because they had no answer for power forward Dave DeBusschere. The Suns had on their roster six-foot-seven-inch Paul Silas, who had just shed some thirty-five pounds to make himself much more athletic, was a great defender and rebounder, and was a perfect matchup for DeBusschere. Seeing Red with Colangelo, I knew then and there that Paul Silas was going to become a Celtic, which he did before the 1972–73 season, and in his four years with the team, the Celtics would win two championships.

A fascinating aspect of the Scott-Silas saga is that within three years they were teammates. The Celtics were defeated by the Washington Bullets in the 1975 Eastern Conference Finals and were facing a new season without starting guard Don Chaney, who had signed a contract with the ABA Spirits of St. Louis. Twelve days after the season ended, before the Golden State Warriors' sweep of the Bullets had even been completed, Red sent guard Paul Westphal and some future draft picks to Phoenix for none other than Charlie Scott. Westphal was twenty-four years old, and though he had been a significant contributor to a championship team in 1974, he had not yet established himself as an NBA regular. Scott was twenty-seven and during his three years in Phoenix had averaged 25.3, 25.4, and 24.3 points per game, respectively. He was an unquestioned talent, but he was also regarded as somewhat high-maintenance.

Scott having been a somewhat combustible personality, Phoenix may simply have tired of having him around. The official Boston explanation was that, however great Westphal's potential, Scott was a major star, a better player, and therefore represented a talent upgrade. I believe there was another reason. I have always felt that with Chaney, a defensive-oriented player, gone, White would have had difficulty sharing the offensive load with Westphal, a backup for three years. But Scott was a star himself and White had a different level of professional respect for his game. Red knew this and he acted swiftly. In so doing, he did something rare for him, executing his first player-for-player trade in nine years, or since September 1, 1966, when he had swapped Mel Counts for Bailey Howell.

For most of the years I knew Red, he pretty much looked the same. He was not so much old as indeterminate middle-aged for at least two decades. In my first year covering the team, Red was only fifty-two. His hair had disappeared on top and what was left had long before ceased to be the color leading to his nickname. What people had a hard time believing is that when he retired from coaching he was a mere forty-eight years old.

He had gone out in classic Auerbachian style, announcing prior to the 1965–66 season that it would be his last. He had famously said he made the announcement when he did in order to give the rest of the league one more shot at him. When he did indeed leave as a winner via a two-point Game 7 victory over the Los Angeles Lakers, he wasn't exactly shy and humble about it.

"Everybody had a shot at me," he shrieked. "Cincy, Philadelphia, the Lakers. But the flag goes up!"

Years later, he expanded on his decision to leave the bench with so many more good coaching years apparently ahead of him, at least three or four of which could be spent coaching Bill Russell.

> What I was doing without any ego attached to it is done today by about eight guys. I was getting a burned-out feeling, and I knew I had to make a decision, one way or the other. And that picture, right there [pointing to the head shot of a haggard, old-before-his-time man on his office wall], I knew I was in trouble. That was taken right before I made the announcement.
>
> I was doing the coaching, and we had no assistants. I was doing all the day-to-day general manager's duties, which means I was making all the decisions about promotions and that stuff, as to whether we'd give away basketballs, or whatever, and when. I was doing all the scouting. So I figured I couldn't go on coaching forever. I knew I could have coached for another five years, at least, but there would have come a time when I'd have to make a decision, so I figured I'd make it at that point.

Among his proudest accomplishments was having written a book in 1952 entitled *Basketball for the Player, the Fan and the Coach*. It was republished over the years in many languages. My own paperback copy (now autographed, of course) is a second edition, purchased a year later. It is loaded with commonsense basketball precepts that would gladden the heart of Gregg Popovich or Mike Krzyzewski today, six decades later. The eleven commandments in the chapter entitled "Attitude of Player to His Teammates" should be posted in every high school and college gym today, not to mention every locker room:

1. You must think of getting along with your teammates because if you are not well-liked it is easy for them to "freeze you out."
2. Show a desire to block or screen for your teammates so they will do the same for you.
3. Show your teammates that you take the good shots. Don't appear too "hungry."
4. Don't hold the ball too long. Look for men cutting.
5. Dribble with a purpose. Don't just stand there hugging the ball or dribbling while your teammates continually cut.
6. Help your teammates on defense. Switch whenever necessary.
7. Don't chide a teammate whose man happens to score. Often it's the fault of the whole team.

8. Don't be too chummy with one or two players. Avoid obvious cliques.
9. Don't discuss the faults of any teammate with the other members of your team.
10. Don't give the impression that you are always hanging around the coach and discussing your teammates with him, unless, of course, you are the captain and the coach asks your opinion.
11. When scrimmaging, don't loaf or take it easy. This will keep the high respect of your teammates. Remember, "There are no friends on the other team, even in practice."

In terms of strategy, that Red wasn't fancy was no secret. He brought seven basic plays, plus options, to Boston and he saw no need to employ any other half-court offense. In a perfect Auerbachian world his teams would constantly fast break and seldom need to run a play. He was a "Keep It Simple, Stupid" guy long before the KISS acronym acquired any currency. As a coach, Red's greatness had more to do with understanding people and with identifying specific roles for players than it did with intricate strategy.

During the 1974–75 season Celtics coach Tom Heinsohn came down with a bug before a Saturday evening game in Atlanta and wasn't able to coach the game. This was way before teams had half a dozen assistants, or, in fact, any assistants in most cases. The Celtics actually did have a rare assistant, John Killilea, but he was out scouting. Somebody had to coach the team and thus Red was summoned while playing cards at his club in D.C. He flew to Atlanta and coached the team to a one-point victory.

The next game was the following Wednesday and Heinsohn was still recuperating. By this time Killilea was back in town, but Red decided he would coach what was going to be the first Boston game against heralded Portland rookie Bill Walton. Prior to the game, Killilea stepped to the blackboard and went over the scouting report. Red watched, impatiently I'm sure, and when Killilea was done he addressed the team.

"All that stuff is nice," he barked. "But you want to win the game? Block out on the boards and play defense. Now get outta here!"

Final score: Boston 128, Portland 110. Heinsohn gets credit in the books. My guess is Red wished Tommy Heinsohn had gotten sick more often.

But perhaps his greatest coaching legacy—even more than his nine championships—was his simple approach to race: he ignored it. He drafted the first African-American player in the NBA, Chuck Cooper, in 1950. He opened up the 1965–66 season with an African-American starting five of Russell, Sam Jones, K. C. Jones, Satch Sanders, and Willie Naulls. No one before had dared start a team that didn't include a white player. The prevailing attitude at the time, crude as it sounds, regarding the use of nonwhite players was, "Two at home, three on the road, and five if you're behind." I've scoured the papers and no one said a word, probably because everyone recognized by that time that all Red wanted to do was win.

When it came time to select his own coaching replacement, he turned his team over to Bill Russell. This, too, established an NBA precedent (George Steinbrenner had hired John McLendon to coach his Cleveland Pipers in the ill-fated ABL five years earlier). Asked about all this years later by *Boston Herald* columnist Joe Fitzgerald, Red said, "I don't even like to talk about that stuff. Really. My feeling was that you take a man for what he is and what he does and disregard everything else about him, including color. Those are feelings I've had because they're right; that's all. So why talk about them? If you sit around and talk about them, it looks as if you did those things just to be able to sit around and talk about them. Personally, I've always felt there's too much talking about it, anyway. We'd be a lot better off if people would shut up about brotherhood and start doing something about it instead."

He wasn't above a little social engineering, however. When I began covering the Celtics in 1969, I discovered that black-white roommate pairings were the norm, per order of Auerbach. Thus we had John Havlicek–Satch Sanders, Don Nelson–Don Chaney, and Dave Cowens–Jo Jo White, among others. Contemporary NBA players will read this and say, "What's a roommate?"

Red had been extremely close to owner Walter Brown, and he was wise enough to know his life would never quite be the same after Brown died in 1964. Owners would come and owners would go. For the most part they knew their place, and that was to kiss Red's ring publicly and grant Red his space privately. They quickly grasped the reality that the public didn't care who signed the paychecks as long as Red Auerbach was there. To the public, Red Auerbach *was* the Boston Celtics.

Things changed in the late seventies. The Celtics were in the clutches of John Y. Brown, a bombastic sort whose résumé included being governor of Kentucky and the business brains behind what was then known as Kentucky Fried Chicken. He had successfully wooed and wed Phyllis George, a Miss America and budding CBS TV star. He also had the requisite basketball DNA of a good Kentucky citizen and had thus become owner of the ABA Kentucky Colonels. Unlike other owners, he was not content to sit back and allow Auerbach to go about his business without getting involved in matters of basketball himself.

Brown cooked up a trade with Knicks honcho Sonny Werblin. Auerbach had craftily accumulated three number one draft picks during the terrible 1978–79 season, two by trade. The Celtics were playing in New York on the night of February 14, 1979. What Red didn't know was that as the game was being played, Brown was sitting in a Madison Square Garden suite with Werblin and giving New York all three number ones for one-time MVP and three-time scoring champ Bob McAdoo, who was not likely to be a good fit in Boston.

This outraged Red, and it nearly led to a cataclysmic occurrence. When the season was over, Red was approached by Werblin, who offered him the keys to the New York kingdom. Yes, indeed, Red Auerbach really was going to do the unthinkable: After twenty-nine years in Boston, many of them spent denouncing New York, and, specifically, the Knicks, he was going to join the enemy!

"I was on my way to see Sonny Werblin and give him a final answer," Red told me, "and sign the contract right then and there. But the cab driver and different people were saying to me, 'Don't go, don't go,' and there were big headlines in the New York papers and I thought, What is money? I just couldn't do it."

Werblin told Red he would keep the door open for three years, and if at any time during that period he wanted to take over the basketball program, it was his. "Believe it or not," Red told me, "with that leverage I went to John Y. and said, 'Look, you can fire me now, but if you don't sell the team in two weeks, I'm leaving.' That's when he sold his interest to Harry Mangurian." A few months later, Red got back two number one picks by offloading McAdoo to the Pistons.

Red was very much a social being. He loved reminiscing about his many travels for the State Department to give basketball clinics or to play foreign opponents during the 1950s and '60s. He was a born haggler, especially when the item in question was an Oriental artifact; his spacious apartment in Washington was decorated almost exclusively in an Oriental motif. Red was also a renowned collector of letter openers, which he owned by the hundreds. He had married the prettiest girl in town, Dorothy Lewis, who, as she reached her seventies, could best be described as an American Sophia Loren. He was a gracious host, popping up every five minutes to get you a drink refill or perhaps another sample of cheese or chocolate. He loved conversation and he loved to keep you off guard. While he wasn't a big fan of other major team sports, he loved all things pertaining to rackets. He had a standard Brooklynite's love of handball, moving on in later life to racquetball. And he really loved tennis. He had a classic Old Guy/Thinking Man's game that frustrated many a younger foe who couldn't understand why he was running around while Red seemed to be anchored in one place, on his way to winning, 6–2, 6–3.

Somewhere along the way, Red moved beyond indeterminate middle age and became a somewhat fragile senior citizen. He had ongoing health issues, often traveling back and forth between his beloved Washington and Boston in the company of a urologist or cardiologist. He got a cane, but he was never what you might call doddering. He always maintained his dignity in public.

New York *Daily News* columnist Mike Lupica loves to recount a conversation he had with Red on the subject of his own father, Ben, an octogenarian who stubbornly refused to use a cane, even though he needed one. Red asked Mike for the phone and rang up Mr. Lupica. "Hello, Ben? This is Red Auerbach. Don't be stupid. Get a cane!"

Red didn't dwell on the subject of aging, with one basic admonition. As Bill Russell entered his seventies, he said he had received one key piece of advice from his old coach and friend: "Don't fall."

About a year before he died, Red was so ill that friends feared he would not make it through the crisis. But he did. He awoke one day and his friend Rob Ades said, "Red, we thought we were going to lose you."

Red looked at him. "I'll decide," he said.

That decision was made on October 28, 2006, five weeks following his eighty-ninth birthday. It did not go unnoticed that his decision had been made less than a week before the opening day of the 2006–07 season, when the Celtics would be falling in line with other NBA teams by incorporating a dance team into the nightly game experience. Dance teams had never met with Red Auerbach's approval. To many of us, therefore, the timing of Red's decision made perfect sense.

CHAPTER 15

ESPN

In the fall of 1989 I received a phone call from Joe Valerio. We had been friendly in the 1970s when I was first with the *Globe* and he was working for the *New York Post*. We had lost contact when he left to become a TV producer for both CBS and ABC, managing, among others, Howard Cosell's critically acclaimed show *SportsBeat*. But though he had been making a living in television he had never lost his appreciation for sportswriters.

He told me he had taken over *The Sports Reporters*, the ESPN show started the year before that I would describe as a sports version of *Meet the Press*, airing as it does on Sunday morning with reasoned conversation about the sports topics of the day. Valerio wanted me to be part of a new cast. Dick Schaap would be hosting. Mike Lupica, a friend of mine since his undergraduate days at Boston College, and Bill Conlin of the *Philadelphia Daily News* would be on as well. I said yes and before long my life would change.

The show would have been worth doing if the only reward were getting to work with, and become a friend of, Dick Schaap. He was a unique figure in twentieth-century sports journalism. People often said that he was a better writer than anyone who worked in television and a better television performer than anyone who wrote, and it happened to be true. He had written more than thirty books, the majority having nothing to do with sports. But he was best known in book circles for his collaborations with athletes. Among others, he had coauthored the classic memoir *Instant Replay* with Green Bay Packer guard Jerry

Kramer. But he was so much more than a guy who could get athletes to talk.

A Long Island native and Cornell grad, he was the quintessential New Yorker, hobnobbing with athletes, authors, artists, politicians, and Broadway stars. He loved to joke that he was the only person who ever voted simultaneously for both the Heisman Trophy and the Tony Award. He liked to say he collected people.

Schaap was the perfect TV host. Thoroughly knowledgeable, quick-witted, and unflappable, he presided over *The Sports Reporters* for twelve years until his shocking death following what was supposed to be routine hip surgery in December of 2001. Most of the time we didn't identify ourselves as being on *The Sports Reporters*. We simply said we were on the Schaap show. And when Dick died, we were phenomenally fortunate that John Saunders could take over as host.

The basic format of the show has stayed the same, with the brief exception of a period when we expanded to an hour and brought in occasional guests. Joe Valerio starts running story ideas by us no later than Tuesday. We come up with ideas for what we call our "Parting Shots," brief observations on a sports topic of our choosing. Schaap's were always the best; he could say more in thirty seconds than the rest of us could say in sixty.

The TV exposure definitely changed my life. When I started, I didn't really think much about who might be watching, but I started to get a grasp at the 1991 American League Championship Series when, for the first time in my experience, an athlete introduced himself to me rather than the other way around. The player was Gene Larkin of the Minnesota Twins, and a short time later his tenth-inning sacrifice fly made Jack Morris a winner in that epic World Series Game 7 against the Atlanta Braves.

That TV exposure got ratcheted up a bit in 2002 when ESPN created *Around the Horn*. It is the first true spin-off of an existing sports TV program: simply put, if *Pardon the Interruption* had never existed, there would have been no *Around the Horn*.

When I first heard that ESPN was planning on giving *Washington Post* writers Tony Kornheiser and Michael Wilbon a half-hour show, I, like many others, I'm sure, said, "They're going to sit there and talk for a half hour? Who's going to watch that?" I had known Tony since the mid-1970s and Mike since the mid-1980s. They were TV naturals. Mike is a normal guy who really knows his sports. Tony is another matter. The best way to describe him is to say that if *Seinfeld* had a sportswriter character, it would have been Tony Kornheiser. But as much as I liked and respected them, I couldn't remotely imagine how they were going to do a successful half-hour TV show with just the two of them.

What I didn't know about was the existence of a flat-out genius named Erik Rydholm, who concocted the show's brilliant methodology, including the idea of listing the topics to come on the side of the screen, a shtick that has been often copied since. The idea of an interview being "five good minutes" was also his.

Tony and Mike came on the air at five-thirty Eastern time in November 2001. I knew something was working the following January when I was watching a college basketball game at Bud Walton Arena at the University of Arkansas and the students were holding up stick faces of Tony and Mike. They were catching on with the kids.

Around the Horn came on the air a year later in November 2002, planning to capitalize on the fan base Tony and Mike had built. The panel of four would rotate among journalists from five newspapers, the five original papers and panelists being the *Los Angeles Times* (T. J. Simers), *Denver Post* (Woody Paige), *Dallas Morning News* (Tim Cowlishaw), *Chicago Sun-Times* (Jay Mariotti), and *Boston Globe* (me). ESPN was in partnership with those five papers and built a studio inside each newsroom, everything state-of-the-art fiber optics. It would be a technically difficult show, with the four daily panelists in their home cities and the host, Max Kellerman, located in Washington, D.C.

The debut was a jumbled mess. The format was cumbersome. We were graded by Max for the quality of our answers, and at the end of the show the winner was the person with the most points. Then we would each get to make a statement at the end of the show, the amount of time we had corresponding in seconds to our point total. Critics killed us. Even worse, T. J killed us in his own column. He didn't last long, as you might expect.

ESPN executives went to work during Christmas vacation to fix the show, and when we returned the format had been changed for the better. The second segment would now be called "Buy or Sell," there would be only one winner, that being determined by the two survivors, who would debate either two or three "Showdown" topics. By the end of year one we had found our footing, settling into roles, and Woody Paige had emerged as the star. He is a natural and uninhibited comedian and he became our combination class clown and funny uncle. He also became something of a folk hero when he came up with the idea of having sayings on a chalkboard behind him on every show.

We had something of a crisis early in year two. Max Kellerman's contract was up and he ultimately left for his own show on Fox. In what was considered a holding action, the job was given to Tony Reali, who already had a job as "Stat Boy" on *Pardon the Interruption*. Tony is still there, managing what I'd consider the toughest hosting assignment in the history of television. In addition to the normal hosting duties of delivering smooth introductions and transitions, and ad-libbing good information and jokes while listening to the panelists, with either or both the director and the producer shouting things into his ear, he must also manipulate the levers governing points for four panelists and control the "Mute Button," which is an integral part of the show. Tony handles it all flawlessly. I am on camera at a studio in Newton, Massachusetts, called Videolink, where I've been going since the *Globe* chose not to renew its original agreement and had the TV studio removed a number of years ago.

Around the Horn has been great to me and I love doing it. But I'd be lying if I didn't admit that appearing on *Pardon the Interruption* is even more fun. In fact I would maintain that doing *PTI* is the most fun you can have in television. It's a matter of simple arithmetic. There are only two of you. There's more time for you to show off.

I was asked to be a fill-in *PTI* host during Tony's and Mike's summer vacations for the first time in 2001 and I've been doing it ever since. The show was created for them, taking advantage of their personalities and their friendship. But it is a perfect format for me, too. (Don't tell Tony I said that.) I've been at home there from the first minute I sat in one of their chairs. When I was first asked if I'd like to do the show, Tony Kornheiser said: "I can only promise you one thing. You will love the people you'll be working with." Tony nailed that one.

Good God, I've been on national TV for twenty-five years. That was never in my plans.

CHAPTER 16

This Guy Ain't No Hick

In my career, I have written more words about Larry Bird than any other individual. I couldn't possibly tell you who's in second place, but Larry is surely in first.

I am lucky enough to have seen him in college. In March 1978 I was off the Celtics beat but still covering basketball, and thus I was in Indianapolis for Providence College's first-round NCAA game against Michigan State and its acclaimed freshman guard Earvin "Magic" Johnson. The night before Indiana State, featuring sensational junior forward Larry Bird, was playing a home NIT game against Illinois State. I *had* to go, and invited *Providence Journal* writers Mike Madden and Jayson Stark to join me on the hour-and-a-half trip west to Terre Haute.

Bird got our attention immediately. Illinois State's first possession resulted in a missed jumper. Bird grabbed the rebound, dribbled up the left side of the court, and, just before reaching midcourt, rocked the ball back off the dribble and fired a forty-foot underhand bullet to a speeding Carl Nicks for a layup. Our reaction was "Nah, we really didn't see that, did we?" But we had. Indiana State won the game. Bird hit the winning basket, and that was my introduction to the One and Only Larry Bird.

The next day Magic led Michigan State past Providence. Bird one night, Magic the next afternoon. Given all that would transpire, that was an interesting tandem.

Drafted by the Celtics with a year of collegiate eligibility remaining, in his senior year Bird led Indiana State to the NCAA championship game, where they lost, fair and square, to Magic and Michigan State.

That said, you will never convince me Bird didn't injure his left hand early in the title game. If you watch the tape, you will see him wince when catching a pass, and Bird, a completely orthodox player, snatched most of his thirteen rebounds with one hand rather than two. But I never heard him complain, not about that or anything else.

I covered that Final Four for the *Globe* and for *Basketball Times*, and when the latter chose Larry as its Player of the Year in advance of the NCAA tournament, I wrote the accompanying story in the edition of March 15, 1979.

"The stopwatch guys and the scouts who rate a prospect in proportion to the number of dunks he makes in a game (not that Bird can't or won't stuff the ball) can criticize him all they want," I wrote. "The smart guys only know that the game is basketball, not speedball or jump ball, and that Bird can play it . . . He has been likened to such varied people as Bob Pettit, Rick Barry, Dan Issel, Tom Heinsohn, Dolph Schayes and Jim Pollard. In time he will be known as the first Larry Bird."

Even before he turned pro, much of the discussion about Bird focused on his background as the so-called Hick from French Lick and his apparently naïve personality. I concluded that *Basketball Times* piece:

"Too much has been made of Bird's off-court Garbo routine and curiosity about his personality will increase should Indiana State advance to the Final Four and complete television exposure later this month. But what matters to the true basketball fan is not Bird's thoughts on love, marriage, the English Monarchy and gas rationing, but his game. And like few before him, it truly is His Game."

Larry Bird was born and raised in a community where education wasn't much appreciated. Orange County was the poorest county in Indiana and in general people scratched out a living there. Until he became a prized basketball commodity during his senior year at Springs Valley High School, Larry didn't expect much more out of life than doing some kind of manual labor and spending his free time fishing and drinking beer with his buddies.

His life became complicated in the immediate aftermath of high school, however. His father, Joe, an alcoholic, killed himself after announcing to the family he was planning on doing just that. Larry had an ill-fated teenage marriage, and a daughter was born during a brief reconciliation period. Then, against his better judgment, he committed to Indiana University, succumbing to local pressure. The idea that coach Bob Knight wanted him was all the townspeople needed to know.

Larry was miserable in Bloomington. He arrived on campus with one decent pair of pants, a few shirts, and $75 in cash that was supposed to last 'til Christmas. He was overwhelmed by the size of the campus and the affluence of the student body. His interactions with the basketball team in those few weeks were not pleasant, either. After less than a month, he walked out to State Route 37, stuck out his thumb, and headed back to French Lick.

Bob Knight had nothing to do with Larry's decision to leave Indiana. His team was loaded and he probably figured he'd be fine without the Bird kid. Knight later told me his failure to intercede was one of his biggest coaching regrets. That Indiana team lost just one game, a two-point loss to Kentucky when star forward Scott May was sidelined with an injury. Bird might have made a difference. The following year Indiana went 32-0.

Larry knew he would go back to college somewhere. He took a job with the local recreation department, where one of his occasional duties was driving the garbage truck. The most ardent suitor for his basketball services was Indiana State assistant Bill Hodges. Larry was comfortable with Hodges and Indiana State in general, and his legendary career began.

By the time he got to Boston, he didn't have much of a worldview. College had broadened him a bit, but his entire experience had been small-town Midwest. That's one reason he so embraced Terre Haute. To him, it was just a big French Lick. He was initially labeled as suspicious, hostile, even ignorant; in time, however, he would reveal himself to be one of the sharpest NBA observers the game would ever know—and that included his interaction with the media.

My first encounter was classic 1979 Bird. I was asked by *Us* magazine to do a story on him that summer soon after he signed a four-year Celtics contract. He had just purchased a house in Brookline, Massachusetts, but he wasn't going to do any interviews there. The sit-down was instead scheduled at the house of his agent Bob Woolf, a catty-corner neighbor. He was pleasant and cooperative enough, but he made a strong point:

He would fulfill all his necessary media obligations, but nobody was ever coming to his house or bothering him away from the arena or practice site. He was very clear about that.

It didn't take long for him to decide that we weren't such bad people, after all. Later that year, after a game in Chicago, I came to the coffee shop at the hotel to get something to eat. Bird was there with some family and friends who had made the five-hour drive from French Lick. He invited me to join them. After a while, he looked at me and said, "Man, I never thought I'd be eating with a writer."

He became so adept at playing the media game that by 1988 I wrote a story in the *Globe* Sunday magazine entitled "The Blooming of Bird." Larry particularly enjoyed his interaction with the media during playoff time, when reporters were covering the games from all over the country. "Whether you're home or away, you're in one spot for three or four days, which is unusual," he explained. "You're in that gym, and when practice is over you've got time for people. If you're on the road, what are you going to do? Go back to the room and sit around? I don't mind staying around and talking to people. They come from all over the country, after all. It's no problem. I'm there, anyway. I'm relaxed. Why not do it?"

This was less than a year after he had bailed out Isiah Thomas with a joint news conference at the NBA Finals in Los Angeles, following the foolish statements by the Pistons' Dennis Rodman and Isiah in the minutes following Boston's victory in Game 7 of the 1987 Eastern Conference Finals. Rodman, who had just been torched by a big Bird fourth quarter, dismissed Larry as "an overrated player," while Thomas piled on by stating, "Bird is a very, very good basketball player, an exceptional talent. But I have to agree with Rodman. If he were black, he'd be just another good guy in this league."

This became *the* postgame story, so much so that Bird and Thomas were asked to have a press conference at the finals. By this time Isiah had backtracked, saying he was referring to "black-white stereotypes." Larry was positively statesmanlike. "Isiah apologized to me," he said, "but he didn't have to. I knew right off the bat those remarks didn't come from the heart; they came from his mouth. And what he said didn't bother me, anyway. If it didn't bother me, and after I explained it to my family [Isiah was his mother Georgia's favorite player not named Bird] it didn't bother them, it shouldn't bother anybody else, either."

Award-winning *Detroit Free Press* columnist Mitch Albom was impressed with the way Bird responded:

> It was just such an enormous controversy across the country and a front-page story here. I remember the look on Bird's face. He had that kind of smirk, like, "What the hell's the big fuss about?" It was like, "C'mon, back to earth." I admired him for that. I thought that was one of the few times that athletes had a better perspective than we did. I'm not sure Isiah ever appreciated how much Bird did for Isiah's career. If he wanted to make it an issue, he could have, but he saw it as something that wasn't worth the attention it was getting and he came to Isiah's rescue. He didn't have to do that.

Larry surprised himself with how much he loved Boston, with one exception—the traffic. In that 1988 article he had told me, "The only thing that keeps me from staying here full time is the traffic. Back home, I drive for twenty-five or thirty minutes from my house and I'm in Jasper. Here I drive twenty-five or thirty minutes and I'm at the Garden."

French Lick was an important off-season sanctuary, however. It was the place where he could always be just plain Larry, Joe and Georgia's kid and Lizzie Kerns's grandson. It was pretty much a closed society, as a writer named Tom Callahan would discover when *Time* magazine sent him there to do the Bird half of a 1985 cover story on the twin megastars Larry Bird and Wayne Gretzky.

When Callahan approached Bird to tell him he was heading to French Lick for some background interviews, Bird pretty much told Callahan, "You gotta be kidding me."

"You want to go to French Lick?" he asked. "I've known Bob Ryan for six years, and it was just last year I let him go to French Lick." But he was just "funnin'," Larry told him. "If you leave my little brother [Eddie] alone, I'll have my big brother [Mark] pick you up at the airport."

He was always full of surprises. For years we all noted that he stared at the Garden ceiling during the national anthem. He never said why and no one asked. Then, during his speech at the dinner to celebrate a statue to him that had been sculpted by Armand LaMontagne and would be placed in the Sports Museum, he got to the subject of his nightly anthem ritual. He explained that he was looking at Bruins great Bobby Orr's retired number 4 jersey as a source of nightly inspiration. "I want people in Boston to think of me when I retire the same way they do Bobby Orr," he said.

Legendary *Sports Illustrated* writer Frank Deford was seated at one of the tables. When Bird explained why he looked at Orr's jersey, the man sitting next to Deford gasped in a loud whisper, "My God." The man was Bobby Orr.

One thing that Bird never kept a secret, but that people were always surprised to learn, was that he played his entire NBA career with a physical impairment that had not been present in college. Larry was always a big fan of baseball and had even played a game or two at Indiana State. In the spring following his senior season at ISU he was playing left field in a softball game. His brother hit a ball that wound up smashing Larry's right index finger.

It was never fixed properly. Swollen and distorted, he played with it for thirteen years. As difficult as this is to believe, he accomplished everything he did as a professional after having to make an adjustment to his shooting mechanics. Anyone who has ever played basketball can understand how difficult this must have been, as the ball rolls off the index finger on every shot.

Making matters even more complicated, he dislocated his right pinky when it was caught in a Chicago Bulls jersey during Michael Jordan's famous sixty-three-point game in 1986. That finger never healed properly, either. Thus, he played the final six-plus years of his career with a shooting hand that was 40 percent messed up and nonetheless shot .496 for his career (.519 on two-pointers, .376 on three-pointers). He never uttered a peep of self-pitying protest.

As he aged, injury became a way of life. Back. Elbow. Ankles. As far back as 1985, when he hadn't even turned thirty, his elbow was a major issue. A bad back would end his career. Just getting him to Barcelona for the 1992 Olympics was an iffy proposition. What bothered him most about the injuries was that they so often prevented him from practicing. He was the anti–Allen Iverson. To him, practice was exhilarating—it really *was*, for him, how you got better. "I'm not happy when I can't practice," he once said. "I used to go out there thinking I'd make every shot because I'd always have the practice. I didn't, but I always thought I would. But without practice I really struggle out there."

Unlike Yogi Berra, who may not have said half the things people think he said, all the following are true.

Larry Bird really did stride into the locker room prior to the first Three-Point Shootout in 1986 and ask, "Which one of you guys is finishing second?"

He really did run by Utah coach Frank Layden one night and ask Layden if he had anyone to guard him.

He really did turn down a chance to reenter a game in Salt Lake City in which he had a triple double, plus nine steals, by the end of the third quarter, saying, "I done enough damage."

He really did say, after Michael Jordan had scored forty-nine in Game 1 and sixty-three in Game 2 of their 1986 playoff series, "If he went from forty-nine to sixty-three, does he expect to score seventy-seven next? If he scores seventy-seven, I'll retire."

He really did say after Red Sox pitcher Bruce Hurst lost in arbitration, "The Mormon church will be on the front steps, picketin'."

He really did say, after learning that Robert Parish had been suspended for punching Bill Laimbeer, "What? For that good deed?"

He really did say, after the Celtics had lost Game 3 of the 1984 Finals by thirty-three points, "We need to go to the hospital and get twelve heart transplants. That's the first thing. Until we get our hearts where they belong, we're in trouble. We're a team that plays with its heart and soul. Today the heart wasn't there."

He really did say, after taking a scant seven shots in a playoff game, "French Lick's shut down today. The whole town is in mourning. Larry Bird had seven shots last night."

He really did say, when asked how he got scratches on his shoulder one particular night, "Tell Dudley Bradley to cut his fingernails."

He really did say to health food advocate Pete Maravich, "Why don't you eat some *American* food?"

He really did say about the difference between playing at home and on the road, "Anybody can play at home. I'll tell you what. My little brother could come in here with us and blend in. But put him on the road . . ."

He really did say, "There's a secret to playin' basketball. I ain't tellin' what it is."

No matter your allegiance you can't name anyone else whose game was a greater microcosm of everything basketball contains than Larry Bird's, if you can eliminate the idea that the essence of the game is jumping. Jumping is an asset. But it is not the most important thing, not even in rebounding, where the keys are positioning, timing, and—by far the most important rule of rebounding—"Do you want the ball or don't you?" Anyone who thinks that what made Michael Jordan great was his tremendous jumping ability must retake the course.

Michael Jordan is the greatest virtuoso who has ever played the game. But he never did something I saw Larry Bird do on more than one occasion—dominate NBA games without taking a shot. Michael Jordan never did. With Michael it always came down to his putting the ball in the basket. With Larry it never came down to any one thing. He possessed a total game, and this is what made him so much fun to watch.

When Larry retired, we needed to pick for the *Globe* some highlight games for a top ten list. Ten? Fifty would have been a start. There was the night he scored sixty against the Hawks. There was his thirty-nine-point, twelve-rebound, ten-assist triple-double in Game 7 against the Knicks in 1984. His twenty-point fourth quarter in the shootout with Dominique Wilkins and the Hawks in 1988 was epic, as was his thirty-six-point, twenty-one-rebound, five-assist, five-block game against the Lakers in 1981, in which he was fifteen for seventeen in one stretch and also broke up a couple of three-on-one fast breaks. His forty-seven-point, fourteen-rebound, eleven-assist game in Portland featured seven left-handed shots.

My two favorites showcased both his ability and his will.

June 8, 1984, was an unusual night at Boston Garden. The Celtics had returned home from Los Angeles with the finals tied at 2–2 and Boston in a serious heat wave. The Garden did not have air-conditioning. At game time the temperature was ninety-seven degrees inside the building. Never in the history of the Garden had so many worn so few garments. They were absurd conditions in which to conduct an NBA Finals game. But the crowd made it a happening.

The Lakers were appalled. But the show had to go on, and Bird was the ringmaster. While players on both sides were incapable of functioning, Bird helped himself to thirty-four points and seventeen rebounds while shooting fifteen for twenty from the floor. Larry just shrugged. "Everybody complained about the heat, but I felt great out there," he said. "I remember running by the Laker bench and seeing them sitting there sucking in oxygen and I felt like I could run forever. The crowd was really into it that night."

Two years to the day later, June 8, 1986, occurred Larry Bird's personal favorite, and mine, too. He had much bigger numbers in other games—in this one he had twenty-nine points, eleven rebounds, twelve assists—but he never made a bigger overall impact at both ends of the floor than he did in this game. The Celtics were up, 3–2, in the finals against Houston, but they had been pushed around in Game 5. Bird had assured the fans that everything was going to be on in Game 6. And then he went out and backed it up. I can't put it any better than I did on the morning after:

> The Houston Rockets were like an unwary couple pulled over on the highway for going 3 miles over the speed limit by a burly Georgia cop with the mirrored sunglasses. It wasn't their day. The cop's name was Bird. The bailiff's name was Bird. The court stenographer's name was Bird. And the executioner's name was—guess what?—Bird . . . He didn't make *every* shot or grab *every* rebound or make *every* steal or sell every hot dog, but he plugged himself into every conceivable aspect of the game to the extent that all the other players had to do was feed off his energy level. "Let's face it," said Kevin McHale, "when you play with Larry Bird it gives you a lot of confidence."

Said Bird himself, "That's the one day I was *totally* prepared."

* * *

The great David Halberstam, author of celebrated works in both the real world and the world of sports, had a word to describe the people he admired most. To him, Larry Bird was "authentic." He had no guile, no pretense. "He is just such a non-fake story," Halberstam said. "There is just such an elemental truth about him."

What greater example of this could there be but Larry's coaching career? He told everyone he would coach the Indiana Pacers for three years. In his third year they went to the finals against the Lakers and lost to a better team. And that was it. Three years, over and out. Everyone was shocked. Who keeps his word in the world of sports? Larry does.

For me, his arrival was as if I were an art student and into the classroom walked the new professor—Michelangelo. Who could be prepared for that? When Larry Bird came to Boston I had been covering the NBA for ten years. I had seen a lot of great things, from both an individual and a team aspect. I didn't expect to be surprised and educated and thrilled by anything new.

Because of his genius, Larry Bird was a writing challenge. As they love to say in sports, he made me take my game to the next level. I hope I was able to do him proper justice.

CHAPTER 17

The Olympics

The Olympics were never part of my thinking. But once I became a full-time columnist at the *Globe* in 1989, I was free to cover a wide range of sports, including the Olympics, and they provided me with some of my greatest memories.

The first Olympics I remember reading about were the Helsinki Summer Olympics in 1952, when I was six. Any huge sports fan must pay attention to the Olympics, and I was a huge sports fan in the making. I really connected with the 1956 *Sports Illustrated* coverage of the Melbourne Summer Olympics, especially the five-thousand- and ten-thousand-meter victories of Vladimir Kuts of the Soviet Union. The 1960 Squaw Valley Winter Olympics brought the surprise American hockey triumph over Canada, and the 1960 Summer Olympics in Rome had plenty of American stories, ranging from the triumphant—such as the overpowering basketball team featuring collegiate stars Oscar Robertson, Jerry West, and Jerry Lucas—and the shockingly negative, such as heavily favored John Thomas being unable to win gold in the high jump. I was certainly aware of marathoner Abebe Bikila: who wasn't moved by the story of the barefoot Ethiopian?

Over the next thirty-two years I followed every Olympics—winter and summer—as a fan. But I was never professionally involved until 1992, when the Dream Team went to Barcelona. I was then privileged to cover the next ten Olympics. They provided me with passport stamps in such places as Spain, Norway, Japan, Australia, Greece, Italy, China, Canada, and England. Travel of any kind has always been one of the truly great perks of the life I've led covering sports. I can't imagine my career without the Olympic experience.

And no offense to Atlanta and Salt Lake City, but having the Olympics in the United States is a letdown. To me, the Olympics is supposed to mean you're going somewhere. Just getting to an Olympics is a feat. You must undergo an elaborate ritual in which you provide personal information that stops just short of ceding your firstborn to the government in question. It is not like going to a sporting event in America.

There is an oft-told story among the American Olympic cognoscenti concerning Dick Young, the legendary longtime baseball writer and columnist for the New York *Daily News* and *New York Post*, a man who I believe changed how we sportswriters go about our business more than anyone in the last seventy-five years. He wanted to cover the 1976 Montreal Summer Olympics while they were in progress. "Tell them I'm coming. I'll pick up my credentials at will-call," he said, unaware that he was supposed to send them passport information six months earlier.

Once you receive your official credential you guard it with your life. It is your passport to everything, and if you lose it you have instantly become a nonperson. I like to kid that the most important thing stateside when seeking to cover an event is a parking pass, and that I can always talk my way into the arena. Perhaps the pope could talk his way into an Olympics, but no one else would have a shot.

My first Olympics, the 1992 summer games in Barcelona, were atypical in that I had one primary assignment—to cover both men's and women's basketball. I only wrote two non-basketball pieces, one on a USA baseball player named Ron Villone, who was of interest to the *Globe* because he was from the University of Massachusetts, and the other on Ben Johnson, the disgraced sprinter.

I have to chuckle every time I glance at that Ben Johnson column. I was never known in the trade as a hatchet man, but I really laid a proper two-by-four on ol' Ben, who was trying a comeback four years after being exposed as having juiced his body in Seoul and who was about to go down in flames the following day. He was a serious candidate for the honor of being the most despised man in Barcelona, and I reflected that in my writing.

After an Olympic contest, writers don't go to the locker room the way we often do in the USA. There is always an interview room with a moderator and as many interpreters as are needed, and these can produce amusing scenarios. Very often a lengthy question in something other than English is followed by an even lengthier answer from the athlete or coach, leading to the interpreter summing up said lengthy reply in about fifteen words. But the real fun takes place in what is known as the "mixed zone." This is where members of the media stand behind barriers as the players walk through en route to the locker room. There is often aggressive jockeying for position by the media, and occasionally moments when incidents threaten to turn journalists into combatants. The track-and-field mixed zone generally gets the gold medal as the most volatile in the summer games. Figure skating usually takes the prize in the winter games.

My first all-encompassing Olympic experience came two years after Barcelona, at the 1994 Winter Olympics in Lillehammer, Norway. I went there with great trepidation. I was hardly a winter sports aficionado. One of the signature events in any Winter Olympics, and by far the most important one for American television audiences, is figure skating. I was not then, am not now, and never will be a fan of figure skating, at least not as a competition. It can be thrilling to watch, but I completely reject the idea that it can be judged properly.

As far as the rest of the winter sports were concerned, the only one I knew anything about was hockey, and even that was far from my strongest suit. I like to write from a position of comfort and supposed expertise. Back home, covering live hockey always filled me with dread because of my lack of experience, but I thought it would have to be my refuge in Lillehammer.

Then, at the Olympic figure-skating trials during the first week in January, something unique in the annals of sport occurred. A hired assailant struck skater Nancy Kerrigan in the knee in the hope this would eliminate her from the competition and help provide a place on the team for Tonya Harding, a skater from Portland, Oregon. It was a bizarre story, to be sure, and a monster story for the *Globe* because Nancy Kerrigan lived in Stoneham, Massachusetts, a community located less than fifteen miles north of Boston.

The NFL playoffs were ongoing, but there was no bigger American sports story in January of 1994 than the saga of Nancy and Tonya, the former an attractive young lady who had thus far fallen a bit short of the greatness that had been predicted for her, and the latter a heartwarming story of a gritty, wrong-side-of-the-tracks girl trying to claw her way to the top. Nancy Kerrigan was a classic skater. Tonya was a more modern athletic skater. Don't think I knew this without the experts telling me.

As a columnist for Nancy Kerrigan's hometown paper, I had to pay attention. I think I wrote six Nancy or Nancy/Tonya columns that January prior to the games. In the end, Nancy's knee healed up in time and the Olympic Committee appointed her to the team despite her not competing in the trials. It was the right thing to do. Tonya claimed the assailant had acted on her behalf, and she also qualified for the Olympics.* The Nancy and Tonya Show was heading to Norway and would remain a big story. I wasn't assigned to cover it, but I couldn't ignore it, either. On February 17 they were supposed to be appearing at the same practice session in the nearby city of Hamar. If I couldn't have gotten a column out of that, I should have been put on the next plane home.

But what had taken place two hours earlier reveals the greatness of the Olympic experience. The young lady on the ice at eleven thirty that morning was Lu Chen of the People's Republic of China. She had attracted a Chinese camera crew, which shot every second of her routine. When she was done, the Chinese packed up and departed. There were somewhere between four hundred and five hundred media folk there from all over the world, and the only reason they were present was to see Nancy and Tonya and hope they would put up their dukes. Not the Chinese.

This drew a laugh from American journalist Tom Callahan. "You know how we always say, 'Well, there's a billion Chinese who don't give a damn?'" he inquired. "I always thought that was just an expression."

I had epiphanies all over Lillehammer. For example, I had never

---

* In March 1994, Tonya pleaded guilty to "conspiring to hinder prosecution of the attackers." Later that year the United States Figure Skating Association banned her for life as both a skater and a coach, concluding that she knew beforehand about the attack and had displayed "a clear disregard for fairness, good sportsmanship, and ethical behavior."

heard of Norwegian Johann Olav Koss. He was a champion speed skater and I had never seen a speed skating competition in person. Unless you live in Wisconsin, that's true of most Americans. He won the fifteen-hundred- and five-thousand-meter races, and so I decided to see if he could win the ten thousand and thus become the first to win gold in all three of those races since Eric Heiden in Lake Placid a dozen years before.

Speed skating is not made for dramatics. Competitors race in pairs against the clock. There is no direct head-to-head competition. But Johan Olav Koss and his thousands of admirers crammed into a building known as the Viking Ship taught me to appreciate a different form of competition. Skating in the fifth pair out of eight, Koss glided over the ice with an unmatched fury. He actually lapped skating partner Frank Dittrich, and that's not the half of it. Dittrich actually skated a personal-best time that day, one that would have left Eric Heiden half a block back. The crowd knew what was going on, too. They cheered the announcement of the split times the way we would have cheered a grand-slam homer or a game-winning touchdown pass.

Johann Olav Koss was basically skating by himself, but I'm telling you it was exciting. It was impossible not to be swept up in the moment. I was a total outsider, a guest at a party where I knew no one. But it was one of the most thrilling athletic events I've ever covered. Koss blew out his own standing world record by an astonishing 12.90 seconds. And when he said afterward he could not have done what he had just done anywhere but in front of these people, I had no reason to doubt him.

"Having the Olympics in Norway is very special, so I have never wanted anything more," he declared. "I have never felt so motivated for doing well. It's been a buildup since '92. The Olympics have been the main goal in my inner mind."

Call it the Home Ship Advantage, but it wasn't the first time I had seen it. The Spaniards had done things they did not seem capable of doing in Barcelona two years earlier. Check it out. They have never come close to their medal count that summer, before or since.

From an American point of view, what I had just seen made some kind of rooting sense. However, that was not the case at Birkebeineren Ski

Stadium, site of the four-by-ten-kilometer cross-country relay race. By this time I had come to the realization that cross-country skiers are as fit and tough as any athletes in the world. Cardiovascularly speaking, they are off the charts. I had been told the 40-K relay race was the Big One, as far as Norwegian fans were concerned. Americans can have no idea what that means in Norway. Birkebeineren Ski Stadium itself holds somewhere between 30,000 and 35,000 people. It had been the first Olympic event to sell out; authorities had received 204,000 ticket requests. But the true spectating action was taking place in the woods, where as many as 70,000 people, many of them having lived in the cold in tents for the better part of two weeks in anticipation of this day, were assembled.

I was being educated on a daily basis. There really is a big world full of people who get along nicely without football, baseball, basketball, or hockey to satisfy their sports itch. It's good to know.

What transpired was worth every numbing second. The home-country Norwegians and the Italians had never been more than five meters apart for the first 39 K and change, and it came down to a sprint between Norway's Bjørn Dæhlie and Italy's Silvio Fauner for the gold. Dæhlie was the greatest of all Norwegian cross-country skiers, but Fauner's calling card was his sprinting ability, and he held off the great Dæhlie, winning by four-tenths of a second.

"I've beaten him a couple of times before with sprints," Fauner said. "But he's also beaten me the same way. So you might say things even out. Just one click of the eye could be the difference."

It was the reverse of the finish two years earlier in Albertville, France. (Nineteen ninety-two was the last time the Summer and Winter Olympics were conducted in the same year. The alternating two-year cycle began in Lillehammer.) And the tremendous rivalry between Norway and Italy in the grueling four-by-ten-K relay continued at the highest competitive level for two more Olympics.

In Nagano, Japan, four years later Fauner would engage in another sensational last-lap finish, losing out to Norway's Thomas Alsgaard by two-tenths of a second, or half a human foot. In Salt Lake City in 2002, Alsgaard fought off Italian Cristian Zorzi to win by three-tenths of a second. This means that three consecutive 40-K races totaling 120 K (74.5 miles) had been decided by a combined time of one-tenth of a second. Let's see if Duke-Carolina or Auburn-Alabama can top that!

Every day in Lillehammer was a delight. These were the perfect Winter Olympics, played out in a fairy-tale setting. When we all began to converge several days before the Opening Ceremony, the snow drifts were who knows how high, but the roads were clear, because the Norwegians knew what they were doing. Right smack in the middle of the Opening Ceremony, a light snow began to fall. It was as if some Hollywood director of a Sonja Henie movie had ordered it up. When the Opening Ceremony was concluded, the snow stopped.

And it never snowed again.

All we were left with was the postcard scenic beauty of Norway. Every drive was beautiful. And the atmosphere could not be topped. The Winter Olympics were being held in a gorgeous country in which their favorite sports were being played. Everyone was in a good mood. Most of all, the Norwegians were winning and winning big. And when they weren't winning the Swedes were, and this was great fun because Norway and Sweden really are Ohio State and Michigan to the max regarding winter sports. I would join the locals at night in a giant tent where the beer was flowing. They would sing when they won and they would sing when they lost, and it seemed as if every one of Norway's 4.3 million people knew all the words.

About the only thing getting in the way of my total bliss was the Nancy-Tonya thing. I couldn't avoid covering Nancy Kerrigan skating for the gold. My rooting interest, however, was Surya Bonaly, the French lady who was the most athletic and acrobatic of all female skaters of her time, though some of the things she could do (backflips, for example) were not point-getters. She tumbled her way out of it early, and the gold came down to a battle between Nancy and sixteen-year-old Ukrainian Oksana Baiul.

An editorial appeared during the Olympics in the *Guardian*, the prestigious British newspaper, triggered by a low score for the British pair Torvill and Dean, which seems apropos of figure skating judging. The pair was eight years post-Sarajevo but still had some gas in the tank and many Brits thought they had been badly judged. "Robbed?" it began.

"Who can say, or possibly bring themselves to care? Were Astaire and Rodgers better than Kelly and Charisse—or even Marge and Gower Champion?" Couldn't have said that better myself.

Nancy skated her Massachusetts heart out. She did what she wanted to do. "In my mind and heart," she said, "I had definitely skated a gold-medal performance. I had peace of mind. I was great." And she was. The judges, however, gave the gold to Baiul.

"Some of the judges favored Ginger," I wrote afterward, channeling the *Guardian*. "Some favored Cyd. The alternate judge might have gone with Marge. That is all you ever need to know about figure skating."

Believe me when I say there are about six people writing about skating who have any real right to an opinion, and despite my statement above, I'm not one of them. On the other hand, my *Globe* colleague John Powers is perhaps the preeminent Olympic writer of our time and a true expert on figure skating. Here is what happens at every figure skating competition at which John Powers is present. Someone skates. A line forms in the stairway next to John Powers. They all ask, "What did I just see?" John Powers tells them. They all go back to their seats and tap out stories on the computer. Back home, people then think they are smart.

I am eternally grateful I lucked into Lillehammer, whose games I believe will go down as the greatest Winter Olympics of all. The International Olympic Committee will never go back to a village of twenty-three thousand. The IOC will never have everything fall into place as it did in Lillehammer, with perfect weather, perfect home-country enthusiasm, and overwhelming home-country success. It was all under the supervision of the Norwegians, who are very capable people.

By contrast, there is one universally held belief among those who have covered the Olympics during the last quarter century: the Atlanta Summer Olympics in 1996 were the worst ever.

I'm not talking about the competition. Great things happen at every Olympics. But in order for it to be remembered fondly a city must offer something else. The memory of Atlanta isn't helped by the fact that it was the site of a horrible incident, one neither the city nor the organizers had anything to do with. The wonder of the bombing at Centennial

Olympic Park on that Saturday night was that it only resulted in one fatality. The shame of it was the phenomenal rush to judgment that initially identified the wrong man. There was absolutely no question that Richard Jewell had planted the bomb, except that he hadn't. The perp turned out to be Eric Rudolph, an antigovernment person well-known to the authorities.

But the truth is that from a media viewpoint Atlanta failed on every count. The transportation for the world media was a mess from start to finish. I was among those staying at the airport, which puts a kibosh on your activities. It was just a blah experience. I had to laugh about the criticism from some that things were "too commercial." Of course the Olympics are commercial. Overall, the Atlanta Olympics felt like work, and the Olympics should *never* feel like work.

One thing I was learning about the Olympics in my third time was that there are two kinds of Olympic experience—the network television version and everyone else's. If you are there in a journalistic capacity, you pay no attention to what the network is covering and instead construct your own personal Olympics, looking for good stories. Atlanta offered a perfect example of the difference, because I am sure that the man I believe to have been the most compelling personality in the entire Olympics was never seen for even a second on American television.

His name was Aleksandr Karelin, and I discovered him completely by accident, which, if you are a columnist at the Olympics, is precisely the way things are supposed to happen. I had taken a cue from my old friend and colleague Leigh Montville, who had written a piece in *Sports Illustrated* about time spent in one giant facility, the World Congress Center, a venue for six sports. I decided to see it for myself. That brought me to the venue for Greco-Roman wrestling, the form that prohibits holds below the waist. I had never seen it in person.

And there stood Aleksandr Karelin. He was from Novosibirsk in Siberia. He had not lost a match in nine years and had only been taken into overtime once. It could be argued that no man or woman, in any sport, had come to the Atlanta Olympics as a bigger favorite to win an event. "To say that he is himself 6-4 and 285 is merely a starting point," I wrote. "He is, as they say around Gold's, cut. Ripped. Put together. Massive thighs. Massive chest. Massive arms. Massive hands. Massive head, out of which stare a pair of deep-set eyes that appear capable of staring into your soul." It also occurred to me he could have been the greatest pass-rushing defensive end of all time.

An American named Matt Ghaffari was obsessed with Karelin. He was Ghaffari's Moby Dick, his White Whale. Ghaffari had wrestled and lost to Karelin thirteen times in sites ranging from Karelin's hometown to a parking lot in Concord, California. "It's like wrestling King Kong," Ghaffari explained. "I've always thought that if you want to wrestle Aleksandr Karelin, you've got to teach a couple of techniques to the strongest animal on earth, and that's a big gorilla."

"He is the complete psychological master," pointed out American Greco-Roman coach Rob Hermann. "Nothing which happens out there bothers him. He wins matches before they even occur. Wrestlers have been known to lose in advance so they wouldn't have to face him."

Talk about hitting the journalistic jackpot! An Aleksandr Karelin is exactly why you come to an Olympics.

I had discovered all this in the afternoon. Of course, I had to return in the evening to see if Ghaffari could bring down the White Whale, and of course he couldn't. The final score was 1–0, but that's all he needed. The story got even better because after the match Karelin waxed rhapsodic, talking about how the music played at the event "is particularly appropriate when you leave the platform, and you are *with* the shield and not *on* the shield, as the ancient Greeks might say." Let me know the next time one of our athletes references the ancient Greeks.

Fast-forward four years to the 2000 Summer Olympics in Sydney. Karelin's unbeaten streak had stretched to thirteen years. This time there was a little advance fanfare, and so when America's Rulon Gardner was able to extricate himself from a hold to manufacture the only point in the gold medal match, he became instantly famous. It was a great story and easy to write, but to me, America and NBC were a little late to the party. I had discovered Aleksandr Karelin four years earlier as part of my own personal Olympics.

Gardner, a native of Afton, Wyoming, had a dramatic life following his triumph in Sydney. In 2002 he and friends nearly died after being stranded in the Wyoming snow while on a snowmobiling expedition. He lost the middle toe on his right foot to frostbite. In 2007 he was in a light airplane crash in Lake Powell, Utah. Gardner and two companions survived an hour swim in forty-four-degree water to reach shore. In 2011, after his weight escalated to 474 pounds, he was a contestant on *The Biggest Loser*, the weight-loss reality show. In 2012 he filed for bankruptcy; Karelin, by contrast, was part of the torch-lighting ceremony at the opening of the Sochi Olympics.

By 2000 I had been to five Olympics and I knew how to get attuned to the rhythm of each particular Games. The frustrating thing about the Olympics for a writer is the obvious reality that you can only be one place at a time. But even when you guess wrong you can sometimes salvage a story if the logistics are good and you can get from Point A to Point B in time.

Sydney was a good example. I was at the swimming venue the night when Lithuania almost toppled the haughty American basketball team. I had been watching the final few minutes on TV. Suddenly, that near upset became the Story for an American columnist, particularly one whose supposed field of expertise was basketball. Fortunately, the basketball arena was nearby. I was one of many Americans who hustled out of the swimming venue over to the basketball arena, where we were able to converse with all the principals from both teams. But if the swimming pool and basketball arena had not been so blissfully close to each other, there would have been no basketball stories for us that night.

Sydney also provided me with a unique story in a sport about which I had close to zero knowledge. Nothing in my sports upbringing had prepared me to cover a women's gold medal match in water polo. About all I knew of this sport was that the 1956 men's match between the Soviet Union and Hungary had left plenty of blood in the pool.

There was no blood involved in Australia's 4–3 victory over the Americans, but there were buckets of tears shed by *both* sides. The ending was beyond stunning. American Brenda Villa had scored with 13.1 seconds remaining to tie the match at 3. But with 1.3 seconds separating the USA from overtime, team captain Julie Swail was called for an "exclusion," the water polo term for a penalty. Amid what could only be described as complete confusion on the part of the Americans, Australia's Yvette Higgins fired a shot past USA goalkeeper Bernice Orwig with no time left. In the history of simultaneous Agony vs. Ecstasy, this has to rank near the top of any list.

The postgame press conference was unlike any I have ever attended. Everybody was crying, and this was forty-five minutes after the conclusion of the match! American coach Guy Baker hugged Australian coach Istvan Gorgenyi. The Australians clapped heartily for American grande dame Maureen O'Toole, who had come out of a three-year retirement at age thirty-nine the instant she heard women's water polo would be included in the Sydney Olympics. Anyone who had not seen the match would have had a hard time figuring out who had won and who had lost. And anyone who had questioned the feasibility of putting this sport, and these people, in the 2000 Olympics needed question it no longer. "All I know is that somewhere up there in that Big IOC In The Sky, good ol' Baron de Coubertin is telling people it sure was a good idea to let these folks into his little soiree," I wrote in my water polo column. It turned out to be the right place at the right time, and that's what you pray for at an Olympics.

Accommodations at the Olympics are rarely memorable. I was put up at Olympic dormitory-style venues in Barcelona, Lillehammer, Nagano, and Torino. They were all fine. Clean rooms. Maid service. Breakfast provided. A bar in each. No problem. Hotels of varying quality hosted us in Atlanta, Sydney, Salt Lake City, Beijing, Vancouver, and London.

At the 2004 Summer Olympics in Athens, however, my accommodations were unusual, to say the least: I was given a room on an upper floor of a fully functioning maternity hospital. There was absolutely nothing wrong with it, and it was conveniently located next door to the complex containing several venues, including the main stadium, the primary basketball arena, and the Main Press Centre. But it was completely fascinating to get off the elevator every day and see maternity patients moving around.

Four years later, the Summer Olympics were in Beijing, which was both predictable and surprising, at least to me. I never doubted for a moment that the Chinese government would put on a dazzling Opening Ceremony or that the facilities would all be beyond first-rate. These games were of paramount importance to the regime. We had all read and heard the stories in the run-up to the games about the displacement of people by the hundreds of thousands to accommodate the new venues.

But modern urban China would be a big shock to Karl Marx, or even Chairman Mao. The government's interest is in maintaining political power, not in advancing Marxism as an economic philosophy. China is what the USA would be if there was but one political party and it allowed not even a smidgen of reasonable dissent. In other words, go ahead and make your money like any good capitalist, but don't challenge us when we tell you something. Just do it and keep your mouth shut.

While that isn't especially surprising, I wasn't ready for Beijing itself. With its tall glass buildings, it's Houston except that the inhabitants speak Mandarin, not Texan. It's got everything any big American city has, including traffic jams and an excellent, if somewhat limited, subway system.

No doubt the Chinese wanted good international press. The hotel where Team *Boston Globe* was staying was a new five-star property attached to the Main Press Centre. Upon arriving we were instantly given our room key and told we could check in in the room. And what a room! There was a problem with my television; I forget the exact nature. I placed a call to the front desk and shortly afterward heard a knock on the door. Two people wheeled in a new large screen! In five minutes it was hooked up and that was the end of my TV issues for the two and a half weeks.

I don't recall encountering any logistical problems in Beijing. I will say this: one thing no one can ever say in China is "We didn't have enough people to do the job." In terms of Olympic competition, during the rest of the twenty-first century it is difficult to imagine any future Summer Olympics in which China will not have both the most gold medals and the most medals overall. They have the manpower, they have the will, and they have the sheer ruthlessness to become expert in just about any sport.

My concluding column from Beijing observed:

> We know that many of the Chinese athletes pay a fearful price for their success. Plucked from their homes at tender ages by roving talent scouts, many of the Chinese are forced to exchange a mother's hug and a father's encouragement for a rigid life in a sports academy where they do nothing but eat/sleep/train 24/7/365. Scores of medal winners have not seen their parents in two years. One little gold-medal-winning girl in something-or-

> other was absolutely terrified at the winner's press conference, having nothing to say. Friends revealed she had not been home in four years. Americans aren't going to do this in order to win medals, nor should they.

China has professional leagues in sports such as basketball and soccer, but they do not dominate the consciousness the way pro leagues do in America and Western Europe. I had renewed my acquaintance with Bostonian Tom McCarthy, president of Beijing International Group and a leading authority on not just Chinese but all Asian sports. He had been living in China for twelve years and he laid it out. "In this country," he explained, "the first priority is the Olympics. Then it's the National Games. Then it's the Provincial Games. And then it's the Asian Games. The pro leagues are nowhere near that level of interest."

The eleven Olympics and four basketball World Championships I covered gave me an invaluable perspective. Americans in general are shamefully parochial. So many other athletic endeavors exist beyond the boundaries of baseball, basketball, hockey, soccer, and American football. The Olympics are a welcome break from the American routine. I love the look and feel of them and the way the Olympics bring out the patriotic fervor of the home population.

This was even true at the 2012 Summer Olympics in London, the announcement of which had been greeted domestically with almost terminal ennui in many quarters of the country. In the end, though, the English astonished themselves with the depth of their fervor for all things Olympic. That English athletes performed splendidly, doing especially well, as the joke was frequently told, in sports where one performs sitting down (rowing and cycling), was of course inspiring. But as is invariably the case in the Olympics, which was the chicken and which the egg was a matter of legitimate debate.

Thanks to the Olympics, I learned about the DACE, the Dreaded Air-Conditioner Effect, which can alter the course of badminton matches.

Thanks to the Olympics, I learned about a sport in which Americans ought to be unbeatable, given our proliferation of superb midsized (six five–ish) athletes, but one in which we are so terrible we seldom even qualify for the Olympics: handball, a sport that combines basketball with volleyball, and one in which we should be internationally competitive. But the sport has never caught on in America.

Thanks to the Olympics, I learned that the great international traveling fans are the Brazilians, Swedes, and Norwegians. The greatest of all are the Brazilians, who cheer loudly and party relentlessly. And this is without their number one sport—soccer—being much of an Olympic factor.

Thanks to the Olympics, I learned that during international competition, American journalists are downright stoics compared to our foreign counterparts, most of whom could not possibly adhere to the American standard of "No cheering in the press box."

In this vein, the seminal moment of my Olympic career came in Atlanta in 1996. You may recall the great to-do over the surprising late-career success of Irish swimmer Michelle Smith de Bruin. Ireland is not a swimming country and Michelle Smith had not made much of an international impact until she hooked up with Erik de Bruin, a coach who had been banned for being associated with performance-enhancing drugs and who would marry her. Amid great controversy about whether or not she was clean, she swam to three gold medals, winning both the two-hundred- and four-hundred-meter individual medleys, plus the four-hundred-meter freestyle.

At one of the postrace press conferences, the Irish media was seated mainly on the left of the aisle and the Americans mainly on the right. Some of the questions posed by the Americans were somewhat, shall we say, leading. It was obviously not a comfortable moment for someone who had just won a gold medal.

Then a member of the Irish media jumped up. He went off on a long spiel in Gaelic. When he was done, he turned to the Americans. "Sour grapes!" he hollered.

I'm going to miss the Olympics.

CHAPTER 18

Beat Me, Whip Me, Take My Picture

When USA Basketball announced that an NBA All-Star Team would represent the United States at the 1992 Barcelona Olympics in place of our traditional amateur team, this was an enormous story in the making. Happily for me, sports editor Don Skwar told me I would be going to Barcelona and that my primary duty would be covering men's and women's basketball. This was one I just couldn't pass up.

I had developed a taste for international basketball after covering the first two McDonald's Opens, in Milwaukee in 1987 and in Madrid a year later. These were the NBA's baby steps into the international arena. The first was simply a three-team round robin featuring the Celtics, the Soviet Union national team, and Tracer Milan from the Italian league. Though the Lakers were the reigning NBA champions, the Celtics were tapped because they had the longest-standing international visibility, the brand needed to give the event clout around the world. The Celtics were again included in Madrid, the other participants being host Real Madrid, Scavolini Pesaro from Italy, and a Yugoslavian national team featuring Drazen Petrovic, Vlade Divac, Dino Radja, and a young Toni Kukoc.

Prior to the initial McDonald's affair, my only direct exposure to high-level international play had been covering an exhibition game in Madison Square Garden in 1973 between a U.S. team coached by Bob Cousy and a team of Russians. Ernie DiGregorio had taken over the game and I wrote something to the effect that while the Russians had steadily improved, the biggest difference between Us and Them was that They had no Ernie DiGregorios.

I remember thinking that the Russians, particularly the guards, were, well, clunky. They were somewhat robotic. They played by the numbers. They had no creativity. That's what I meant when I said they had no Ernie DiGregorios. Ivan Edeshko was not a bad player, but the Russian guard exemplified what I was talking about, moving around the court as if he were following a blueprint.

In Madrid, it was all about goodwill and business—expanding the NBA brand. The Lakers were the reigning NBA champions, but that didn't matter to the Spaniards. The Celtics were still the team that most represented the NBA in their eyes. "It was important for the Celtics to come," explained Scavolini Pesaro coach Valerio Bianchini. "Los Angeles may be a better team now, but for Europeans, the Boston Celtics mean more than L.A. The style of the Boston Celtics is something closer to our mentality."

The Celtics players had been reluctant. "I didn't want to come," said Kevin McHale. "This is our exhibition season. We have a new coach [Jimmie Rodgers having replaced K. C. Jones]. We need the work we can get at home. Other teams are getting ahead of us. But the people were so nice, and everybody was trying so hard to please us that you develop a different feeling."

Larry Bird was at the zenith of his popularity. The crowd assembled to get a Bird autograph at the Corte Inglés department store broke a record set by Sophia Loren. He was totally overwhelmed by his reception. "I enjoyed every minute of it," he later said. "As soon as we got here the players realized everything was going to be first class. The games themselves were a new experience."

They were played by international rules, and don't think that doesn't make a difference. All balls on the rim are live. Throw-ins do not have to be handled by an official, and advancing the basketball often involves a combination of dribbling and a maneuver that could best be described as hop-skip-and-jumping. Yugoslavia's Zarko Paspalj continually advanced from Point A to Point B in a manner Americans assumed *must* be illegal on all seven continents and any number of galaxies. Except that it wasn't.

The Celtics were given some competition as a result. Yugoslavia led them with a 40–36 score with five minutes remaining in the half. Real Madrid was hanging around with forty-seven seconds left in the third period, trailing by a doable six points. But the Celtics did rouse themselves sufficiently to win both games.

The local press recognized the team was only playing as hard as it needed to. *Marca*, a national sports daily, observed: "When Larry Bird came back to play with nine minutes to play, the game was about to be decided. The blonde one was back to tip the balance, to shake the *madridistas* out of their sweet dreams, to ruin what could have been the greatest success in the history of the club. The wakeup was brusque and at the three-point line. Larry placed himself there, let his teammates move the ball."

I wish I'd said that.

This was all taking place soon after a Soviet Union team had won a surprising basketball gold medal in Seoul in 1988. That was accomplished at the expense of the traditional group of American college kids, but it was already becoming clear that the level of international play was rising at a rapid rate. The Yugoslavia team we saw in Madrid featured a group of young players whose names would indeed become known to NBA fans: Petrovic, Divac, Radja, Kukoc, Paspalj, and Stojan Vrankovic. They were not on a level with the Celtics, but their raw skill was evident. Basketball was becoming a fully international sport.

With the McDonald's Open the NBA had put its foot into international waters. Now, of course, they go swimming there on a regular basis. There had been NBA involvement internationally going back to the 1950s, with Red Auerbach giving clinics in Europe and Asia and also bringing NBA All-Star teams over for exhibitions. But the McDonald's Open set the forces in motion that would make the NBA the international conglomerate it is today.

In addition to the opportunity to see a great European city and try out my *español*—nowhere near as proficient as my *français*—the trip to Madrid gave me an itch I will never stop scratching. I fell in love with international basketball.

Anyone interested in the definitive story of the first group of NBA players to represent the USA in the Olympic Games need only pick up a copy of Jack McCallum's 2012 book *Dream Team*. It's all there: how the idea was hatched, how the team was picked, how it all played out, and how everyone feels about it now, twenty-plus years later. If you care at all about the subject, it's a must read, especially if you are of the opinion that the Dream Team came about because a frustrated United States was determined to right the wrong that was the Soviet Union's triumph in Seoul.

The progenitor of the One and Only Dream Team was not an American, but rather a Serb, Boris Stankovic, who at that time was secretary general of FIBA (Fédération Internationale de Basketball), the governing body overseeing all "amateur" basketball outside the United States. In a prior life he had used his degree in veterinary medicine from the University of Belgrade to create a career as a meat inspector. Thus, in his book McCallum delights in continually referring to the FIBA chief as "the Inspector of Meat," doing so with all due respect and admiration for a man he clearly likes.

Boris Stankovic knew that the best basketball on earth was played in the NBA, and his goal was to see the rest of the world rise to that level of basketball expertise and artistry. He reasoned the only way that could happen was if the rest of the world experienced playing against the very best, to feel the fire of the dragon, if you will.

America would have been content to go about its Olympic basketball business as usual. The truth is more criticism was heaped on 1988 Olympic coach John Thompson and the committee that had selected the team than it was on the players themselves. We didn't have enough shooters. We walked it up. John was not even interested in offense. Etc. An effort would have been made to seek different types of players and place them in the hands of a more flexible coach for the Barcelona games in 1992. The overwhelming American sentiment was that the Olympic experience should be reserved for collegians.

No one was asking NBA commissioner David Stern to help restore America's basketball honor, nor was he asking for that responsibility. Some of us have been trying to explain this to people for the past two decades. Jack McCallum summed it up nicely:

> But whatever revisionist history might eventually be written, remember this: the Dream Team resulted from the vision of Boris Stankovic. It was not a secret plot hatched by David Stern to "grow the game," one of the commissioner's favorite phrases.

It was not the result of a crusade by the NBA's marketing demons to sell $200 Authentics in Europe, even though that was an eventuality. It was not frustration built up by the increasing reality that inroads were being made on the United States' claim of basketball supremacy. The idea germinated in the mind of the Inspector of Meat from Belgrade.

That is how I found myself in La Jolla, California, in late June of 1992. The newly formed Team USA was beginning its road to Barcelona by practicing and scrimmaging against a group of eight standout collegians. It was the beginning of what I have jokingly referred to as the greatest boondoggle summer of my life.

I cannot verify how many people can say they were present for the first bounce of the ball at the first practice in La Jolla right through the final buzzer in Barcelona. All I know is I was one of them. It was a great personal experience, but it was also fulfilling journalistically, even if it seemed every game was decided by a hundred points. Again, I repeat: the USA dominance, far from a problem, was totally welcome. Believe me on this, please: the theme of the entire 1992 Olympic basketball experience for the rest of the world was "Beat Me, Whip Me, Take My Picture."

The picture thing began right away, at the pre-Olympics Tournament of the Americas in Portland, Oregon. The first USA opponent was Cuba. They knew they had no chance to win the game, but merely being on the same ninety-four-by-fifty-foot expanse of wooden real estate as the Dream Teamers was going to be a thrill, so the Cubans did the logical thing: they asked to have a joint team photo taken before tip-off. And so a ritual was under way that continued for the remainder of the Tournament of the Americas.

The Cubans did what they could. Final score of the first official competition for the Greatest Basketball Team Ever Assembled: USA 136, Cuba 57. Such was the scope of USA weaponry that Cuban coach Miguel Calderon Gomez was inspired to wax poetic. "In Cuba, we have a saying," he said with a smile: "'You cannot cover the sun with one finger.'"

Legendary American coach Chuck Daly was impressed with his

counterpart's wisdom. "I like that line," he said. "That's something I'll take home with me this week."

There was, of course, no semblance of competition in Portland, Oregon; only Puerto Rico, among the USA's other opponents, lost by fewer than forty points. We did learn a few things about the American team. The first was that Michael Jordan was only going to play hard when he felt like reminding everyone he was Michael Jordan. Second, on a team with Michael Jordan, Magic Johnson, and Larry Bird, the star of stars *this* competition was Charles Barkley. Unlike Michael, he had every intention of playing hard every minute he was on the floor. Unlike Magic Johnson, and especially Larry Bird, he was fully healthy. At age twenty-nine, he was at the peak of his physical powers and he was sufficiently motivated to put on a nightly show, on and off the court. He was, by far, the dominant personality on the Dream Team.

The third thing was the discovery for some, and reminder for others, of just why Chris Mullin was on this team. If Barkley was the most effective player night in and night out, Chris Mullin wasn't far behind. His game consisted of running the floor, coming off picks, and firing up jumpers, mixing in occasional back-door cuts. In this company he was unstoppable, shooting 63 percent from the floor in Portland (50 percent on threes) and 62 percent in Barcelona (54 percent on threes). I know it's almost sacrilegious to cite statistics in reference to the Dream Team, but for some people that's the only way to get a point across. You'll have to take my word on the Chris Mullin Eye Test, but the numbers are irrefutable. He was a spectacular sight on the Dream Team.

I did my due diligence with the Americans, reporting on each game of the Tournament of the Americas as if it really needed dissection. How seriously can you take the thing when Larry Bird jumps up against Venezuela and checks himself into the game? He hadn't played for a few games due to his bad back. With 2:41 remaining and the crowd chanting "La-ree! La-ree!" Magic Johnson yanked his warm-up and Larry bounded to the scorer's table. "I was almost asleep when Magic pulled my pants off," Larry laughed. "I really had no plans to play, but I figured it would be just for a few minutes." He further explained how he was not going to make any hero plays or do anything stupid, but he also had a message for Coach Daly. "Don't worry," he said. "I can still get some shots up."

This was my first live exposure to legitimate international competition. This is when I first saw the daily exchange of gifts, the way internationals salute their fans after a game. And I saw some displays of passion we don't ordinarily see in the States.

I was instantly fascinated by the Uruguayan radio broadcast team. I had never seen such exuberance or so much gesticulation on the part of broadcasters. It would not have surprised me if one of them had jumped over the scorer's table to congratulate a Uruguayan player. One of them seemed even more gonzo than the other two. I was amused, therefore, when informed that the gentleman in question was not actually a part of the official broadcast team. He was a fan, a friend of theirs who had been invited to sit in! That type of passion, I was to discover, was hardly exclusive to the citizens of Uruguay.

The basketball tournament was an opportunity to gauge just where the sport outside the U.S. stood in relation to the Americans. I came to the conclusion that the best way to evaluate the other teams was in reference to American college basketball. "Four questions," I wrote then.

> 1) Could the team win a conference? 2) What would be its NCAA tournament seed? 3) Could it reach the Final Four, under any circumstances? 4) Could it win the whole thing?
>
> Take Mexico, for example. This club had good overall size and was loaded with three-point shooters. Its best player, 30-year old swingman Jose Luis Arroyos, was, in addition to being a Tony Orlando reminds-me-of, a very clever scorer. The man is an experienced pro, after all. He is very wise to the ways of international basketball.
>
> Mexico, which took second in the 1991 Pan Ams, would win the Mid-American or Ohio Valley Conference. It would get a 13th or 14th seed in the NCAA Tournament. It would play the Big Ten or SEC runner-up in the first round and it would either play them close or pull off an upset. Yes, Mexico could get to the Final Four. That's not bad. And Mexico finished seventh in Portland. Brazil or Puerto Rico are in an even higher category.

This was five years after Brazil had beaten the USA in the Pan Am Finals and four years after the then–Soviet Union (in actuality, the

Lithuanian All-Stars) had taken down the Americans in Seoul. The idea that we could send American college kids to these competitions and think a gold medal was a lock was now ludicrous. The world had not caught up to the NBA, but the world had caught up to the collegians.

When I went to Portland that week for the Tournament of the Americas I was at one level of basketball understanding. When I came home from Barcelona two months or so later, I was immensely wiser. And I submit it made me a better writer.

You meet people. You learn things you can put into practical use. In the 1987 Pan Am Finals, most people aware of the outcome have pretty much determined that Brazilian star Oscar Schmidt had an unstoppable game with forty-six points, and that was that. I know I did. But there had been more to it. Brazil guard Manny De Souza, a key player on that team, schooled me one day during the week in Portland. The subject was experience and how it can often trump sheer talent.

"Look at what happened in Indianapolis," he said. "The American kids look up and they are behind by eight points with ten minutes left. *This is not supposed to be happening.* You could see it in their faces. Panic. They score. We score. They score. We score. We trade baskets the rest of the game. They could not handle the rest of the situation. Now let me ask you this. Do you think David Robinson isn't a much better player now than he was then? You know the answer to that question."

Once upon a time, the skill gap between America and the rest of the world was so large that the only way our college kids could lose was via sheer robbery, as took place at the Munich Olympics in 1972. Gradually, though, we started coming up short in various international youth tournaments. Then came Seoul, where the two best players on the floor were the Lithuanians Arvydas Sabonis and Sarunas Marciulionis, each of whom would have success in the NBA. A healthy Sabonis, in fact, was one of the great players in history. One of my real regrets as a basketball fan is that I never got to see the young Sabonis, who was said to be "Bill Walton with a three-pointer." There is no higher praise for any center in my book.

I hadn't thought out the value of experience before having that conversation with Manny De Souza. It was an "Aha!" moment in my ongoing

Little Bobby Ryan catching and little Joey Giangrosso batting, in the window of George Case's sporting goods store in downtown Trenton, N.J., circa 1948.

Bobby Ryan, son of Mr. and Mrs. William P. Ryan of 214 Ellis Ave., is shown above, decked out in full regalia as the "Littlest Dodger of Them All." To meet the convenience of the photographer, Bobby condescended to go to Dunn Field, the home of the "hated" Giants. His proud father is the popular Bill, one of Trenton's outstanding sports figures.

Staff Photo

My picture in the *Trentonian*, age two. Why a Dodgers uniform, rather than a Giants uniform, is a mystery for the ages.

My dad, Bill Ryan.

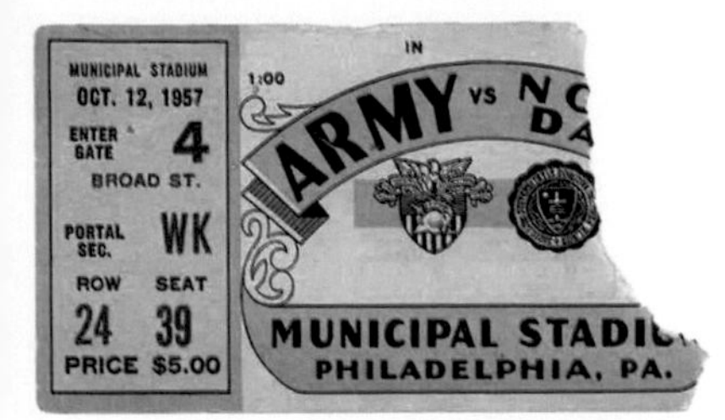

My Mom obtained tickets for the historic 1959 resumption of the Army–Notre Dame rivalry (they had ceased playing after the 1947 clash) five months after my father died.

That's me, the well-dressed Lawrenceville football manager, on one knee. In the foreground is head coach Jack Reydel, who christened me "Scribe."

Air Scribe en route to a three-point play and a career-high 18 against Princeton High. As sports editor of the *Lawrence*, I was shameless enough to put this photo in the paper, albeit alluding in the caption that Jack Purd "was waiting for a pass that would never come."

The twenty-year-old me interviewing Red Auerbach at halftime of a 1966 Boston College game. He had come to scout our star, John Austin. When I saw him being led across the floor, I almost had the Big One.

Tommy Heinsohn in high dudgeon at Madison Square Garden, early 1970s. Hank Finkel and Dave Cowens on the left, me at the table.

Churning out courtside copy in the early 1970s with instant critics checking things out. And players think they operate under pressure! A nightly occurrence back then.

The reporters' table used to be right at courtside.

Me grilling Earl Weaver. Like that hair? I told Earl it was my Ross Grimsley look.

Boston College was playing Vanderbilt, which was on the schedule of both Florida State and Bradley. Dave Cowens (Florida State) and Steve Kuberski (Bradley) were asked to scout on an off night for their respective alma maters. Whatever had just happened on the court must have been pretty funny.

Why is it that athletes who retire, always allow other people to write their career obituary? Isn't it important for the fans to realize, first hand, the factors and thoughts behind the decision to hang it up? How could an athlete possibly sever the emotional bond between him and his loyal supporters without giving an explanation for his actions?

Before I present the evidence in the case of Cowens athlete vs Cowens Private Citizen I would enjoy sharing some rather ideological concepts with you concerning my approach to basketball.

Since day one, other coaches and authorities have tried to ingrain into my thought processes the values of loyalty, discipline, responsibility, dedication and fairness in ones day to day behavior. Of course, we all fall way short of living by these high standards, especially when ones job, financial situation, ego and security is in jeopardy or threatened. But you know, I always felt a slight tinge of guilty when my behavior was the I didn't live up to the expectations set upon me by myself or others. I think this underlying pressure to be guiltless or blameless, caused to develop into the competitor I have been over the years. And it is for this primary reason and others that I will mention that I am going to retire from basketball.

An original sheet from Dave Cowens's hand-written retirement letter, which he handed to me in my hotel room.

I emceed a few *Boston Globe* dinners to honor local scholastic athletes. This guest speaker was famed Olympian Wilma Rudolph.

Renewing acquaintance with fellow 1968 *Boston Globe* intern Peter Gammons, at the Toronto airport during the 1992 American League Championship Series.

Oscar Schmidt, the legendary Brazilian basketball star, asked for Larry Bird's autograph and I obtained it for him. This is us at the Barcelona Olympics in 1992.

My Mom, Mary Ryan, with Larry Bird, at the dinner celebrating his statue dedication in February 1988.

Portrait of Henry James
Crayon drawing on paper
by Abbott Handerson Thayer, c. 188
Collection, American Academy of Arts and Letters
New York City

MIDDLESEX-ESSEX
MA 018 3 L
05 OCT 2008 PM

Dear Bob –

Everybody keeps telling me about your terrific piece on Ted Williams and me. You have made me momentarily famous among people who don't read much. To those who do, you have always been a hero.

Many thanks,

John [Updike]

Mr. Bob Ryan
Editorial Rooms
Boston Globe
Morrissey Blvd
Boston, MA
02107

John Updike communicated via postcard. This one is thanking me for a column I wrote extolling his legendary 1960 *New Yorker* piece on Ted Williams's final game. Note the brackets surrounding "Updike." In case I was wondering.

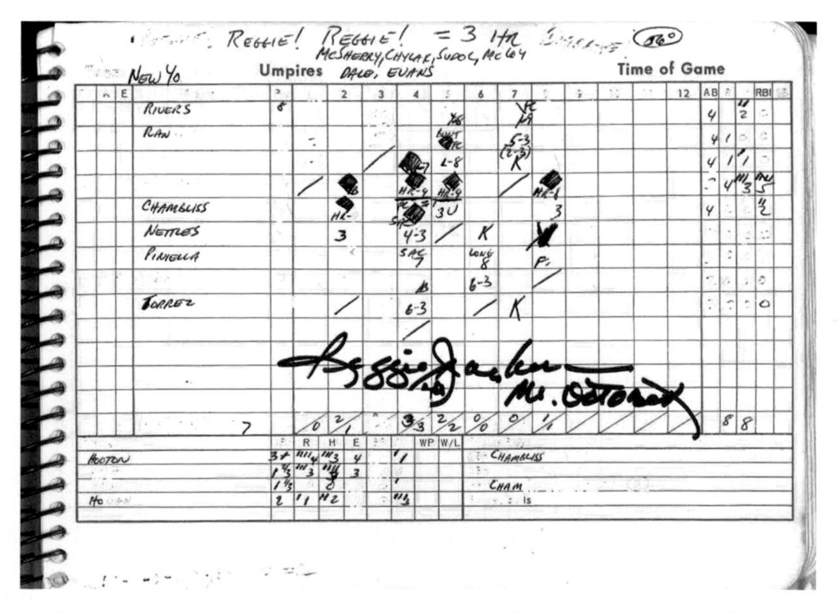

I asked Reggie Jackson to sign my scorebook from his unforgettable three-homer outburst in Game 6 of the 1977 World Series, and this is what I got.

Elaine and me, with Bill and Lori Walton.

Me and the truly great *Globe* columnist Ray Fitzgerald, flanking *Globe* All-Scholastic Dinner speaker Al McGuire. I remember the punch line in Al's speech was "Eat the banana." Whatever that meant.

Me and the great Tigers announcer Ernie Harwell in Tiger Stadium during the last year of its existence, 1999.

Me, Magic, and Larry in Monte Carlo, 1992, before the first game of the Dream Team. If the house is burning down, this gets saved first.

basketball education, and I couldn't have had it sitting home in Massachusetts watching it all on TV.

Despite the fact the USA team was far from healthy, its fortunes were still assured. Larry Bird was an old and battered thirty-five, and his participation beyond Portland was in the "if" category. He had to see his physical therapist, Dan Dyrek, after the Tournament of the Americas was over. But while the flesh was weak, the spirit was totally willing. He loved being a part of this team. "I should be all right in another week," he said when he got back to Boston. "I can't wait to get to Barcelona."

Magic Johnson was dealing with a bad knee. He wound up pretty much willing himself through the entire Dream Team experience. Clyde Drexler had achy knees. Patrick Ewing, who had sprained an ankle late in the playoffs, injured his right thumb during an intra-squad scrimmage. John Stockton, however, had the most serious issue, sustaining a fractured fibula in a collision with Michael Jordan thirty seconds after entering the Cuba game. In a normal NBA circumstance, a Hall of Fame point guard would not be on the floor during mop-up time of a seventy-nine-point game. But on this team everyone was a Hall of Famer–to–be with the exception of Christian Laettner, and if the Hall were going about its business the way it should, he'd also be there by virtue of being one of the top ten collegiate players ever. Even without Stockton and the impaired Magic, the team had the floor leadership it needed from Scottie Pippen.

In the end, my biggest personal takeaway was a relationship with Oscar Schmidt. Savvy American basketball fans knew who Oscar Daniel Bezerra Schmidt was even before he had that forty-six-point game against the USA in the 1987 Pan Am Finals. He had begun his professional career in 1974 at age sixteen in his native Brazil and by the time he was twenty was on the NBA radar screen. He was six eight, he could handle the ball, and he could really shoot. More than that, he loved to shoot. Loved it, adored it, lived for it. Not for him the subtleties of moving without the ball, setting a screen, or setting up someone else to shoot. For Oscar Schmidt, shooting *was* basketball. He reveled in his image as a gunner, as we used to say back home in Trenton.

"Some people are piano movers," Schmidt said, "and some are piano players. *I* am a piano player." I used to think Oscar Schmidt was the person who first said that, but I'm told he borrowed it. I can only tell you he embraced it as much as any player I have ever known.

Knowing full well Oscar Schmidt's concept of basketball, the New Jersey Nets chose him in the sixth round of the 1984 draft. It was a throwaway pick, to be sure, and the team did not exactly move heaven and earth to sign Schmidt, who at that time was making a nice living throwing up jumper after jumper in Italy. "They offered me one hundred thousand dollars," he told me. "The minimum was sixty-five thousand dollars. It was only for one year. It did not show the proper respect." Oscar obviously felt the Nets had confused him with some piano mover.

This may have been the best thing that ever happened to Oscar Schmidt. He did not have an NBA sensibility, and not just because he would have had a hard time playing defense to even a minimum NBA standard. Oscar Schmidt was just too sweet, too human, to get caught up in the cutthroat NBA world.

After his Brazil team had lost a Tournament of the Americas game to Venezuela, in so doing losing its chance to play against the USA in Portland (they would get their chance in Barcelona), Oscar nonetheless lingered on the court to sign autographs, mainly for small children. At the postgame press conference he was asked how he could have remained to sign those autographs after such a tough loss.

"This is not war," he said, shrugging. "The children were not at fault."

My own Oscar Schmidt story began at his first postgame press conference. He stated that one of his objectives in coming to Portland was to get Larry Bird's autograph. "Larry Bird is my idol," he declared. I figured I could facilitate this when the competition was over. I even secured Oscar's mailing address in Italy. I'd take care of it in due time. But Oscar was relentless.

After Brazil defeated Mexico, the only thing on Oscar's mind was Larry Bird. He practically wailed into the microphone, "Who will get me get me Larry Bird's autograph?"

Oscar had company. Marcel De Souza got into the act. "I know *everything* about Larry Bird," he told me. "His birthday is December seven. Mine is December four. I read his book. I want to play against Larry Bird."

Now I had no choice. I was the one who could get the gaga Brazilians Larry Bird's autograph, but it had to be more than just an autograph. I had to get two copies of *Drive*, the book of his life story I had coauthored with him three years earlier. Fortunately, Portland has one of America's great bookstores. Powell's is practically big enough to be the fifty-first state, and it had one hardbound and one paperback copy in stock. I decided Oscar would get the hardbound and Marcel the paperback.

I called Larry at his hotel and told him what was going on. There was no chance of my penetrating security at his hotel, but he said that was okay: "I get to the arena early to shoot. I can do it then." This had become important to me because I had developed significant attachments to Oscar and Marcel. I couldn't take a chance on Larry scribbling out a perfunctory "Best Wishes," so I concocted the inscriptions for each man. All Larry had to do was copy.

To Oscar: "I want you 1-on-1 in French Lick!"

To Marcel: "You're lucky I wasn't in Indianapolis." That was the site of the historic Brazil triumph over the USA in the 1987 Pan Am Games.

The next morning Brazil beat Uruguay, 139–93. Oscar had a routine thirty-five on thirteen-for-nineteen shooting. Marcel, a six-six guard, had twenty-one. The postgame press conference started and about seven seconds in Oscar asked who would get him Larry Bird's autograph.

The press conference ended and I called them over. I handed Oscar his book. He read his inscription with eyes bulging. "Marcel, look at this!" But he had an inquiry. "What is this French Lick?"

I handed the paperback to Marcel. He went off on a Bird riff after reading the inscription. "I first saw Bird at the 1978 World University Games in Bulgaria," he explained. "I had heard about him from a friend of mine from Kansas I met when I played a year at Bradley. My coach at Bradley, Joe Stowell, had told us that there was a player at Indiana who was going to change the game."

"So, Oscar," I asked, "how long have you been a fan of Larry Bird?"

"Since forever," he exclaimed. "He is the perfect forward. Every shooter, every player like me, has Larry Bird for his idol. He is the perfect player. He has no failures. He does everything. I have three idols: Oscar Robertson, Bob Morse [former Pennsylvania star and longtime Italian League mainstay], and Larry Bird. I have the other two autographs. Now I have Larry Bird's."

Oscar showed off the book to Spanish-speaking journalists for a half hour. The two combined must have thanked me a thousand times. I, in turn, was most thankful for the existence of Powell's.

That was clearly the personal highlight of the week, but there was always something fascinating going on. The number one on-court happening took place in the game between Team USA and Argentina. The Argentines had a pretty good six-five guard named Marco Milanesio. At one point in the game Milanesio set himself up in a low post position on the right box, on the same side of the court as the Argentina bench. When he realized Magic Johnson was guarding him, he waved excitedly to his mates on the bench.

"*Aquí! Aquí!*" he yelled. "*Fotografía!*" He begged someone to snap his picture as he was posting up the great Magic Johnson.

Such things do not happen on a languid Tuesday evening in February in Milwaukee. By the way, though he never played in the NBA, Oscar Schmidt retired at age forty-eight having scored more points combined, at all professional levels, than anyone in history. The number is 49,737.

The Americans had come to Portland to put the car on the road and chart the best route to take to Barcelona. Everyone else had come to qualify for the Olympics. Unexpectedly, however, this gathering of NBA All-Stars captured the imagination of the rest of the world, even if the domestic audience was underwhelmed. Many Americans, ignorant about the whys and wherefores of the Dream Team's very existence, seemed embarrassed. They couldn't get it into their heads that being dunked on or otherwise athletically abused by the Americans was an honor. They couldn't possibly imagine an American gushing about an international athlete the way Messrs. Schmidt and De Souza had fawned over Larry Bird.

"They *want* us to dunk on them," marveled Magic.

When the Tournament of the Americas was over, and the routs were in the books, the contest was on to describe the reality of the Dream Team:

Bronze medal: Former Soviet coach Alexander Gomelsky to Chuck Daly. "You no win gold? I give you ticket to Siberia."

Silver medal: Canadian center Bill Wennington, an NBA player himself. "Can anybody beat the USA? The world will end before that happens, and if it does, the United States will end with it."

Gold medal: Venezuela coach Julio Toro. "The United States team is two hundred light-years from the rest of the world. If you got an All-Star Team from the other teams here, spot us thirty points and we will still lose. This is a clinic and it will be a clinic in Barcelona."

I've now reconsidered and think I should have awarded Gomelsky the gold.

I rather liked one other line. Horacio Lopez, a six-five forward from Uruguay, was a hardworking guy who knew how to play, and particularly how to score. He led all competitors in Portland—yes, even Brazil's piano player—by dropping in thirty-four points a game. I introduced myself to him one night at the hotel bar and complimented him on his game. As we downed our *cervezas* he summed up the experience on the part of the non-Americans with one precise phrase.

"They are putting us in our place," he sighed.

From Portland, the Dream Team traveled to Monte Carlo for a week of practice before heading to Barcelona. Whose idea was that? Remind me to include him or her in the will.

Monte Carlo is a fascinating place. They say it could fit into Central Park, but you'd never know it since it is layered and its general design is vertical, not horizontal. So it doesn't seem that small.

The work routine, if you can call it that, was simple. Chuck Daly's practices were around eleven thirty or twelve noon. We weren't allowed in until the final five or ten minutes, so there was no need to get to the arena much before one thirty. We then had a half hour to interview people (they were all available), after which we hustled back to our rooms, banged out our stories—I had decided in advance there wasn't going to be any need to convene the Pulitzer committee as a result of anything I would write that week—whipped on our bathing suits, and headed to the beach or the rooftop pool. The hardest part of the week was trying not to feel guilty about doing this for a living.*

We missed what has been called the Greatest Game Ever Played, the

---

* One more Monte Carlo vignette: Prince Albert pulling up to the front of the hotel in a spiffy sports car, hopping out, and casually flipping the keys to a valet. Ah, Monte Carlo.

intrasquad scrimmage at Stade Louis II in which all these A-listers brought their egos and their A-games to put on a display of basketball virtuosity many of the participants swear to this day was the best basketball they have ever seen. Jack McCallum's *Dream Team* offers the play-by-play in vivid detail. I recall Chuck Daly telling us we had just missed something special.

We weren't socializing with the players there, but we heard the stories, many of them revolving around Michael Jordan's golfing escapades. He played thirty-six holes. No, he played fifty-four. As Chuck Daly would famously say about this and that, "Whatever." Michael did what Michael wanted.

We heard that assistant coach P. J. Carlesimo's duties included being the team's social director and booker of Michael's tee times. Mike Krzyzewski, another assistant, seemed to have an affinity for the slots. I did take note that Scottie Pippen, a notoriously fragile individual when dealing with the suffocating and strident personality of Jordan, would not sit at the same blackjack table as number 23. I couldn't get out of my head the factoid told to me by one who knows: those spectacles Pippen favored away from the arena were clear frames. In this he was a man ahead of his time.

I took full advantage of the festive atmosphere. One day I asked NBA PR honcho, and longtime friend, Brian McIntyre if he would do me a gigantic favor and take a picture of me with Bird and Magic. Forget that detachment crap. This was history. I was wearing a special T-shirt I had purchased on the final day of the Tournament of the Americas in Portland. It was black, with a picture of each hoop demigod on the front. On the back their career accomplishments were listed on matching tablets, Ten Commandments style.

I don't know whether Bird or Magic did it first, but one of them put his forearm on my shoulder. The other one followed suit on the opposite shoulder. The result is a treasured photo that hangs in my home office. It is one of the first two keepsakes I will pluck from my office if the house is ever burning down. The other is a copy of John Updike's *Hub Fans Bid Kid Adieu*, the one signed "from an admirer."

In Barcelona I wasn't staying in a luxury hotel overlooking the Mediterranean, but rather in standard Olympic press dormitory-style accommodations, complete with a roommate, my *Globe* colleague Ron

Borges. He had arrived first and happily had purchased a fan, which ran 24/7 for our entire stay. Summer in Barcelona.

Ronnie and I hardly saw each other during our stay. He had the boxing beat and we seldom arrived back at our room at the same time. In deference to the different time zones in which the Olympic press corps operates, the people in charge of our complex ran a twenty-four-hour bar. The only problem was that some of the four and five A.M. revelers seemed to forget that many of their international counterparts were trying to sleep at those hours. Not blaming anyone in particular, but you Germans know who you are.

As far as the basketball was concerned, the Dream Team was nothing less than a major rock band on tour. Nothing on the court changed, and as always Charles Barkley kept things interesting. He made headlines immediately when he planted an elbow in the torso of a bewildered Angolan named Herlander Coimbra, claiming he had been provoked and laughing it off by saying, "Hey, how did I know he wasn't carrying a spear?" Only Charles could get away with that line. But as we have learned in the last two decades, only Charles can get away with a lot of the things he says and does.

On the court, he continued his dominance of the international basketball community. Charles led Dream Team scorers with eighteen points a game on 71 percent shooting. He posted up at will. He shot threes. He ripped down rebounds and routinely blasted coast-to-coast for shattering dunks. He reduced Karl Malone, who would retire as the second leading NBA scorer of all time, to caddy status.

Charles went to games when other teams were playing and told future foes just what he was planning on doing to them. He became famous for his three A.M. excursions down Barcelona's famed Rambla, a thoroughfare leading from the heart of the city to the waterfront. No one had a better time or made more out of the Dream Team experience than Charles Barkley.

I was looking forward to the USA's game with Brazil, because Oscar Schmidt would get a chance to play against his idol, number 33. Oscar was no longer the consistent player he had been and I knew that if the Americans had chosen to target him, as they had Croatia's Toni Kukoc in an early round, they could embarrass him. I was counting on Larry Bird to make sure that didn't happen. They let him off gently. Team USA won by a predictable score of 127–83, but Oscar had a late flurry and finished with twenty-four points in the presence of his idol. Believe me, getting to twenty mattered to Oscar.

If anyone doubted that the Dream Team needed something of a stimulus to up their intensity, consider the Lithuanian game. The key to this was Jordan. Michael had probably played only thirty-six holes, or a mere twenty-seven, that morning and afternoon. He was in the mood against a Lithuania team led by Arvydas Sabonis and Sarunas Marciulionis. Someone must have reminded him about the role these two had played in defeating the Americans four years earlier in Seoul. David Robinson, perhaps.

Larry Bird was also feeling good that night. Dedicating himself to passing (he took but one outside shot), Bird orchestrated the attack, putting on an all-around passing clinic after intermission, sparking the Dream Team to a seventy-eight-point second half—and that was in twenty minutes, the standard international half.

The final score was 127–76. "There was a sense of competition," Jordan said by way of explanation.

Everyone knew who would win gold in men's basketball in Barcelona. The games were not so much legitimate athletic contests as they were demonstrations of basketball artistry put on for the edification of an adoring public by the world's greatest practitioners. I suppose it would have been appropriate had the Dream Team saved its best performance for last.

That did not happen, but there was one dramatic moment in the gold medal game against Croatia. Each of the seven previous contests had been wire-to-wire destructions. The USA had never trailed, not once. They were leading Croatia, 23–22, with 9:44 remaining in the first half when Franjo Arapovic finished off a fast break with a dunk, drawing a foul on David Robinson as a bonus. He made the free throw and thus the world saw a magic moment on the scoreboard: "CRO 25 USA 23."

Some enterprising Croatian should have snapped a picture of that scoreboard. He would have had fifteen seconds to get the job done before Charles Barkley drilled a straightaway three to restore the American lead for good. The USA was off on a 33–13 run, ending the night's competition.

"It was exciting at that point," agreed Croatia's Drazen Petrovic. "But all we can do at that point is try to play the best we can. It is impossible to beat that team." The final score was a rather respectable 117–85. When it was over Magic Johnson basically apologized for a somewhat lack-luster effort in the gold medal game. "Our problem was that we had played Croatia already and we weren't up for this one the way we were for Lithuania. I think if we had played CIS [the former Soviet Union entry] we would have been up."

Larry Bird, who had shared the co-captaincy of the team with Magic, spoke a harsh truth. "If the games were closer, I might have been more excited on the medal stand. But when you're up there and you win by fifty every night, it takes something away."

Bird loved the overall experience. He certainly wanted to be a part of it. But the element of suspense that gives any athlete a buzz was missing. Larry did one thing no one else did, however. He seized the opportunity to thank the eight collegians who had provided the Dream Team its first competition back in La Jolla. "I think our best basketball was against the college guys in San Diego," he said.

The circumstances Bird alluded to were the scrimmages between the Kids and the Stars. In the first game the Kids prevailed 88–80, and it was just the get-their-attention coaching tool that Chuck Daly needed. The Stars arrived at practice the following day with game faces plastered on. After a few minutes of play it was Stars 30, Kids 2, the 2 being a pair of free throws. "Those kids opened our eyes up pretty good," Bird recalled. "From that day on, we picked up."

The players knew they had just had an amazing experience, but I doubt if any of them had completely grasped the extent to which they had elevated their sport internationally. Their elders knew, however. The shooting and passing far surpassed any known standard. The rest of the world now had a clearer understanding of just how high the bar was.

"People may say it's overkill and all that," said Mike Krzyzewski, who would later be called upon to rescue a faltering Team USA program. "But there is no way anyone who professes to like basketball couldn't appreciate that. Anyone who doesn't isn't a true basketball fan. You must understand what this team is doing, and its impact on the game. This is history—and we'll be seeing the benefit of it for the next decade."

No one was puffing his chest out farther than the Inspector of Meat. "Only by playing against the best teams can people improve," said Boris Stankovic, the proud head of FIBA and the man whose stubborn insistence that the American professionals be included in the Olympics had transformed the sport forever. "Open competition [i.e., bringing in NBA players] is absolutely necessary to bring new blood into international basketball."

While the world knew who was getting the gold, the real competition was for the remaining two medals. These were the first Summer Olympics since the breakup of the former Soviet Union three years earlier. It was also the first Summer Olympics following the breakup of the former Yugoslavia. In 1988 the Soviet Union had defeated Yugoslavia for the gold medal. Four years later neither of these countries existed as we had known them.

Americans being sadly deficient in basic international understanding, few United States citizens realized that the core of the great Soviet Union team had been players from Lithuania, one of the three Baltic republics swallowed up by Josef Stalin's Soviet Union in 1940. In no way, shape, or form did those Lithuanians identify themselves as fellow Russians. But if they wished to play basketball on an international scale, they had needed to put on uniforms saying CCCP (USSR to us).

Nor did Americans understand what Yugoslavia was and wasn't. A political creation of World War I, an amalgam of republics, two of which, Serbia and Croatia, were ancient enemies, Yugoslavia was headed for years by Marshal Tito (Joseph Broz), whose amazing political skill was clear after his death, when his Yugoslavia was torn apart and the entities started killing each other. Tito was, for me, the most fascinating politician of the twentieth century. He somehow managed to keep the lid on factions that despised each other, all the while thumbing his nose at the Soviets, his official superiors.

By 1992, independence had been restored to both Lithuania and Croatia and each was a basketball-loving and basketball-proficient nation. Winning a medal would be viewed as a major step toward gaining prestige and notoriety in the world at large. Neither the Lithuanians nor the Croatians were much concerned about losing to the Dream Team. Playing that team was an honor and keeping the margin of defeat under forty was a goal. Of far more importance were games against everyone else. Desperate to win a medal, the Lithuanians and Croatians didn't mind whether it was silver or bronze, because that was out of their control. Whoever wound up playing the Americans first in the medal round would be in line for the bronze. The other one would aim for the silver. All understood that winning the silver in this competition did not make a team better than the bronze medal winner. Lithuania drew Team USA first in the medal round. When that 127–76 affair was over, Lithuania knew bronze was the hope. Croatia, having defeated the CIS, or Russian, squad in the semis, would be taking home silver after losing to the USA.*

We think we have rivalries in America: Red Sox–Yankees. Celtics-Lakers. Duke-Carolina. Ohio State–Michigan. Alabama-Auburn. We have *no* idea. In order to get the bronze medal, Lithuania would have to defeat the team from Russia! Only one American knew exactly what was at stake. Donn Nelson—son of Don Nelson, the onetime Celtics fan favorite who would become the all-time winningest NBA coach—had spent many years in Lithuania and was an assistant coach on its Olympic team. He knew on that afternoon basketball was merely a vehicle. In the eyes of the Lithuanian nation this was payback time. Nelson knew what this game meant on many levels to such Lithuanian stars as seven-two center Arvydas Sabonis and six-three guard Sarunas Marciulionis, who had led their CCCP team past the USA in Seoul while carrying Lithuania in their hearts.

I do not remember much about the specifics of the game, only that it was difficult to imagine anyone playing harder than the Lithuanians did, unless it was the CIS team, whose players, after all, were not responsible for the wrongs that had been perpetrated on the Lithuanians and who themselves very much wanted one of those precious medals. I felt privileged to be in the building. When it was over, and Lithuania had defeated the CIS team with an 82–78 score, I wrote very little about basketball. I

---

* The CIS was what was left of the Soviet Union after the pullout from Lithuania, Estonia, and Latvia. The remaining twelve republics competed under one banner in both the 1992 Winter and Summer Olympics. They were known as the CIS, or Unified, team.

pretty much let Donn Nelson have a forum in which he could educate Americans.

"You have to know the history of the nation," he said. "The people killed in the Stalin regime. The three hundred thousand people extradited to Siberia. The feelings really run deep. There are players on this team [Alvydas Pazdrazdis and Gintaras Einikis] who were in [Lithuanian capital] Vilnius when the tanks rolled in, trying to protect the parliament building. This is kind of a vindication of everything the country has gone through in the last fifty-one years."

Nelson said he had seen many happy locker rooms, but none like this. He described how Lithuanian president Vytautas Landsbergis had come into the locker room to congratulate the team and departed with a champagne shower and a Grateful Dead T-shirt (the Dead had actually helped sponsor the team). He told how the players sang their national anthem.

"There was not a dry eye in the audience at that moment," Nelson reported. "It was like a wedding and a funeral rolled into one. It was awesome."

Lithuania's head coach spoke through an interpreter. "When we are on the court, we were assured the eyes of three million people. Almost all of the Federation of Lithuania was watching on the television screen. They were rooting for us and so we felt our hearts beat together on the court." I love Gregg Popovich, and he has had some interesting postgame press conferences, but I have never heard him explain a big W quite like that.

Imagine being one of the players in such a circumstance. It's a little bit bigger than winning one for ol' State U. "We're tired," Marciulionis explained. "Last night we could not sleep. We could not lose. It would be a tragedy."

Granted, not all international competitions become this politically tinged or are this emotional. But many of them I have seen over the years do have an extra layer of passion that transcends the actual basketball. It's an experience you don't get back home, no matter how heated the rivalry. And it's hardly limited to basketball. You can immerse yourself in it at any Olympics, summer or winter. If you think a pennant race or playoff game has some buzz, international competitions will give you a *real* jolt. I cannot imagine my professional life without them.

National honor seemed to be at stake everywhere you turned. One of my favorite moments came at the press conference following Angola's surprising 86–63 conquest of Spain. The first question posed by a Spanish journalist to Spanish coach Antonio Diaz-Miguel, a respected international figure, was:

"Coach Diaz-Miguel, are you going to resign?"

Perhaps sparked by a phone call from his old college coach, Dean Smith (a friend of Diaz-Miguel), Michael Jordan made a show of greeting him and putting his arm around him when the Dream Team came up against the Spaniards.

There was, of course, another basketball competition going on, and it, too, became enmeshed in international geopolitics.

Our women's team was pretty good. Team USA had won gold in 1984 and 1988 and entered the competition in Seoul as a significant favorite. Coach Theresa Grentz had at her disposal such female luminaries as Teresa Edwards, Cynthia Cooper, Katrina McClain, Medina Dixon, and Suzie McConnell.

Game 1 was a 111–55 destruction of Czechoslovakia (this was four months before the country was dissolved and split into the Czech Republic and Slovakia). China was supposed to provide a sterner test in Game 2, but the final score was still USA 93, China 67. That was followed by a 114–59 annihilation of Spain.

At this point the great former Soviet coach Alexander Gomelsky declared the competition over. "Great team," he declared. "Same team. This is *two* gold medals. No question." I did wonder if this was a sandbag attempt—after all, the coach of the CIS team was Alexander Gomelsky's brother, Evgeni.

The CIS women were experienced and a definite medal candidate. But they were not supposed to be much more than any bug on the windshield for the mighty Americans. Keeping the margin under double digits would have been a triumph. I have maintained for years that through six Summer Olympics and four men's world championships, I saw a lot of enjoyable basketball games. But my favorite one, without question, was the 1992 USA-CIS women's semifinal game.

The Dream Team oohed and aaahed us with their exquisite passing and shooting, to be sure, but what Evgeni Gomelsky's CIS team did in defeating the USA in that 1992 semifinal game was far more meaningful, because it involved artistry that translated into victory. Absent the artistry, there would have been no win for the CIS women.

The Americans had overwhelmed their first three opponents with a killer press, deriving a disproportionate percentage of their offense from their defense, allowing their inherent athleticism to carry the day. The CIS ladies absolutely shredded the press. It seems that big brother Alexander had given Evgeni a tutorial in press breaking, and the CIS players were able to carry out the plan. And any time they settled into a half-court game, the CIS squad spread the floor and kept the ball moving.

"They attacked us with the pass, rather than the dribble," said Medina Dixon, who was so distraught she said she was not interested in taking home any medal other than a gold. I'm not suggesting that the Americans weren't well coached, but this was a triumph of pure basketball players over superior athletes, and it was a joy to watch. Team CIS shot 50 percent from the floor, attempting a scant four three-pointers. No hoop purist could have asked for more.

Mike Fratello worked the game for NBC. "What a coaching job," he said. "That was an almost perfect execution of a game plan. I don't know what it was for sure, but I bet if I wrote it down beforehand, that would have been it. They attacked the press without fear, they limited turnovers, and they were the first team the USA had faced which had the size, the strength, and the mental toughness to get on the boards with the Americans."

The score was CIS 79, USA 73. It was a moment in time. The CIS team was the flip side of the Lithuanian dynamic. The letters "CIS" meant nothing to them. You often hear a coach explain after a nice victory that his players had just silenced the doubters and were playing for "the twelve people in this room, and nothing else." It's usually empty rhetoric. But if ever a group of basketball players had no reason for an allegiance to anything other than their own individual and collective happiness it was that collection of young ladies. It had nothing to do with three million people back home hanging on every possession. It had to do with pleasing themselves, and nothing else.

When the 1992 Olympics were over, those twelve women were going back to a very uncertain circumstance. They had no idea what their athletic futures would be. There was no more Soviet Union state-funded sports machine. There were only former Soviet republics, with limited resources. The breakdown of the squad was seven Russians, two Latvians, one Azerbaijani, one Kazakh, and one Ukrainian. The only bond they had was basketball.

I mean it when I say this game is my favorite Olympic basketball memory. I don't have time for males who don't have time for women's basketball. If you need dunks and a game played in the air then you have a very limited concept of what constitutes proper basketball. I'm sorry, but after a while dunks get old. To me, if you truly love basketball you can appreciate it at all levels. It's simply a matter of expectation. You see ten-year-olds play and you set your mind at that level. The same holds for high schools, Division 3, Division 2, Division 1, international ball, the NBA, and the women's game.

The NBA is the best brand but may not provide the best entertainment value on any given night. You might walk into a Division 2 gym and discover a six-three kid who's an absolute maestro, or into a Division 1 gym to discover one of those wonderful six-five guys who may not be the world's greatest athlete but who really knows how to play. I've been around long enough to know when a kid has a reasonable chance to make it in the NBA and when he doesn't, and I always cheer on those six-five tweener clever kids who I'm pretty sure aren't going to make it but whom I would rather see play than the next hundred first-round picks. West Virginia had just such a player in Mike Gansey a few years back. I saw him play and told everybody I wanted to adopt him. A few years after that I saw a kid at George Mason named Luke Hancock. He transferred to Louisville and helped them to the 2013 NCAA title. Those two are welcome at my house for dinner anytime.

I do not expect to see a woman in the NBA during my lifetime, nor even see one play Division 1 basketball on a men's team. The physical gap is just too large. But women can play an exceedingly entertaining brand of basketball that just doesn't happen to include high flying or dunking. Some of the best playmakers I have ever seen are women. I saw Dawn Staley four years later in the 1996 Olympics, and I was totally captivated.

"What they saw," I wrote afterward, "was a typical Dawn Staley game, a seven-assist performance that included two bring-'em-out-of-their-seats backward passes to fast-break trailers. They saw her go from zero to

60 in about 1.5 seconds every time she touched the ball in the backcourt. They saw her take a somewhat tentative and nervous US team, and just plain kick it into offensive gear. They saw her put the crowd right into the game. If there had been a game ball to award, the vote would have been 4,869 Staley and 0 Everybody Else."

Don't you wish you had seen that? And I was talking about a five-foot-six-inch woman. I'll say it again: my favorite Olympic basketball game ever was played by women.

CHAPTER 19

The Sub Heard Round the World

August 12, 1994. That's the day international basketball changed forever.

The 1994 World Championship in Toronto was the first competition for Team USA following the Barcelona Olympics. No player or coach of the Dream Team was involved. There were twelve new players, the youngest being twenty-two-year-old Shaquille O'Neal and the oldest being thirty-four-year-old Dominique Wilkins, and a coaching staff consisting of head coach Don Nelson plus assistants Don Chaney, Pete Gillen, and Rick Majerus.

It was a formidable team on paper. Reggie Miller, Joe Dumars, Larry Johnson, Kevin Johnson, Shawn Kemp, and Dan Majerle were all in their primes. O'Neal and Alonzo Mourning were on the rise.

Team USA was expected to win, and it did. The average victory margin in its eight games was 37.8 points. That may sound like Barcelona Redux, but the reality was something else. It was a far different scenario, and not just because the American team did not exactly conduct its business in an appropriately classy manner. That is, unless you think clutching one's genitals in a show of disrespect for an opponent is the right thing to do.

The fear factor that had permeated the 1992 basketball competition was gone. No more pictures, no more "Oh, gee, Mr. Jordan, it's such a thrill to play against you." Now it was about competition, not artistry, not ceremony. The Dream Team had trailed just once during all its Tournament of the Americas, exhibition, and Olympic games. This USA team had to work a little harder. They trailed Australia, 17–10. They trailed Russia, 25–24. They trailed Greece, 15–14. Fourteen minutes into the game with Spain, they were down by a point to a team that would not make it to the medal round.

Fear? A Greek guard named Efthimis Bakatsias took it to the hoop on three straight trips downcourt. Russian Sergei Bazarevich blew by Kevin Johnson, then the gold standard of quickness. Soon enough the historic moment arrived when international basketball was moved from the kiddie table to the real dining table, the one where the grown-ups sat with all the sparkling silverware.

At 2:34 into the second half of the preliminary-round game between Team USA and Russia, the score was USA 59, Russia 54. Coach Nelson did not like the way things were going, and so Shaquille O'Neal was sent in to replace Alonzo Mourning.

Chuck Daly had never as much as called time out in either Portland or Barcelona. That was widely known. But the other thing he had never done was make a substitution based on need.

Shaq for Zo was a historic moment in the story of international basketball because it was a substitution for need, not for rest or politics. Boris Stankovic had to be smiling. It had only taken one cycle to prove that his basic theory was correct. The Americans hadn't regressed in two years. The rest of the world was catching up.

"It's different than it looks on TV," Bazarevich said. "When you play against them, you see they are human." Two years earlier, opponents referred to the Americans as "heroes" or "idols." Now they were referring to them as "very good players."

The countdown had begun. When would America lose? Surely not 1996 and probably not by the 1998 World Championship in Athens. I didn't think it could happen any earlier than 2008. But I believed firmly it *would* happen.

Kevin Johnson, who had seen the look in the foes' eyes up close and personal, had a sobering thought, however. "It could be as early as 2000," he suggested. "The competition is getting better. By playing against us, they have benefited so much. They see how we do it, and they go back and work on things. They ask, 'How can we get better?' and they do something about it. The whole experience is great for them."

I'm surprised the Inspector of Meat didn't file adoption papers, right then and there.

There wasn't much evidence to think that things had changed by the 1996 Olympics in Atlanta unless you studied the fine print. The Americans roared their way to the gold. Barkley was back, bolder and more intimidating than ever. Reggie Miller and Mitch Richmond made the USA an even better pure shooting team than the original Dream Team. Hakeem Olajuwon, who had become an American citizen with the help of famed Boston attorney Alan Dershowitz, was at his peak and Shaq was ready to take over as the world's best big man.

But there was definitely no fear factor and Barkley himself was on record as saying that people should refrain from referring to this squad as a "Dream Team." "Please change the name to Team USA," he instructed. Buried inside the hype was a first half of play against Argentina, which had not been considered among the world's elite aggregations. The Argentines led, 44–42, at intermission.

"Note that we're talking about *futebol* Argentina here," I wrote, "and not more familiar basketball entities such as Lithuania, Croatia, Yugoslavia or even long-time South American power Brazil. If Argentina had gotten this good, then something uplifting is going on."

Mention of the former Yugoslavia, whose players were now playing for split-off countries, made me consider the possibility that even the Dream Team might have had a hard time with that bunch on a given night. A team consisting of Vlade Divac, Dino Radja, Toni Kukoc, Zan Tabak, Arijan Komazec, Zarko Paspalj, Stojan Vrankovic, the late Drazen Petrovic, Sasha Danilovic, Sasha Djordjevic, and Dejan Bodiroga, playing before a maniacal Belgrade home crowd in Game 3 of a 2-2-1-1-1 best-of-seven series against the Dream Team, and perhaps benefiting from some home-cooked officiating, might have been able to pull off an upset.

We didn't learn much about the talent gap in 1998 because the team the U.S. sent to Athens for the World Championship was a JV squad consisting of Continental Basketball Association players, Americans playing in Europe, and a few collegians. The NBA was having one of its labor–management contretemps involving a player lockout and couldn't provide its necessary complement of players.

Thus, the American team was actually an underdog and it was easy to pull for them, especially since they weren't getting a lot of respect from the local press. One Greek writer had likened these non-NBA players to "lint at the bottom of a washing machine." Making journalistic life easier for me and the one other American journalist there, Eddie Sefko of the *Houston Chronicle*, was the fact that, given the paucity of American media, the players were practically lined up after each game to converse with us, something that would ordinarily be unimaginable. Coach Rudy Tomjanovich, coach of the two-time-NBA-champion Houston Rockets, was himself a good story. He had long been on every writer's "Five Nicest Guys in the NBA" list.

Team USA was always vulnerable. An 84–82 early-round loss to Lithuania had proven that. But it was very much in the gold medal hunt, and with 3:09 remaining in the semifinal game they led Russia, 64–54. The team never scored again.

In a perfect storm of bad decisions, clutch play by the opponent (two monster threes by Sergei Babkov), and an artfully crafted flop by Vasiliy Karasev on a Michael Hawkins maneuver with ten seconds left, the score was tied at 64. Then Sergei Panov took an inbounds pass and went two-thirds the length of the floor for the winning layup with 2.9 seconds left.

By this time I was learning why some international players turn out to be much better than an American might have thought. "The international players perform so much better over here," explained Del Harris, a Team USA assistant coach. 'They're playing the game in their surroundings. There's a definite comfort level. Take a guy like [Australia's] Shane Heal. He couldn't do anything when he played with the Timberwolves. But in this game he's a great player." As proof, Heal hit Team USA for thirty-one.

A scout also told me: "You see a guy in his regular Spanish or Italian league, and he might take a night off. They don't take any nights off when they're playing for their country."

Yugoslavia, which had plenty of missing stars itself, had enough talent left to win the tournament with a 64–62 triumph over Russia. The atmosphere, as usual, was totally festive. These internationals know how to celebrate. Five minutes after the game was over, the *losing* fans were singing and chanting.

Three times a year, USA Basketball publishes a magazine entitled *USA Basketball News*. A headline in its issue of December 2000 declared: ALL IS GOLDEN FOR USA TEAMS IN SYDNEY.

That was hardly the case.

The U.S. women's Olympic team was the unquestioned class of the tournament. Russia provided a bit of competition, leading by eight late in the half, but the USA wound up winning by eleven (88–77). South Korea was down two with fourteen minutes left, but Team USA answered the challenge to win by thirteen (78–65). The women did all Americans proud.

The men? Well, they won, but they embarrassed us all.

Kevin Johnson had been proven correct. The USA was still winning basketball golds but here in 2000 the games were no longer formalities, and the Americans didn't seem to like it. Rudy Tomjanovich was still the coach. USA Basketball owed it to him after asking him to coach that ragtag bunch in Athens. And while he didn't have either Shaquille O'Neal or Kobe Bryant at his disposal, he appeared to have a formidable group featuring Alonzo Mourning, Kevin Garnett, Ray Allen, and Vince Carter.

But after early blowouts against China and Italy, Team USA ran into a rugged foe in Lithuania and needed a major effort to subdue them. It was a five-point game with 1:45 left and nothing was assured until Allen hit two free throws with 24.9 seconds left. The final was 85–76.

There was no postgame talk from the other side about playing against heroes or idols. It was more like playing against punks. "I think they're gonna lose a game," said Lithuania's (and the University of Maryland's) Sarunas Jasikevicius. "And I think they're gonna lose a game here. They are treating this like a vacation."

Team USA struggled against France, hardly a major power, and then a stunner took place in the semifinal rematch with Lithuania. No matter what the Americans did, Lithuania would not go away. And so it came down to an amazing sight: the USA bench players kneeling on the floor while Lithuania's Jasikevicius was taking the last shot, looking very much like those kids on fifteen seeds hoping to upset the twos on the first day of NCAA competition.

The shot was short. Team USA was saved. Final score: USA 85, Lithuania 83.

Instead of being humble and professional, team USA was ridiculously arrogant. The ringleader was Vince Carter, who had obviously allowed the acclaim for his dunks to go to his head. Here he was, pointing to the crowd after making a sneak-away dunk to put the USA ahead by three. Here he was, snorting after the game, "We *didn't* lose. I don't care what the world thinks. Look at the scoreboard."

Lithuania's roster that night included no NBA players, and of the three on American college teams, only one, Jasikevicius, had much of an impact. Lithuania was not considered an elite European power. Instead of looking at the scoreboard, Vince Carter and the Americans should have looked in the mirror. That's pretty much what we disgusted Americans were saying that night in Sydney.

It wasn't about winning or losing. It was about playing the game properly, and with respect, and the team doing that was Lithuania, not the United States. The USA players thought gold medals were a birthright. The rest of the world thought they were something you were supposed to work for.

Donn Nelson was still on the Lithuania bench, and after that game he gave me a primer. "We were definitely the best team in the [Olympic] Village to play the U.S.," he said. "One, we are the best defensive team of the others. Two, we follow a game plan religiously. Three, we play as a team." Nelson also said that the duality of being so close to the Lithuanians while still being a red, white, and blue American was wearing on him. "I can't do this anymore," he declared. I don't think even an internationally savvy basketball guy such as Donn Nelson thought the gap would get closed so quickly.

The gold medal game was coming up and I had decided which team I was rooting for. "The shame of all this," I wrote, "isn't just that the USA might lose. That would only be justice. The shame of it is that a team doesn't even have to be very good to expose them as people. What's happening here isn't really a basketball story. It's a people story as old as mankind. The rest of the world is simply standing up to a classless bully.

"The US plays for the gold Sunday. An awful lot of people around here are shouting 'Vive La France!' Some of them are carrying American passports."

I didn't get my wish. The gold medal game was lackluster, one the USA could easily have lost. France was four points down (76–72) with 4:26 left but simply did not have the wherewithal to get the job done. The final was USA 85, France 75. Team USA was free to go on a real vacation.

With this as a setup, what transpired at the World Championship in Indianapolis two years later was not a total shock. The Worlds have always been a very big deal to the rest of the world, but not to Americans. World Championship golds in any sport resonate just as much elsewhere as do ones captured in an Olympics. That is not the case in America. The time had come when in order for the USA to win an international basketball championship it needed an A team, or, at the very least, an A-minus team. Anything less would be in trouble.

At the 2002 World Championship the USA sent a team of B All-Stars. With headliners such as Kobe Bryant and Shaquille O'Neal spurning invitations, coach George Karl had to defend America's undefeated streak in open competition with a squad led by thirty-seven-year-old Reggie Miller, along with Elton Brand, Antonio Davis, Baron Davis, Michael Finley, Raef LaFrentz, Paul Pierce, Ben Wallace, and Andre Miller. They were wobbly from the beginning—nip and tuck with Germany for twenty-five minutes, trailing China by twelve at the quarter, huffing and puffing to stay even with New Zealand for fifteen minutes. Barcelona was many light years away.

The inevitable happened on September 4, 2002. Eight years and a month after Don Nelson felt compelled to substitute Shaquille O'Neal for Alonzo Mourning, a team of NBA stars fell to an international foe, and not the one many would have supposed would have gotten the honor. It wasn't one of the traditional European powers. It wasn't even Brazil. No, it was a country whose most famous athlete was a five-foot-five-inch *futebol* star named Maradona. "We still don't know what we've done," said Argentina's Fabricio Oberto, who had just scored eleven points and grabbed nine rebounds as his team defeated Team USA, 87–80.

It wasn't fluky. It didn't require a miracle shot or one man on an insane scoring binge. It didn't need cheating referees. It was fair and square. The

Argentines came within fifteen seconds of going wire-to-wire in victory. The game was tied once, at 2–2. They led by sixteen at the half, and when Team USA closed to seven with 8:11 left, they responded with a 9–1 run and that was that.

Good-bye fifty-eight-game international winning streak for the NBA guys. I'm guessing the Inspector of Meat made a congratulatory phone call to the Argentines.

I was both sorry and glad the American coach was George Karl. I like him a lot and didn't want him to have the distinction of having coached the first NBA group to lose in major international competition. But I thought he might grasp the enormity of the moment and not just explain it away as a Bad Day at Black Rock for the Americans, or pretend that it had no greater context. I was right.

"The symbolic importance of this is that basketball is a great game," he said, "a game the world has fallen in love with. In the time of feeling poorly, there's a part of me that feels this is a really good celebration of basketball."

Team USA would lose to both Yugoslavia and Spain before they could get out of Indianapolis, thus finishing an astonishing sixth, at least in the eyes of people who were not aware of what had been going on the previous decade. The experience in Indianapolis was the complete vindication of the Boris Stankovic theory.

The next few years were sobering for the American basketball community. The 2004 Athens Olympics got off to a rousing start when the Commonwealth of Puerto Rico, always operating under a separate Olympic charter despite all its athletes being American citizens, absolutely crushed Team USA in the opening game. The score was 92–73, but it looked and felt like 192–73. This time the head coach was Hall of Famer Larry Brown. His appointment was a reward for lifetime achievement, and turned out to be just shy of a disaster. He had his likes and dislikes and didn't appear to have much use for younger players such as LeBron James.

Team USA did come out of Athens with a bronze medal, after losing to Lithuania again in the preliminary round, but this was the first time the U.S. had not won the gold, unless you count that preposterous heist in Munich in 1972.

But we had yet to bottom out. By the time the 2006 World Championship was beginning in Tokyo, there had been significant changes in USA Basketball, the governing entity supervising our involvement in international competition. Ultimate responsibility for putting USA Basketball back on the right course was given to Jerry Colangelo, a man who had worn many hats in his time, including general manager, coach, and president/owner of the Phoenix Suns, and owner of baseball's Arizona Diamondbacks. He was probably the second-most famous man in Arizona. I'm guessing Senator John McCain is number one, and I'm sure the late Senator Barry Goldwater would still get some write-in votes.

I've known Jerry for forty years or so, and he is a born take-charge guy. He reasoned that USA Basketball needed a fluid coaching and roster situation, that rather than going from competition to competition with a different coach selected on the basis of distinguished service as much as current relevance, we should appoint a permanent national coach, as exists most everywhere else. There would be a core group comprising a national team. These were big departures from the way things had always been done, but when you lose to Argentina, Yugoslavia, Lithuania, Spain, and Puerto Rico, the old way needs revision.

After the semifinal game of the 2006 World Championship in Tokyo, a new name was added to the list of American conquerors—Greece. I was there, and I could not believe what I was seeing. The USA defense was shredded time and time again, and could not defend Greece's pick-and-roll. Most specifically, we could not stop six-foot-eleven, three-hundred-pound Sofoklis Schortsanitis, a.k.a. "Baby Shaq," a large fellow who was very light on his feet. He was a 2003 Los Angeles Clippers draft pick; 'tis a pity he's never come over here. You'd like him.

The new coach of the team was Mike Krzyzewski and he made no excuses. "Their offense beat our defense, and I'll take responsibility," he said. "You win together and lose together, but when there's a big loss, the coach has to take more responsibility."

We didn't know it at the time, but the U.S. team had really now bottomed out. Mike Krzyzewski was the right coach and had the program on the right path, figuring out who we needed, who we didn't, and how we should play. The results are in. Team USA won back the gold at both the 2008 and 2012 Summer Olympics, both times over Spain, and both times by having to work extremely hard for it. In Beijing Spain was trailing by four with two and a half minutes to play. The final was 118–107, but it was really much closer than that.

"I knew that we had a tough road ahead of us," said Chris Bosh.

"We played with great character in one of the great games in international basketball history," proclaimed Coach K.

In London Spain pushed Team USA even harder. The final was 107–100, and that barely tells the story. "We knew it wasn't going to be easy," said LeBron James. "We didn't *want* it to be easy." Larry Bird and his fellow Dream Teamers would have liked it to be a little harder themselves. But that wasn't possible in 1992.

Boris Stankovic, the Inspector of Meat, has lived to see his dream come true. It doesn't matter if the Americans are still on top twenty years from now. It matters that when they win now it is something to be proud of.

CHAPTER 20

Smitten by a Lady of Low Repute

Have you ever been in love with a hooker?

It can happen, I guess. I can't speak from personal experience, but I must confess to something that is reasonably analogous: I remain a fan of college sports, specifically college basketball and football, the two marquee, revenue-producing sports.

They have been a part of my sporting consciousness since my father was hired by his old army buddy Ambrose "Bud" Dudley, the director of athletics at what was then Villanova College (now, of course, a university), to become his assistant, in 1952, when I was six. We would spend practically every winter weekend over the next two years attending college basketball doubleheaders played at either the Pennsylvania Palestra, where Penn and Villanova played, or at Philadelphia's Convention Hall, where Saint Joseph's, La Salle, and Temple played.* I can also say I was in attendance when Rio Grande, led by the legendary scoring machine Clarence "Bevo" Francis, played Villanova at the long-demolished Philadelphia Arena.

In addition, I was taken to many Villanova football games, some of which were rather a big deal because they involved a promotion my father had concocted in which someone purchasing ten dollars' worth of groceries at an Acme Market would get a ticket to a Villanova football

---

* The Big Five as we know it was not formed until the 1955–56 season. That was the first year Saint Joseph's, La Salle, and Temple joined Penn and Villanova to play the preponderance of their home games at the Penn Palestra.

game at Philadelphia's mammoth Municipal Stadium, which seated nearly one hundred thousand people and which was the site of the Army-Navy game for many years. The promotion was nicknamed the "Grocery Bowl," and Villanova actually played to crowds of more than ninety thousand against such intersectional foes as Kentucky and Ole Miss.

I was hip to the NCAA tournament as early as 1953, and was very interested in the great Tom Gola–led La Salle teams whose achievements during Gola's three varsity seasons included winning both an NIT and an NCAA championship, while finishing second to Bill Russell's San Francisco team in yet another NCAA championship game.

There were well-documented recruiting abuses in those days, and college basketball had to deal with the shocking point-shaving scandals of 1946 and 1951. For some, there was always something off-putting about the idea of big-time college athletics, but compared to the way things are today, it was all a relatively low-key enterprise that was always manageable. Players were expected to go to class, and it was a bigger story when someone failed to graduate than when he didn't. And, of course, in those days it was always a "he."

America is the only country in which college sports are a vital part of the national sports smorgasbord. No one else does what we do, and that includes Canada, whose collegiate sports system is equivalent to our Division III.* In the rest of the word, such competition is at the private club level, or perhaps under governmental control (see the People's Republic of China). In England, Cambridge and Oxford engage in competition, but their players are true *student*-athletes. At day's end you will find that stroke or coxswain in the library. When Sir Roger Bannister broke the four-minute-mile barrier in 1954, he did so as a full-time medical student who trained during his infrequent off-hours. Hear! Hear!

No European, South American, Asian, African, or Australian has seen collegiate competition at the level of Alabama football or Kentucky basketball, or what it would mean to the entire psyche of those two states if those activities ceased to exist. They could not image the Big House in

---

* Simon Fraser University in Burnaby, British Columbia, did become the first Canadian member of the NCAA, but it is at the Division II level and we shall see how it goes.

Ann Arbor or Thompson-Boling Arena in Knoxville. Institutions of higher learning in other countries have no need for such structures. And multimillion-dollar salaries for *coaches*? What are actual professors, people who actually matter, paid, they might ask.

America has focused on college sports for a long time. By the beginning of the twentieth century the concept of the so-called "tramp athlete" was well-known. Superior football players were selling themselves to the highest bidder. Injuries were a major concern, and no less a figure than president Theodore Roosevelt felt supervision was necessary. He even threatened to have college football outlawed.

In late December 1905, New York University chancellor Henry MacCracken convened a meeting of thirteen universities, and from it the Intercollegiate Athletic Association of the United States (IAAUS) was created on March 21, 1906. Four years later it was renamed the National Collegiate Athletic Association (NCAA), and that remains the primary governing body for intercollegiate sports today.

Perhaps you've heard of a little thing called "March Madness." It is otherwise known as the NCAA tournament, with the words "men's" and "basketball" being somewhat superfluous. This is the NCAA's most significant piece of business, and it has evolved into the last true communal activity, short of a presidential election, that binds this country. Once upon a time, "everyone" watched the Miss America Pageant from Atlantic City, and "everyone" watched *The Ed Sullivan Show*, even if the Beatles weren't performing, and "everyone" watched the Oscars (hosted by Bob Hope) and "everyone" gathered in front of the TV set at two o'clock Pacific or five o'clock Eastern to watch the Rose Bowl on New Year's Day. With the advent of cable television and with changing lifestyles, those old viewing habits have changed. But the NCAA tournament has gotten bigger and bigger, if only because of the ubiquitous brackets, which, legal or not, are filled out in every office in America.

I covered twenty-nine of those Final Fours, beginning in 1970 at College Park and concluding in 2012 at New Orleans, my favorite American city. I loved the entire month of March, starting with the Big East Tournament in Madison Square Garden and then continuing with the subregionals and regionals. Starting in 1999 I established a personal policy of driving from the regionals to the Final Four. On occasion I could stay on the road for the better part of two weeks, driving from the subregionals to the regionals. March was truly *my* month.

But I was always troubled by the realization that the idea of the participants all being legitimate "student-athletes" was a farce. The classic example was the 1996 Mississippi State Final Four team, which included at least one documented felon and another player, Dontae' Jones, who had miraculously accumulated thirty-six summer school credits from a correspondence school in order to establish himself as a legitimate Mississippi State student. He had somehow passed muster with the vaunted NCAA clearinghouse, the arm of the NCAA overseeing academic eligibility, and there he was, in the Final Four.

The term "student-athlete," as opposed to "player," is a running joke among the media. We are instructed over and over to refer to the young men as "student-athletes," and woe be to the moderator at any NCAA tournament press conference who forgets himself or herself and lets slip the dreaded "p-word" in reference to one of the participants. The term "student-athlete" was the brainchild of legendary NCAA president Walter Byers, whose iron-fisted rule of the organization lasted from 1951 to 1988. He came up with the phrase in order to insulate the NCAA from any labor-management implications with regard to the players, who, he wanted the world to know, are not employees in any sense, but, rather, recipients of athletic scholarships. Very clever.

It became an annual personal ritual for me to seek forgiveness in advance for even being at the Final Four, given the fraudulence and hypocrisy connected to the event. I would write that while we all know many of the participants are only tangentially student-athletes, the time to express moral outrage had passed. Once at the tournament, we are here, I'd write, to absorb the pageantry and enjoy the competition. And, by the way, some of the kids really *are* legit.

Who doesn't know there is something inherently wrong with the system? But people like myself have come to an accommodation with it, because once they throw the ball up we aren't worrying about how they got here. We are all, frankly, enablers. Any writer who can't deal with this should stay home. This is America. We *want* this activity, warts and all. It means too much to us to consider losing it.

Despite its problems, I can't imagine my life without the enjoyment I have derived from college sports, starting with the games my father took me to, followed by the excellent basketball teams at BC during my four years there, a bonus I had never counted on when I enrolled. I got to see BC play against Lew Alcindor, Wes Unseld, and Bob Lanier, but the most fearsome opponent of all was Jimmy Walker of Providence, who had, in this order, twenty-nine, fifty, forty, and thirty-three in his four games against us and who was the manliest man among boys I have ever seen in college basketball.

As a writer I got to cover the ballyhooed Bird vs. Magic finals in 1979, the unforgettable Villanova conquest of mighty Georgetown in 1985, and the epic Duke 104, Kentucky 103 East Regional Final in 1992, won by Christian Laettner's miracle shot, which many, myself included, maintain was the greatest college game ever played. Those are highlights. But equally important to me is being able to say that my love of college basketball had, by the end of the 2013–14 season, taken me to 181 separate venues to see college basketball games. I am hoping to add significantly to that list.

I have done some crazy things in order to see a college basketball game, but the showstopper was an excursion in January of 1986 to East Tennessee State University in Johnson City, Tennessee. I was working on a story about Oak Hill Academy, which is located in Virginia's far southwest corner, where it converges with both North Carolina and Tennessee. I had a night off and I read in the paper that East Tennessee was playing Furman in a clash of Southern Conference powers, and when I looked at the map Johnson City appeared to be quite reachable.

I was told that there were two ways to get there by car, the short way being over the mountain and the long way being around it. Of course, I opted for Option A. Things were fine until I neared the top of the mountain and a sudden snow squall hit. I mean, we're talking whiteout. I was panicked. I've done really stupid things, I thought, but this one wins the prize. I pulled over and waited. In less than ten minutes the snow stopped.

I got down the mountain, checked into a Holiday Inn, received directions to the school, and followed the crowd to the gym. I bought the best ticket the vendor had left. It cost five dollars and was right behind the home-team bench. The game went into three overtimes. It was terrific.

This is what being a *fan* of sports is all about. I had no allegiance to either team, only to the sport of basketball and to fandom itself.

The NCAA is now tearing itself apart, with the big schools asserting their right to what they feel is their fair share of the money. The old conference affiliations, which were originally grounded in geography and common interests, are constantly changing. It really is impossible to keep track of what school is in what conference. All this upheaval does take something away from the enjoyment. Throw in the ongoing "student-athlete" shenanigans, and it becomes a hard system to defend. It's an absolutely illogical, almost embarrassing spectacle. Try to explain the lunacy of "Signing Day" to your European visitor.

Perhaps twenty years ago, I honestly thought college sports were getting so far off the track that surely the country would recognize the folly of it all and college sports would fade away within a generation or two. And here I am, talking about more college gyms for my collection. The hooker still has *me* hooked, and there is nothing I can do about it.

CHAPTER 21

Bob Knight

To anyone who has followed sports closely in this country over the past forty years, when I say that on the short list of Most Interesting People I have met the name of Bob Knight is near the top of the list, it should not come as a shock.

In my experience, he is neither lovable nor hateable. He is exasperating. He is entertaining. Most of all, he is contradictory. I think it is also safe to say that if there is a sports person in my experience who is most assuredly "comfortable in his own skin," it is Robert Montgomery Knight. He is not plagued with a shred of self-doubt. Apology is an abstract concept for him.

I first saw him in action as the mercurial, precocious coach of the Army basketball team. Boston College played the Cadets in the 1966 Holiday Festival in Madison Square Garden and again in the 1969 NIT, both won by BC. He put on some memorable shows, once kicking the end of the Army bench, much to the shock of the be-medaled occupants seated there, minding their own business.

The first time I met him was a brief encounter, and I assume a handshake was involved. I was covering the Celtics and after a game in Cleveland I was introduced to him by his old Ohio State teammate John Havlicek. What I recall is how downright—I know these are difficult concepts to contemplate when the subject is Bob Knight—shy and even humbled he seemed to be in Havlicek's august presence.

The second encounter took place on the night of the 1976 NCAA championship game in Philadelphia. Knight's Indiana University

Hoosiers were preparing to put the finishing touches on an undefeated season against Big Ten foe Michigan. This was the first year the tournament had been expanded to allow conference teams other than the champion to participate.

Two hours before game time in the Spectrum, the great broadcaster Curt Gowdy, who had taken a liking to me, asked me if I'd like to take a walk around the arena with him. That seemed a nice way to work off some of the emotional energy that builds up—yes, even for broadcasters and writers—before a major event. Today I would have to decline. I'd be blogging or tweeting.

Somewhere along the way we bumped into Knight. Gowdy innocently asked if he knew "Bobby" Ryan. Wrong move. Knight glowered at me and mumbled something about "[naughty word] people who write things they don't know anything about," or some such thing. Poor Curt was mortified. I knew Knight was referring to what was known in the trade as "the Wisman Incident." A few weeks back an angry Knight had grabbed Jim Wisman by the jersey and jerked him into a seated position on the Indiana bench. It was well noted that the Hoosiers were up by a large margin at the time. But Knight had seen the occasion as a teaching moment, only with him sometimes words were not enough to convey the message. Scores of columnists had written derogatory things about Knight in that context, me among them. I recall ending my treatise with the not-too-original line "Would you want your son to play for Bobby Knight?"

Judging from Knight's reaction, he was well aware I had been one of his critics. Yet, a couple of years later I received a very nice letter from him at home complimenting me on something I had written in the pages of *Basketball Times*.

He has twice called me at home, and that is never a good thing. The first time concerned what I thought had been an innocuous (but accurate) reference to him in a 1986 piece I had written about Clarence "Big House" Gaines, the celebrated coach at Winston-Salem State who had been on the job since the dawn of time. Coach Gaines, a thoroughly delightful gentleman, had mentioned how proud he was of his association with many big-name college coaches, among them Bob Knight. At that time I had reason to believe I was in good standing with Mr. Knight (you can never be entirely sure), so I reached out via phone, hoping that a few complimentary quotes from him would spruce up the article.

He was gracious on the subject of Big House and was in an expansive enough mood to offer additional observations I could incorporate into other stories. I wrote the Big House story, and by way of attribution I referred to the head coach at Indiana University, Mr. Bob Knight, as the enfant terrible of college basketball, albeit in an affectionate manner. Let's just say it was not to the coach's liking. He focused on the word "terrible," and I admit that when you Anglicize the reference it doesn't sound too good. So much for trying to flaunt that prep school French. Anyway, his effective reaction was "You do this to me, after I went out of my way to help you?" Forgotten, I guess, was the fact that it had taken me several days to get to him, and that he was, after all, only being asked to speak about a man he professed to love and admire.

The second time he called me at home he was far angrier. In the book I had coauthored in 1988 with Bob Cousy, entitled *Cousy on the Celtic Mystique*, the topics extended beyond the Celtics, and a chapter was called "College Basketball and Bobby Knight." It was not what you might call an unqualified endorsement of the methodology Knight had employed while winning three national championships.

The Cooz had personal experience with Knight, since he was the head coach of those two BC teams that had beaten Army in Madison Square Garden back in the sixties. Cooz also talked about a preseason scrimmage against the Cadets that had taken an immediate violent turn and had caused Cousy to call it off after ten minutes or so. And he recalled an incident in which his assistant Gerry Friel almost had fisticuffs with Knight. There were passages such as this:

"He brings Quinn [Buckner] back like a conquering hero. A lot of them swear that Bob Knight is great. It is like boot camp. You are proud you have been through the experience. It's a macho experience you can tell all your friends about, and you're a tough man if you can survive it. But for those who can't stand to be humiliated, it is a stupid approach."

I still don't know whether he's ever had it out with Cousy, but I was chastised for my collaboration. He presented an alternate version of some of the things Cousy said, such as denying the circumstances of any BC-Army scrimmage in his own book with sportswriter Bob Hammel, a longtime friend. He said I was wrong to take Cousy's word for it. I'm afraid I've got to stand by the Cooz on that one. More than anything, Bob Knight just couldn't understand why he had to be included in a book by Bob Cousy.

A few years passed and I think there might have been another letter giving me his approval on something I had written, because I felt comfortable enough with the relationship to take a stab at an interview at a big December doubleheader in Indianapolis featuring Indiana, Kansas, Kentucky, and Notre Dame. I inquired if there was any possibility of speaking with him. A day or so later, the call was returned. "Coach says come to the [RCA] Dome around six, after our practice, and you can go to dinner with him and some friends." I was about to be exposed to the Charming Knight.

Dinner was at a local steak house. I rode in a car with Knight and a friend and the conversation included his saying he was much more welcome in West Lafayette, home of Purdue, than anyone thinks. At some point he began a discourse on fly-fishing in Russia with Ted Williams, Knight being an avid outdoorsman and Williams being one of the most acclaimed fishermen in American history.

At the restaurant we were seated in a small function room, about twelve of us, including assistant coaches, managers, a friend or two, and me. The waiter entered and the Coach called the meeting to order. "Onion rings and ribs!" he roared. "If they don't like 'em, they'll learn to like 'em."

Back at the hotel Knight invited me to watch his team perform a brief walk-through in a large function room, after which we headed to his suite and what turned out to be a thoroughly enjoyable ramble through the years. The most interesting topic was Knight's 1981 flirtation with CBS.

"If they had handled it right, I would have gone to CBS, you know," Knight declared. He practically worshipped Ted Williams, who had mastered two disciplines, hitting a baseball and fishing. He figured he had already mastered the art of coaching and could likewise master the art of broadcasting.

"I told them I didn't want any screwing around," he said. "Just make me an offer. I never wanted to get an agent. Red Auerbach had told me to go get a New York agent, but one of my goals was to get through life without ever having an agent. I probably should have listened to Red."

He spoke about how the negotiations had dragged on. "Two months later they were offering me twice as much as the original offer," he explained. "That pissed me off. That's exactly the way I didn't want it to go."

He said it had all worked out for the best, however. "I came to one meeting with a notebook," he recalled. "In it I had written down some ideas for stories. I was talking about an interview with [then Supreme Court justice] Whizzer White, who was a member of the Colorado team in the very first NIT. Did you know that? I didn't think so. I wanted to talk with [UN diplomat] Ralph Bunche, who had played at UCLA. I wanted to see Billy "the Hill" McGill, who at the time was working as a janitor in a school system. I would see Bill Bradley. Good stuff, right?

"Well, I could see they had absolutely no enthusiasm for any of this. I thought, 'Wait a minute. Even if they aren't ultimately interested in me, they should have been interested in stealing my ideas.' I figured that if this is the way it's going to be, I couldn't get along there."

And then something happened that made it all moot. Landon Turner, a key member of his 1981 championship team and an almost certain NBA player, was seriously injured in an automobile accident. He would be wheelchair-bound for the rest of his life, and Knight just could not leave Bloomington, Indiana, for the foreseeable future.

That was one fascinating evening. He was then fifty-two years old. I asked him, if he had given thought to leaving the coaching ranks eleven years previously, what was he thinking at that point in his life?

"Good question," he said. "No, not really. I think it's because I've enjoyed the kids I've had for the most part. And you know when I really knew I had done the right thing? The [1984] Olympics. I remember thinking how grateful I was that I had stuck around so I could coach that team. Someday I will quit, but then I'll follow the advice given to me by Ara Parseghian. He told me, 'When you quit, don't quit thinking you're going to do something else, or like it better. Quit and then worry about what you're going to do."

He would leave Indiana under duress in 2000. So was that the case sixteen years later when he left the Texas Tech job voluntarily, eventually winding up in what would turn out to be an unfulfilling gig at ESPN? I really don't know, but I think he's too proud and stubborn to tell anyone the truth about such a delicate personal matter.

Following that night in Indianapolis, was I now an official Knight Insider? Did I want to be? After all, some of my best friends in the business detested him then and detest him now. But I always like to say that good friends should be able to agree to disagree, and so I continued to regard him in a generally positive light.

That interview led me to place a call for a boilerplate pregame interview the week in 1994 when Boston College was to play Indiana in the NCAA round of sixteen in Miami. This time I had no trouble getting through. We talked about his team and then he turned the tables a bit, assuming the role of inquisitor. "Tell me," he said, "what's going on at BC with Jim O'Brien?"

O'Brien was in need of a new contract, and, not for the first time, he was having trouble securing a proper deal from BC director of athletics Chet Gladchuk. Let the record show that the last time this had happened I had sprung to O'Brien's defense. It was hardly a secret that I was an admirer of Jim O'Brien, who was two years behind me at BC and one of the best players in school history. I truly believed he was an excellent coach, and in terms of the so-called fit that is so often spoken of in college sports, he was beyond perfect. But Chet Gladchuk was not a paid-up member of the Jim O'Brien Fan Club.

Knight knew very well who Jim O'Brien was. He had coached against him in a losing effort during that 1969 NIT, and no smart basketball coach would forget such a clever player. He knew O'Brien had done a good job at Saint Bonaventure, one of America's toughest places to recruit (you go there in January and think the Iditarod will soon be passing through). And he knew the job O'Brien was doing at BC.

"Are you going to be at the press conference Thursday?" he asked me, the game being scheduled for Friday night. I said yes. "Here's what I want you to do. You ask me a question about BC. I'll take it from there."

I don't even recall the exact wording of the question, but Knight replied: "A lot of people around the country ask me who would be a good candidate to coach their team and who they should talk to. And if I was going to hire a coach today, Jimmy O'Brien is the guy I'd want to talk to. I mean, here's a guy who went one and fifteen with these kids as freshmen [in the Big East] and he works with them and keeps them going—hoping one day will be your day. And that day is here for Boston College."

Knight had done his homework. The fact is that BC seniors Bill Curley, Howard Eisley, Malcolm Huckaby, and Gerard Abram had started for O'Brien together as freshmen, and they had won their first league game against Providence and lost their next fifteen league games. And now they were in the round of sixteen as seniors, those same four, plus freshman Danya Abrams. I didn't tell him that. He either knew or had somebody find out, but he laid it on the media that Thursday afternoon in Miami.

BC beat Indiana, 77–68, before losing to Florida in the regional finals. But Knight had been a mensch, and Jim O'Brien did get a new contract. Irony of ironies, he would leave BC for coach Knight's alma mater, Ohio State, with whom he went to the 1999 Final Four.

The last time I saw Bob Knight was in 2007 in Winston-Salem, North Carolina, for a first-round confrontation between Knight's Texas Tech team and Boston College, this time coached by Al Skinner. All I did was ask a simple get-the-conversation-moving question at the press conference.

ME: Coach, what do you most like about the makeup of the team, and what concerns you most about them?

KNIGHT: Where the hell did you get that tan?

ME: Florida. Spring training, hanging out with your buddy LaRussa. So what do you like most about your team?

KNIGHT: What did you like most about the Cardinals?

ME: Albert Pujols.

KNIGHT: That's a brilliant answer for a writer. I'm not kidding you. You kind of stuck it to me with that answer. I didn't think you'd come up with anything that good.

He then sort of answered the question, but he quickly returned to his more preferred topic.

KNIGHT: I'm not sure that's as good an answer as Albert Pujols. It kind of pissed me off that you came up with such a good answer. I had a lot of great retorts, but you screwed me out of all of them.

He talked about what might happen on his deathbed and what he would say if his wife asked him what he was thinking about: "You cannot believe that son of a bitch Ryan came up with Pujols."

After leaving the podium, he was heard saying "Albert Pujols" as he walked down the hall toward the Texas Tech dressing room.

I guess it meant he liked me.

Most of the truly distasteful Bob Knight stuff I've either read or heard about, or, in the case of the famous thrown chair, seen on video. It's a long list. The 1976 Spectrum hallway scene and the angry home phone calls were pretty tame. I read John Feinstein's great book *A Season on the Brink*, and some of the things recounted, especially his verbal and mental abuse of Darryl Thomas, all under the guise of trying to make him a better player, are pretty ugly.

The worst thing about Bob Knight is that, while he seems to have high standards for other people's behavior and actions, he does not seem to be able to hold himself accountable. About the closest thing to a regret I've ever heard him express was that, if he had to do it all over again, he would have attempted to stop a 1974 Indiana freshman named Larry Bird from heading back home before practice even began.

He said this for two reasons, one being a genuine feeling that he should have reached out to an overwhelmed kid and the other being that he could have used him. He didn't think he was going to need him, but he also didn't think he was going to lose Scott May to a broken arm, either. Indiana lost one game in the 1974–75 and 1975–76 seasons, that being by two points to Kentucky, with May injured. Given the talents of Larry Bird, he'd have been the last coach to go through back-to-back undefeated seasons.

He's always going to blame the late Myles Brand of the NCAA for forcing him out of Indiana, but the fact is he messed up and will never admit it. He wound up at Texas Tech, with a toady athletic director in Gerald Myers—the only kind of "boss" he could possibly have at that stage of his career—and a constituency that really didn't give a damn about basketball, not even when he was on the verge of breaking Dean Smith's career victory total.

As Knight closed in on the record, the Texas Tech athletic department saw fit to post the following message on its website: "The TTU Athletic Department would like to put as many fans in the United Sprint Center for the next four games as Coach Knight will hopefully tie and break Coach Smith's record here in Lubbock in front of his home fans. The TTU Athletic Department Ticket Office will have special ticket prices for the historic events."

Good God, they were begging for fans.

He should have broken that record at Indiana. But he'll never say mea culpa and has been resisting for years all attempts to bring him back to Bloomington. Too proud. Too stubborn. But consistent.

He is not the only person about whom I would say, "Why do you do these things? Why do you make it so hard to defend you?" But he's one of them. I know millions of people won't believe this, but he can be fun to be around. I know what he did that Thursday afternoon for Jim O'Brien. But he really doesn't care what you or I think. Never has. Never will.

There is a Sinatra song that should be played endlessly wherever he is laid to rest. C'mon. Do you really have to ask which one?

CHAPTER 22

I Can Hardly Believe It's Legal

If they stopped playing football in the next five minutes it wouldn't bother me at all.

I mean, what if someone came to you with the proposal for a new game called "football"? It's a territorial game, you'd be told. The object is to advance an oblong leather ball down a one-hundred-yard-long field into an expanse of land called the "end zone." Well, you'd say, I've heard of worse premises. Tell me more.

Okay, there are eleven men on a side. A whole bunch of big people, and I'm talking about participants who might weigh as much as 350 pounds, smash into each other at a place called the "line of scrimmage." The object of the team not in possession of the ball is to find the person on the other team who has possession of it and bring him to the ground in as violent a manner as possible. The object of the team with the ball, of course, is to prevent that from happening. Now, the offensive team can throw the ball to someone, but the man who catches it had better be ready to sustain a very hard blow designed to make him drop the ball.

Wow, you'd say. Sounds pretty rough.

Oh, you don't know the half of it, you'd be told. Injury is not only possible, it is *expected*. You cannot play this game without the understanding that, sooner or later, you will sustain an injury to your knee, ankle, arm, shoulder, neck, back, or, worst of all, head. The injuries are often not short-term issues. Countless people who have played this game, especially at the highest level, suffer debilitating injuries that will last their entire lives. Oh, and their life expectancy falls somewhat short of the norm for American males.

Wait a minute, you'd say. This is legal? It not only is legal, you'd be told, it is America's sport of choice. Autumn Saturdays, Sundays, and Monday nights are given over to this. The climactic game each season is called the "Super Bowl" and is the highest-rated television program of the year, every year. America comes to a stop for that game.

This can't be, you'd say. Has the country gone mad?

Apparently.

Perhaps you don't think of football that way. But you should. Football is a barbaric game. In a more civilized, more genteel society, no one would even think of sanctioning such an activity. Yet as the twentieth century came to a close, I found myself out of step with frightening numbers of my fellow Americans: football was not my favorite sport.

That said, I wouldn't dream of missing the Super Bowl or the National Championship football game. I never said I don't enjoy watching football. I've been watching it for more than sixty years. But I'm talking philosophy. How do we as a nation reconcile having chosen football as our new national game? Is the trade-off in body carnage worth the type of entertainment the game provides? For most people the answer seems to be yes, and that includes some of the aforementioned participants who have been maimed—there is no other word—by this brutal game.

In the end, I'm torn. I can roll up my mental sleeves and talk collegiate and professional football history with just about anyone. I have enjoyed many a football game. I think I understand its subtleties and nuances. But the older I get the more mystified I have become with the easy acceptance of football's inherent brutality and viciousness by so many who love it above all other sporting endeavors. How can people justify the very existence of this game? Why did it take so long for people to arrive at the conclusion that using the head as a battering ram was not such a good thing?

I addressed this issue as far back as 1989 in the aftermath of an incident where San Francisco 49er defensive back Jeff Fuller speared New England Patriots running back John Stephens, launching headfirst into Stephens's helmet. He was not the tackler who first met up with Stephens; that was 49er linebacker Jim Fahnhorst. Fuller decided he would finish off Stephens, who was about to go down. The twist here was that

Fuller got the worst of it. When they took him off the field he had no use of or feeling in his right arm. Initial fears were that Fuller had sustained a broken neck; nonetheless, he sustained spinal damage. That was the last hit of his career. Jeff Fuller never did regain use of his right arm.

Bill Walsh, the former great 49ers coach, was working on TV that day. Walsh was supposed to be a thoroughly erudite individual, a man whose approach to the game was almost professorial. Surely, he would decry Fuller's actions. Here, however, was Walsh's take: "Fuller is one of the really devastating hitters in football. He's like [David] Fulcher or [Dave] Duerson, those kind of safetymen. And he's probably as big a hitter as they've had, and he has the reputation, not only of being fast, explosive, play the ball well, but his run support has been the best in football."

His broadcast partner that day was Dick Enberg. He, too, had a reputation as a thoughtful, sensitive man, but he was also working a football game. As an ambulance arrived, Enberg observed, "This is one positive out of how we've progressed in terms of how we handle injuries on the field. In the old days, just dragging a player off and tending to him, and here they're not going to take any chances, and how carefully they'll move Fuller to the stretcher and then to the emergency vehicle."

Yup, we were all so darn happy they weren't going to just drag Fuller off the field. Bill Walsh had a further positive spin on the proceedings: "Sports medicine," he said, "has been a real science in recent years . . . there's a real career for 'em now, for many doctors."

After Fuller had been tended to, and both an IV bag and oxygen mask had been produced, Walsh summed it all up for his viewers: "And let's hope Jeff's okay and can return to action, most likely not in this game, but in the near future."

I was appalled at the general casual nature of the public response and pored over the game tape extensively to verify what I had seen and heard. How could people so badly miss the point? Jeff Fuller had been spearing. And he paid a terrible price. But football life just went on, with minimal commentary about the reckless and vicious nature of what Fuller had done. Few saw this as a cautionary tale. There was no crusade launched to denounce spearing.

I wrote a column in the *Globe* lamenting this but got very little response. It was a journalistic tree falling in an enormous forest. I was messing with football, and perhaps worse than being vilified, I was being ignored.

In recent years public consciousness has been raised on the subject of head injuries. The NFL has learned to address neurological concerns. Of course, it's way too late to help many former players, whose innumerable "dings" were actually concussions, the effects of which would surface in later life.

Football's most ardent proponents have decried many of the attempts in recent years to lessen the violence in the game. They call it "girly ball" or "glorified flag football," with much of their ire directed at the measures that have been instituted to protect the quarterback. They fear the game they have come to know and love is being defanged. The game continues to appeal to people with a thirst for violence I just don't share. I get far more enjoyment from seeing an acrobatic catch along the sideline or a successful double reverse than seeing someone hit hard enough to leave the game. To this, many will say I just don't get it. Oh, I get it, all right. I just don't accept it.

When I became a full-time columnist in the fall of 1989, a few weeks before the Jeff Fuller incident, I was pleased to be working in one of the few big markets in America, if not the only one, in which the local professional football team was a distant fourth out of four in the local pecking order.

The New England Patriots are one of the most interesting franchises in the history of the National Football League. There is an abundant literary treasure chest awaiting the man or woman enterprising enough to attempt writing the definitive history of the franchise. The most logical person to have done this was the late Will McDonough, my colleague at the *Boston Globe*. He was there at the birth of the franchise in 1960 and no writer was ever more plugged in to the goings-on in that then-goofy enterprise. The fact that he had a low regard for the team founder and first president, Billy Sullivan, would have made for some provocative reading.

Regrettably, Will McDonough passed away in January of 2003. There have been many worthy and talented writers assigned to cover the team since then, but none with the historical background only McDonough possessed. But I'm telling you, the story is sitting there for someone brave enough to tackle it.

Billy Sullivan was quite a character. His family was in the printing business. He was a Boston College graduate who had befriended Frank Leahy. He was the publicity man for the 1948 pennant-winning Boston Braves. Somewhere along the way he got into the fuel oil business. And all along he had cultivated a deep love for football.

He got in on the ground floor of the American Football League—barely. The story is that he had to scrape around to get the $25,000 he needed to secure the final spot in the eight-team league when it came into being in 1960. He always had partners, but we seldom heard about them. Let's just say Billy seldom was put off by the sight of someone holding a camera, microphone, or notebook.

Some people of quite substantial means were involved with the AFL. Billy Sullivan was not one of them. The Patriots were created on the cheap and in a real sense things never changed during Billy's stewardship. He was a man of vision and ambition, but he never had enough real money to run a franchise the way it should be run. Nonetheless he was a fighter, and he managed to keep his hands on the team for thirty years.

The Patriots never had a proper playing field during their AFL existence. Their first game was played at Braves Field, which by that time, eight years after baseball's Braves had left Boston for Milwaukee, had been stripped down to a seating capacity of perhaps fifteen thousand. For many years they played home games at Fenway Park. Football games had been played at Fenway for decades, but that doesn't mean it was a good idea. Before the decade was out, they would also play home games at both Boston College and Harvard. They would even play a "home" game in Birmingham. That's Alabama, not England, although the latter might have made more sense.

Despite their penurious existence, the Patriots were a reasonably successful AFL franchise, even though far too much of the news that emanated from the team was the kind to make someone smile. My first personal encounter with the buffoonery came in the fall of 1969. The new head coach was Clive Rush, who had been the offensive coordinator for the 1969 Super Bowl champion New York Jets. Calling Mr. Rush "eccentric" is a massive understatement. The man was wacko. Bizarrely, he was almost electrocuted in a mishap as he was mounting the podium the day he was introduced as head coach.

After losing their first seven games the Patriots defeated the Houston Oilers to give Rush his first NFL head coaching victory. I was sent the next day to get an off-day story. By this time tales of his eccentricity had become a nonstop topic in the Boston sportswriting fraternity. I was told to be prepared for a quiz given to me by the coach.

"He will ask you whether you are 'fact' or 'flair' in terms of your writing approach," I was told. "And the correct answer is 'fact.' He will then ask you what NFL writers you like and admire. The correct answers are Dave Anderson of the *New York Times* and Bob Oates of the *Los Angeles Times*."

I never directly covered the Patriots throughout the 1970s and '80s, but I was present at one of the most famous games in franchise history, the 1976 first-round playoff game with the Oakland Raiders in Oakland. The University of San Francisco Dons, led by seven-foot center Bill Cartwright, were also in town, playing in the Cable Car Classic at the famed Cow Palace. I figured I'd cover the Pats-Raiders in the afternoon and go back to the Cow Palace for the championship game that night. That's a real Bob Ryan kind of day.

I was sitting next to Will McDonough, and as the game unfolded he told me that the Patriots were the best team in the AFC that year and were heading to the Super Bowl. Lo and behold, they went up, 21–10. But then powerful running back Sam "Bam" Cunningham went out of bounds, rather than fighting for a first down. Oakland linebacker Phil Villapiano did a good steer-roping imitation on Pats' tight end Russ Francis in a crucial third-down situation and there was no call. Defensive tackle Ray "Sugar Bear" Hamilton nailed Raiders quarterback Ken Stabler for a big loss, only to see referee Ben Dreith call him for roughing the passer.

This was the single most famous call against the Patriots in their history. And you just knew what was going to happen. Thus reprieved, Stabler led the Raiders into the end zone. Final score: Oakland 24, New England 21. And who would win the Super Bowl but the *second*-best team in the AFC. At least, that was the way we saw it.

It took twenty-five years, but the Patriots would get their revenge in the infamous "Tuck Rule" game.

That game in Oakland represented the high point of the first twenty-six years of the Patriots' existence. And having it end in anger and outrage was somehow appropriate because most things concerning the Billy Sullivan regime were off-kilter. A typical Patriots fan knew that when the Big Moment came it would be like Lucy snatching the football from Charlie Brown. Nothing ever went right for long. When they finally found a good coach in Chuck Fairbanks, his tenure ended in chaos when Sullivan discovered on the eve of the playoffs that, with four years remaining on his contract, his head coach had negotiated a contract with the University of Colorado to become their head coach. Infuriated, Sullivan suspended Fairbanks for three days, this but a week in advance of a playoff game against the Houston Oilers. Sullivan reinstated Fairbanks in time to coach the game; the Patriots were hammered, 31–14; and that was Fairbanks's last game with the team. He explained that he had fulfilled his desire to coach in the NFL, that he had left the organization in better shape than he had found it, and that he preferred a collegiate lifestyle. He also admitted he hadn't gone about things in quite the right way.

Billy Sullivan took everything personally, good or bad. I had trailed him around New Orleans at the 1972 Sugar Bowl when he was in pursuit of Penn State coach Joe Paterno. A year or so later I was standing in P.J. Clarke's in New York with him following a New York Football Writer's Dinner, when he said he was sorry he hadn't been more forthcoming back in New Orleans, called me a "nice young man," and said that someday he would reward me with a big scoop. This was somewhat offset by his later declaring me to have "the balls of a snake." What I had done to arouse him was write a column in which I labeled his son Patrick as "the Good Sullivan." This was in contrast to Patrick's bumbling big brother Chuck, who would almost bankrupt the company in a foolish attempt to be a rock entrepreneur.

Will McDonough was definitely not a Billy Sullivan fan. Listening to Will on the phone in the newsroom was always entertaining, but the showstopper might have been the day I heard him tell Billy Sullivan,

"When you die, I will be in a long line of people waiting to piss on your grave."

Billy wound up having to sell the team, and when he did it was to the totally unlikable Victor Kiam, who was famous for doing his own commercials as owner of Remington Products, the gist of which was that he liked the Remington razors so much he bought the company. His three-year stewardship bottomed out in the 1990 Lisa Olson incident, when the *Boston Herald* reporter became embroiled in a controversial locker room incident in which, it came to light, she had been harassed by certain players. She was trying to deal with the consequences privately, but when the story broke it became a major national incident. No one on the Patriots came off well, and that included Kiam, whose major public response was to make light of the situation.

Speaking at a male-only banquet, the owner of the New England Patriots joked, "What do the Iraqis have in common with Lisa Olson? They both have seen Patriot missiles up close."

Kiam bailed out after three years, selling the team to James Busch Orthwein of the Saint Louis Busches. In some ways he was my favorite Patriots owner. And in one very important way he was the single most important owner in the history of the franchise.

James Orthwein was an heir. They are not like you and me. Mr. Orthwein was sent straight from central casting. He could have been portrayed by Edward Everett Horton. There would be occasions when he would summon the media to an impromptu press conference prior to, or at the halftime of, a Patriots home game, and when we arrived at his box there he stood, in a double-breasted blue blazer with the gold buttons and an appropriate drink—martini or vodka and tonic, perhaps—in hand. I nicknamed him "James Busch Chatsworth Osborne Junior Orthwein," after the preppy character from the great *Dobie Gillis* TV show.

But before he handed the team over to a longtime season ticket holder named Robert Kraft, Orthwein performed a major public service for Patriots fans. Just as 1967 is the dividing line in Boston Red Sox history,1993 is the dividing line in New England Patriots history. For that is when Orthwein hired Bill Parcells as the new head coach of his team.

The Patriots had been in existence since 1960. They had suited up such excellent players as Babe Parilli, Larry Eisenhauer, Jim Nance, and, best of all, Gino Cappelletti, a pass-catching end who also was a first-rate place kicker. They had a serious cult following. But if you had stopped the average person on the street and asked for a one-word association for the Patriots, the winner would have been "joke." There was a comic-opera aspect to the entire organization. They were an NFL outlier franchise, perhaps the only one whose local ranking was a distant fourth behind baseball, basketball, and hockey.

No success was ever sustainable. The Patriots had actually gotten to the Super Bowl in 1986 under coach Raymond Berry, but they were left for dead by that great Chicago Bears team (46–10), and the Pats fell back quickly. As it was revealed, the team had a drug problem. Rod Rust went a disastrous 1-15 in 1990 and Dick MacPherson, a sweet man in way over his head (he was a college man through and through), was a dismal 8-24 in his two years.

The rest of the NFL was thriving, but the Patriots were stuck at a paltry eighteen thousand season tickets. Fans feared Orthwein would move the team to Saint Louis, and who could have blamed him? By that time the Patriots had been in business for thirty-three years and all they would have left behind was a very tiny footprint.

As soon as Bill Parcells arrived, the phones started ringing. There is no other way to put it: Bill Parcells provided a truly desperate franchise with instant credibility. The team's win-loss line will never reflect his full impact. In his four years, the Patriots were 32-32. But in year four its record was 11-5 and the team went to the Super Bowl, and long before that he had made the Patriots a local force by the sheer impact of his personality. Bill Parcells put the Patriots on equal footing with the other three Boston major sports franchises all by himself, even at the height of the Larry Bird/Celtics mania that had engulfed all of New England.

I wish I had had the foresight to have secured a transcript of every Parcells media session during those four years. He could talk football, he could talk Broadway. Every day he stepped up to the podium, whether at training camp, at an off-day press conference, or after a game, was a command performance. By the time Parcells left the season ticket base had more than tripled. Every game was a sellout. Football talk was in the air twelve months a year, and that had never been the case in Boston.

A coach needs players to execute, of course, and the player who did the most to make Bill Parcells a success in New England was someone who is in danger of falling through the cracks of Patriots history, which would be a big injustice. Before Tom Brady, Drew Bledsoe was the quarterback. He and Parcells were joined at the hip because the first big decision Parcells had to make when he took over was whether to take Bledsoe of Washington State or Notre Dame's Rick Mirer in the 1993 draft. Parcells guessed correctly, and Bledsoe rewarded him by getting him to the Super Bowl. Bledsoe would throw for 44,611 yards in his career, most of them for the Patriots. He threw 256 touchdown passes. He was a quality player and a total stand-up guy. He happens to be the second-best quarterback in the history of a team whose best may well be the best of all time.

Bill Parcells being Bill Parcells, he would come into inevitable conflict with a new owner who wanted to share the glory in a way that would infringe on Parcells's turf. And that's what Parcells's departure after the 1996 season was all about, in my view. The man in the middle was Player Personnel Director Bobby Grier, but he was strictly collateral damage. Bob Kraft insisted he was all about Organization. Parcells interpreted that to mean Bob Kraft. It was not a match made in heaven.

Bill Parcells, as good a coach as he was, just was not Bob Kraft's kind of guy. Pete Carroll was. Bill didn't schmooze. Bill coached. Bill did everything *his* way. Pete Carroll would schmooze. Pete was a nice guy. Pete made people feel good. Bob Kraft thought he could get along without Bill Parcells, but he was wrong. Pete Carroll did a decent job, but the team regressed during his three years, going from 10-6 and a division championship to 9-7 and 8-8 and out of the playoffs. The slide would have continued because Carroll just did not command sufficient respect among his troops. He hates hearing that, but one reason he has enjoyed better success with Seattle on his third NFL go-round (the Jets being the first) is that he learned a few things from the Patriots experience.

After firing Carroll, Bob Kraft made his own brilliant decision and hired onetime Parcells assistant Bill Belichick. He was about to succeed Parcells as head coach of the New York Jets. It was a done deal. Until it wasn't. On the day he was supposed to be announced as the new Jets coach, Belichick stopped himself at the one-yard line. He issued a cryptic note saying he was not going to be the "HC of the NYJ" for reasons unknown. I happened to be in Hempstead, Long Island, at the Jets facility that day, and one line of thought was that Belichick was somewhat unhinged.

I don't think Bill Belichick is all that hard to understand. He is a smart, well-educated man with a degree in economics from Wesleyan. If forced to earn a living using that degree in economics or in some other capacity, I'm sure he could have done very well. But he has never wanted to, and he will never have to.

He loves football. All he has ever wanted is a life in football. He loves everything about it, including its history. It is said he may very well have the largest private library of football books in the world. He can talk T. Truxton Hare just as easily as he can talk Tom Brady. He may know more about Paul Brown than Brown's son Mike does. He loves the planning and the scheming. He can discuss the technique involved in every position on the field in minute detail.

Steve Belichick's son was a prodigy. Steve was a football insider phenomenon, known, if at all, by the public as an assistant coach at the Naval Academy, a post he clung to because it provided stability and continuity for his family. He was also well-known throughout the larger football community for his teaching expertise at camps. Everyone in the NFL who knew about Steve Belichick had probably heard something about that smart kid of his, too.

Bill Belichick entered the film room with his father as a child. He had found his calling. He would have a playing career in football and lacrosse, but there never was a millisecond's doubt that his entire adolescence and young adulthood was spent preparing to become a football coach.

Most football coaches live nomadic existences. Wives learn the art of packing. Kids learn how to make new friends on something approaching an annual or biannual basis. Not Mrs. Belichick or Bill. He was born in Nashville, Tennessee, but he was raised in Annapolis. Listen to him speak. You'll hear it.

He made his name as Bill Parcells's defensive coordinator for the 1986 and 1990 Super Bowl–champion Giants, and he later worked a year with Parcells in New England. This was a natural segue for a head coaching post. But his tenure guiding the Cleveland Browns was not so much a coaching experience as it was a scorched-earth campaign. He had no people skills and didn't seem to think he needed any. Players were treated as nothing more than commodities and the media would have been pleased to have been treated as pond scum, which would have been an improvement. So when Bob Kraft let it be known that the man he wanted to replace Pete Carroll was Bill Belichick, people thought he was crazy. But Kraft had gotten to know Belichick during his time as a Patriots assistant in 1996 and had a firm belief in him.

The reality is that the Bill Belichick we came to know in New England had either received tips on media management or had figured it out himself, with one exception, that being the immediate postgame session with the media. Win or lose, he is close to useless on Sunday or Monday night. He is Mr. Cliché, always alluding to happenings in "all three phases of the game" (i.e., offense, defense, special teams) and little else. Those banal clips and sound bites are all the nation at large sees.

All anyone has to do is come back Monday, after he has decompressed and after he has seen the game tape. He can be riveting. Football beat people have forever groused about how he refuses to be forthcoming on the subject of injuries or other daily nuts-and-bolts information. But he has never been less than a bonanza for a columnist. We aren't hung up on the mundane daily stuff. Ask the right general football question and he is a one-man seminar. He loves dispensing football knowledge. He's not so good about dispensing team knowledge.

One of the fascinating things about sports is the way one incident can affect the big picture for days, weeks, months, years, and decades to come. One play both changed Bill Belichick's life and altered the history of the New England franchise. It took place in the 2001 first-round playoff game between the Patriots and the Oakland Raiders, who were leading 13–10 with just under two minutes to play. Tom Brady was sacked by a blitzing Charles Woodson. The ball hit the ground and Oakland linebacker Greg Biekert recovered. The Raiders were going to be able to run out the clock. The Patriots' season was going to end.

However, referee Walt Coleman ruled it not a fumble but an incomplete pass. He was invoking a rule even the most seasoned and astute press box observer did not know existed: Rule 3, Section 21, Article 2, which has forever become known as the "Tuck Rule." Brady's right arm had been up, but he had not yet begun to throw the ball. According to the rule, however, because he had not yet "tucked" the ball into his body, when the ball came loose it was an attempt to throw and thus an incomplete pass.

This was a colossal break for the Patriots. We had all seen what we had seen. That was a fumble, period. Brady's arm was not in any kind of forward motion. But a rule that was put in specifically to reduce the number of decisions a referee might be asked to make was now saving him from a disastrous fumble.

Given that reprieve, Brady made the most of it, taking the team through the snow that had covered Foxboro Stadium to the twenty-eight-yard line, whereupon Adam Vinatieri kicked what might very well have been the most difficult field goal ever kicked in NFL history. Another Vinatieri field goal won it in overtime. That was the beginning of a run that culminated in a Super Bowl triumph over the Saint Louis Rams.

The poor Raiders had been screwed by an abominable rule. But New England was the last place they could look for sympathy. This was a classic case of what goes around comes around.

Remember Sugar Bear Hamilton and Ben Dreith? Revenge was ours, sayeth the Patriots. The only difference was that twenty-five years before the Patriots had been done in by a flat-out bad call. This time the Raiders had been done in by the correct call of a truly bad rule.

With the Patriots as Super Bowl champs, the image and culture transformation that had begun to take shape under Bill Parcells was now a fait accompli under his onetime chief acolyte. Football interest in Boston surged. The Patriots now challenged the Red Sox for local sports supremacy. Bill Belichick made himself so indispensable in the minds of New England fans that he was able to survive an episode called "Spygate" with little loss of popularity.

Belichick was caught filming Green Bay defensive signals in 2006, which is a breach of the rules. He was caught a second time on Opening Day against the Jets in 2007. He has never admitted it properly, choosing to issue disingenuous explanations that he had "misinterpreted" the rule, as if he didn't know every NFL rule forward, backward, and sideways, far better than any coach in the league.

Some say he gained a competitive advantage from the practice, others that he didn't. I guess he did it because he thought it was clever. It was the kind of thing the Smartest Kid in the Class would do. The end result tarnished his accomplishments in the eyes of the outside world. Spygate is a bright memory in the rest of the country but is verboten in Boston.

I wrote a column in 2008 in which I said that Bill Belichick "has been exposed as monumentally disingenuous at best and utterly duplicitous at worst." Not everyone in my town was pleased.

Belichick is a very compartmentalized man. First, there is the Football Coach, who frames everything in terms of how it will affect his team and its chances for success on the field. He is very good at this. That is why he gets the big money. Second, there is the Private Citizen, who is close friends with rocker Jon Bon Jovi. People are always amazed to learn he once made a European tour with the Bon Jovi band, serving as a cross between a roadie and a groupie.

He is a fan of other sports and was a frequent spectator at Celtics playoff games during the Paul Pierce/Kevin Garnett/Ray Allen era. If anyone had a doubt as to whether or not he had an ego, all they had to do was see the gigantic grin on his face every time he was shown on the Jumbotron during a time-out while the crowd chanted his name.

The Private Citizen is seldom on display during the football season. One major exception took place in July of 2013 when he made a practically mandatory visit to the podium to address the Aaron Hernandez situation for the first time. He and Bob Kraft had each been out of the country when the former Patriots tight end was arrested and charged with murder a week or so earlier. This was not a normal situation involving a fallen athlete in trouble with the law and Bill Belichick is not an ordinary football coach, so he needed to be heard from.

He read from a statement, but he did ad-lib, and he came off as downright human. Reporters get few glimpses of the Private Citizen Belichick, and the public never gets any. Some observers felt he got way too much praise for simply doing what should have been done. I chose to take him at face value. I think he did grasp the grim reality of the situation and how it far transcended any technical issues the loss of Hernandez would create for the team. I don't think it was an act.

One of the by-products of the Patriots becoming such a major part of Boston's sports dialogue after so many years of being an afterthought was the concurrent canonization of Tom Brady. Prior to Brady, the greatest Patriot had not been a skill position player, but rather an offensive lineman—John Hannah. Brady ended all that.

While Belichick is neatly compartmentalized, Brady is even more amazingly so. He is at the top of the food chain among athlete/celebrities, but he has always managed to keep a good balance between being Tom Brady, all-time quarterback, and Tom Brady, *People* magazine celebrity and husband of the richest model in the world, that being Gisele Bündchen. Brady had always gravitated to public people, but he never made a public misstep, until he got caught in a bit of a mess with a pregnant ex-girlfriend, Bridget Moynahan, and a fiancée, Bündchen, simultaneously in his life. Only Tom Brady could have finessed that well enough to escape with practically zero damage to his pristine image, except, perhaps, among Moynahan relatives and any fans in convents.

The fact is he figured out how to be a celebrity without being smothered by the ravenous media. He was never a recluse. The key, however, was that he never once forgot that the basis of his fame and fortune was being a quarterback. He was always one of the boys. He never shirked his off-season work, so much so that he was a longtime winner of one of the prize parking spaces given to the best workout guys. And I'm sure he never played the "I'm married to a supermodel and you're not" card inside the locker room, either.

The Patriots have always been a bountiful subject for writers. Theirs is a unique NFL tale.

But I'm not the one who will write it. That's because, as I've said many times, it's only football, and I can hardly believe it's legal.

CHAPTER 23

Ending the Curse

I was never into the "Curse of the Bambino" business. That was Dan Shaughnessy's thing. The first time I heard the theory espoused was circa 1983 or 1984. My friend Henry Hecht of the *New York Post* had a fellow Vanderbilt Commodore friend named Darrell Berger, who was a Unitarian Universalist minister with a parish in Scituate, Massachusetts, two towns below me on the South Shore of Boston. While visiting Darrell one day, he mentioned that he had heard about a premise whereby the Red Sox' sale of Babe Ruth to the Yankees in 1920 had been an Original Sin from which there could be no absolution, and that it had been nicknamed "the Curse of the Bambino." He couldn't recall where he had heard it. As far as I know, its origin is still unknown.

Losing World Series Game 7s in 1946, 1967, 1975, and 1986, with all but the 1967 loss being of the heartbreak variety (1967 was just too much Bob Gibson), made for great melodrama and lamentation. Throw in losing the 1949 pennant to the Yankees after leading by a game with two to play; the Bucky Dent playoff-game homer in 1978; and the infamous game in which Grady Little left Pedro Martinez in too long in Game 7 of the 2003 American League Championship Series, and it's easy to see how many people bought into the idea that the Red Sox were terminally jinxed.

So, was winning it all in 2004, in the manner in which it was done, worth the wait for Red Sox fans? I think that's a valid question. I killed the team in print after the Yankees had taken a 3–0 lead in the 2004 American League Championship Series. Game 3 had been a particular disaster, with the Yankees winning 19–8, and there weren't a lot of happy people walking out of Fenway Park on the night of Saturday, October 16, 2004.

Eleven nights later the Red Sox were World Series champions, having improbably won eight games in a row.

When people ask me to choose my various favorite this and favorite that during my forty-six years at the *Globe*, I always explain that in the case of baseball it's not one game, or one event, but a combination. In this respect, I can't talk about Games 4 and 5 of the 2004 ALCS as separate entities. I think of them in tandem. They represent a combined ten hours and fifty-one minutes of spectacular baseball, and they both ended on the same day.

The bottom of the ninth inning of Game 4 appeared to be inevitable. The Red Sox were down, 4–3, the Yankees having taken the lead with two runs in the sixth off Derek Lowe and Mike Timlin. Mariano Rivera was on to nail down the series as he had done countless times before. Kevin Millar led off the Red Sox ninth by drawing a rare walk from Rivera, and speedy Dave Roberts was sent in to pinch-run. You didn't need to be a diamond scholar to know he was going to attempt a steal of second. He would tell me a year later that legendary base stealer Maury Wills had once told him that someday he would be in a situation just like this and he would succeed. He waited out Rivera, whose best weapon in preventing steals was simply holding the ball. But he eventually did run, catcher Jorge Posada made a strong throw, and Derek Jeter, a master of the swipe tag, made a very good attempt to fool second-base umpire Joe West into thinking he had made a successful tag. Fortunately for Roberts, the team, Red Sox fans everywhere, and right-thinking fans the world over, Joe West was not fooled. The replay vindicated West's judgment. It was close, but Roberts was clearly safe.

Bill Mueller, a good contact hitter, hit one up the middle. Rivera kicked at it, but the ball shot through into center field. There was no play at the plate. The Red Sox were alive. They went to the twelfth, tied at 3. Manny Ramirez singled. David Ortiz, busy constructing his own legend, homered off Paul Quantrill, and the Yankees now led the series 3–1.

It was well past midnight. Game 4 would commence at five P.M. It would prove to be nerve wracking.

The Red Sox led, 2–1. The Yankees led, 4–2. The Red Sox tied it, 4–4, with two in the eighth. Each team went seven pitchers deep as the game passed through the ninth, tenth, eleventh, twelfth, and thirteenth with no further scoring. The Yankees had a great chance in the thirteenth. Tim Wakefield, who had been victimized by Aaron Boone's pennant-winning Game 7 homer the year before, had come into the game in the eleventh. His usual catcher was Doug Mirabelli, but Jason Varitek was playing full time in the playoffs, and he was having trouble with Wake's knuckler. Hideki Matsui had reached first base via a fielder's choice, but now he was on third with two outs, representing the go-ahead run because two of Wake's knucklers had eluded Varitek. Manager Terry Francona ordered both Bernie Williams and Jorge Posada walked intentionally to load the bases and thus create the possibility of a force out to end the inning.

Veteran slugger Ruben Sierra, once an MVP runner-up, was at the plate. Wakefield struck him out.

In the bottom of the fourteenth inning, Yankee pitcher Esteban Loaiza walked both Johnny Damon and Ramirez. David Ortiz fouled off five two-strike pitches and blooped a single to center on the tenth pitch of the at-bat. The Yankees now led the series, 3–2.

Time of game: five hours and forty-nine minutes. In the history of baseball, there may never have been two consecutive postseason games with such drama.

Game 6 was the famed Curt Schilling Bloody Sock Game. Game 7 was a breeze. Damon hit a second-inning grand slam off Kevin Brown, and the Red Sox won, 10–2. They were going to the World Series after becoming the first team in baseball history to erase a 3–0 series deficit.

The World Series was pure anticlimax. The Red Sox wiped out the Cardinals in four. Curse that! But the real drama had taken place in those ten hours and fifty-one minutes of baseball. For me, it will never get better than that. I would have been happy to retire from baseball writing right then and there.

But I'll never retire from talking about it. No other game has so many nuances, so many interesting situations, so many what-ifs. No other game can reward a cheesy feat such as a twenty-foot dribbler down the third-base line that might bring home the winning run, even as it punishes a seemingly great feat, such as a four-hundred-twenty-foot fly ball to the deepest point of a ballpark. No other game is played in arenas of different proportions, allowing for such discussions as whether or not a ball hit off the left-field wall in Fenway would have been a home run in Baltimore. No other game routinely allows you to connect a player born in 1995 with a player who died in 1908, and have the comparison make any kind of sense at all.

Yes, baseball has its problems: labor issues, steroids, crazy salaries, postseason games played at night that prevent many young people from watching. I'll let somebody else take those on. In this book, however, I just want to celebrate the great game baseball is. It rewards us over and over. As to the Curse of the Bambino, if it really existed, I hope the 2004 victory, and the two subsequent Red Sox World Series wins in 2007 and 2013, have banished it forever.

CHAPTER 24

Violence Mixed with Chivalry

I wish I knew more about hockey.

I like to think I know something about basketball. It's the one sport I could play at an interscholastic level. It's a sport I've been exposed to in different ways since I was a five-year-old kid turning the numbers on a manual scoreboard in the Mercer County Parochial Basketball League right through the gold medal game of the 2012 London Olympics.

I like to think I know something about baseball. I've been reading about it ever since I started reading, and I have been a passionate follower of the game probably since I was born. The modern analytics guys can speak over my head, but I can articulate what I see and get it down on paper pretty well.

I like to think I know something about football. I have firm memories of watching games as far back as age seven. I'm a good American: when fall comes, it's football season. I do have some major reservations about the game, but that doesn't prevent me from being a fan from September through the Super Bowl. I chose not to play football in prep school in order to preserve my body for basketball, but as the football manager I learned a lot about the game by hanging around the coaches as much as I did.

But I'm confessing right here and now that I am very shaky when the subject turns to hockey, the final member of the Big Four team sports in America.

I knew about the mighty Canadiens growing up and even saw them play the Rangers in New York once. Lawrenceville had hockey and I was the sports editor, so I went to hockey games, and I even assigned myself to write the story of our game with archrival Hill, which appeared on the front page of the *Lawrence*. We won, 2–1, with goals provided by Graham More and John Gorringe. I said of Moore's winning goal that "after skating around the cage, he emerged at exactly the right moment from a tangle of players and beat the goalie at the upper right hand corner of the nets." But the highlight of the day was a waved-off goal for the home team. Sometime in the third period "an ardent female fan's scream, which sounded like a whistle, halted play, and a subsequent Larrie goal was nullified." Now, there's a line I'm certain my *Globe* hockey colleagues, Messrs. Fitzgerald, Rosa, Powers, Dupont, and Shinzawa, have never written. The story actually reads better a half century later than I would have expected, but there's so much about this game I'll never know.

For years I kept promising myself that one year I would ask the Boss to free me up in order that I could immerse myself in a Bruins training camp. I'd go to practice every day, and to the exhibition games, and would emerge from this crash course with an undergraduate degree in puck-ology. This would all be in the hope I could develop a proper feel for a game that is so important to the psyche of the area where I've lived since 1964.

I never did.

It would have been nice because I have never played hockey in my life. I have been on skates and I have held a hockey stick in my hands, but not at the same time. There are things I know simply from playing baseball and especially basketball that I will never know about hockey. I have been forced to study the game from the outside, and I have never been able to learn anything resembling a hockey nuance. I'm so impressed when hockey analysts can telestrate how a certain play developed since I can only see the end result, and even then I can be confused.

Not knowing hockey may not be an issue in some cities, but it's definitely a problem in Boston, which I would argue deserves the nickname "Hockeytown" above all other cities.

Detroit likes to call itself "Hockeytown, USA" but the plain and simple fact is that no city in the United States has the deep reservoir of hockey history, passion, and competition that Boston has.

The Boston Bruins, established in 1924, were the first American team in the National Hockey League, but the region is perhaps even more passionate about high school and college hockey. Does anyone else have a Beanpot Tournament? The Beanpot is a Boston tradition that began in 1952—an annual tournament played on the first two Mondays in February among Boston College, Boston University, Northeastern, and Harvard. The great thing about it is that the four schools are located within a three-mile radius. No other city can even dream about a Beanpot.

I admire anyone who can write hockey well. Hockey is, by far, the hardest of the four big mainstream team sports to write about. The very fact that so few goals are scored in many games means a writer must have full command of the game's nuances to write a full hockey story.

A one-period score of 0–0 does not faze good hockey writers because they see things in a hockey game I can't see. They know what people are trying to do and why they either succeed or don't succeed, much the way I used to amuse myself during Celtics routs in the 1970s by seeing which opponents, if any, knew how to counteract the Celtics' plays. In those days, having been in attendance at daily practice for years, I really did know all the plays.

I, on the other hand, agonized over writing hockey stories. I prayed for goals, lots of goals. Failing that, a goalie making spectacular save after spectacular save—"standing on his head," as they say—was an acceptable alternative. I'm not usually all that big on quotes, but when it came to writing hockey, the gabbier the player the better I liked him.

All this said, I did have a couple of priceless hockey moments. The first one came about by chance. The 1968–69 Bruins won the first two games of their opening-round Stanley Cup series with Toronto by scores of 10–0 and 7–0. The first game was punctuated by a big hit by Toronto defenseman Pat Quinn on the sainted Bobby Orr, as well as a madman performance by the Maple Leafs' Forbes Kennedy, who personally accounted for twenty-two penalty minutes. The *Globe*'s Tom Fitzgerald was in high dudgeon, writing that the Maple Leafs were "a parody of a major league club. Since they were outplayed in such essentials as shooting, passing and skating, the Leafs resorted to the last refuge of the humiliated. They gave a pretty good impersonation of a vengeful gang, dedicated to any consolation to be derived by provoking violence."

After the Leafs lost Game 2 7–0, their coach, Punch Imlach, decided he would speak to only one Toronto writer, and to no Boston writer at all. I don't remember what I was doing at the game. I wasn't yet on staff; I was a mere copy boy. But I obviously had a press pass, and after the game I was in the corridor outside the Toronto locker room when Imlach emerged. He didn't know me from, as I later put it in print, Wilt Chamberlain. He was talking as he walked along the corridor. I tagged along, and thus got an exclusive for the evening *Globe*, the headline being GLOBEMAN SNEAKS ONE OVER ON PUNCH.

The funny thing is, Punch sounded completely reasonable, not like a crazed press-hater. "We've been down two–zip before and come back," he said. "We're in the same boat as the Rangers, two down and coming back home ... Our kids are giving away too many goals on defense ... They [the Bruins] are doing everything right, but we're not working, either. [Norm] Ullman and [Floyd] Smith haven't scored, and you see what that means to our offense ... Total goals means nothing. If that were the case, I would have quit last night."

I had my first true scoop. Within two years, however, I would resent hockey.

This was the heyday of the Big, Bad Bruins and they truly owned the town and New England. By this time I was covering the Celtics and I viewed myself as in direct competition with the Bruins and their fans. Mine was an immature attitude and it was petty, but I must confess it was very real. When Ken Dryden led the Canadiens back against the Bruins in 1971, I smirked.

Even though I was not very rational on the subject of the Bruins, I was as enraptured by the singular talent of Bobby Orr as the next hundred thousand New Englanders. There had never been, and, in my opinion has never been, a better hockey player than number 4, Bobby Orr. Hockey may be lowest in my pecking order of team sports knowledge, but my most firmly held sports conviction is that Bobby Orr is the greatest hockey player who has ever laced up a pair of skates.

I have a hard time containing myself when people automatically anoint Wayne Gretzky as the greatest, simply because he scored all those points. Yes, his numbers are staggering and I doubt will ever be surpassed.

He should be on your all-time six. But the Greatest of All-Time (GOAT)?

The essence of hockey is hitting and being hit, and Wayne Gretzky was involved in neither. He is the greatest scoring specialist ever, but no player has ever controlled the entire game from his position in a manner to equal or surpass Bobby Orr. As a defenseman, he won eight Norris trophies as the best at his position, and three consecutive league Most Valuable Player awards. At the same time, he scored 120, 139, 117, 101, 122, and 135 points between 1969–70 and 1974–75, this at a time when 30 points for a defenseman was quite a haul. No defenseman has ever come close to those numbers. Bobby Orr was a monster on the power play and he was perhaps the greatest penalty killer ever. His skating was superior, his vision and anticipation were uncanny, and his end-to-end rushes are legendary. He also never shied away from a fight if necessary. Sadly, Orr was done by thirty, his knees shot. With today's medical advances, he might have had eight to ten more productive years. We were all deprived too early of incomparable artistry on ice. But the memories live on, and so, fortunately, do the videos, proof that he played the game in a manner not seen before or since.

The late Fred Cusick, the Bruins broadcaster for many years, was the most scrupulous and objective of hockey observers. In a 1990 interview, he said: "Bobby Orr changed the game. Most of all, he controlled the game. Doug Harvey controlled the game by slowing it down. Orr was the only one I saw who could do it by speeding it up."

I realize how contradictory it may seem for me to first proclaim how much I don't know about hockey and then say I have not the slightest doubt that Bobby Orr was the GOAT in that same sport. I can only say I know what I know.

Happily, I eventually outgrew my irrational hostility toward the Bruins and their dominance of Boston winter sports. Perhaps this happened in May 1979, when the Bruins, on the verge of what was then a thirty-six-year run of playoff frustration against the Montreal Canadiens, had managed to snatch defeat from the jaws of victory thanks to what has become the most dreaded six-word combination in the English language to people in Boston: "too many men on the ice." In Game 7 of the 1979 semifinal series against the Canadiens, having not won a playoff series against Montreal since 1943, Boston was leading by a goal with 2:34 remaining when, during a line change, they were whistled for too many men on the ice. Like passionate fans anywhere, those watching and listening had an instant feeling of dread. And for good reason. Guy Lafleur tied the game with 1:14 remaining and Yvon Lambert won it in overtime. I can truthfully say it hurt to hear that news.

Somewhere along the way I had been sent to Montreal, where like so many others I fell under the spell of the great Montreal Forum, a true cathedral of the sport. I soaked it all up, from the classic French sayings on the walls to the snappy dress of the patrons to the bilingual announcement of goals and penalties. And in my first game there Lafleur, as if sent by central casting, won the game for the Canadiens with an overtime goal.

But what I was most struck by was what I like to refer to as the Picture. It hung in the Forum pressroom, portraying the legendary Maurice "Rocket" Richard scoring a goal, but not just any goal. You may not realize it at first but when you count the players in the picture you come to a startling revelation: there are six members of the opposition team and no one from the Canadiens except the Rocket. He had just scored in a one-on-six situation!

This is my favorite sports picture of all time.

Sadly, the Forum is no more. Like the old Madison Square Garden, Chicago Stadium, and Boston Garden, it was no longer good enough for modern fans. But each of these arenas had a charm and intimacy that can never be replaced. They put the fans in the game. The new buildings have better creature comforts and nowadays those things are paramount. But something precious and irreplaceable has been lost.

I just hope the Montreal organization has taken good care of the Picture.

Harry Sinden, variously Bruins coach, general manager, and president, once said: "If we're down one, I want Orr; if we're up one, I want Bourque." The best player the Bruins have had since Bobby Orr was Ray Bourque, like Orr, a defenseman. He was a rookie the same year as Larry Bird, and the fact is he was overshadowed by number 33. During Ray

Bourque's best years the Celtics were actually a bigger deal in Boston than the Bruins, largely due to Bird's unmistakable charisma and swagger, as well as his fascinating persona off the court.

Bobby Orr was overtly spectacular. Ray Bourque was a player of great economy and efficiency. He had zero charisma. He just showed up, played a mistake-free game, and went home. It was wash, rinse, repeat. For twenty-two years. He was nothing special at first glance—five eleven, weighing two fifteen to two twenty, he had that blocky hockey build. On the ice, in uniform, he looked like a hundred other guys. But he was better than those guys. And the next hundred. And the next hundred.

Ray Bourque had a quiet dignity. He was never outspoken, but he was always stand-up.

The most extra attention he ever attracted was the night Phil Esposito was brought back to have his jersey retired. The only problem was that Bourque had actually been wearing that number 7. No one was sure how this was going to play out. The question was answered when Bourque skated over to Espo and pulled off his number 7 jersey to reveal a 77 on his back. That's the number he wore for the remainder of his career.

Ray Bourque was ridiculously and unobtrusively brilliant. He was named a first-team All-Star thirteen times and to the second team six more times, to go along with his six Norris trophies. One has to dig very deeply into a great many sports to find a record of high-level longevity to match it.

However, the one thing he could not get as a member of the Bruins was a championship ring. He had played in a pair of no-hope Stanley Cup Finals in 1988 and 1990, when nobody was beating the Gretzky-led Edmonton Oilers (the Bruins lost 4–0 and 4–1). This became more and more of an issue as Bourque passed into his late thirties, with both fans and media lamenting the idea that he might conclude one of the great careers of all time without having his name inscribed on the Stanley Cup, largely because of the penuriousness of owner Jeremy Jacobs, who never seemed willing to put winning a championship ahead of selling more hot dogs and beer, the concessions business being his actual livelihood.

By the 1999–2000 season everyone realized the only way Bourque would ever skate around the rink holding a Stanley Cup was if he was playing on a team other than the Bruins. Thus, with almost universal approval, they dispatched their franchise icon to the Colorado Avalanche late in the season. The Avalanche fell short that season, but Bourque later admitted that was a good thing for him, as he had only played fourteen regular-season games with the Avalanche. If he were going to win a cup, he wished to do it as a 100 percent, all-in member of the team—which is exactly what came to pass in the spring of 2001.

At age forty-one, in his twenty-second NHL season, he was a first-team All-Star for the thirteenth time. He had achieved what he described as a "shared goal" with his Avalanche teammates. Team legend Joe Sakic ceded the honor of being the first Avalanche player to skate around with the precious cup to Ray Bourque, an Avalanche for fifteen months. Afterward, Bourque brought that same Stanley Cup back to Boston in order to share his happiness with the fans who had supported him. Who ever heard of such a thing? But because he was Ray Bourque, it somehow made sense.

If Ray Bourque was the best post-Orr player the Bruins have known, Cam Neely was the most dynamic. Like Orr, Neely was all about pyrotechnics. He *exploded* in your face. You could not divert your attention from him from the moment he stepped on the ice.

Obtained along with a number one pick from the Vancouver Canucks in May 1986 in exchange for Barry Pederson, the six-one, two-hundred-twenty-pound Neely became one of the great offensive forces in the NHL, with a swashbuckling style of play that combined classic goal-scoring with classic hitting, a rarely seen combination. "He's a hockey power forward," Harry Sinden declared, and no player has since come along who has replicated his peculiar package of skill. Until further notice, Cam Neely is sui generis.

He was sailing along with back-to-back seasons of fifty-five and fifty-one goals when, in Game 3 of a 1991 playoff series against the Rangers, he was the victim of two cheap open-ice hits by New York's Ulf Samuelsson. Neely was then a month shy of his twenty-sixth birthday and he would never be the same again, having sustained knee and thigh injuries that wrecked his career. He played but nine games in 1991–92 and thirteen the following year. He launched a comeback in 1993–94, scoring fifty goals in forty-nine games. But it was not sustainable, and he retired at the conclusion of the 1995–96 season. He was thirty, the same age as Bobby Orr when he was forced into premature retirement.

How good was Cam Neely? Harry Sinden says: "If we had won a championship, if we had ever won a Stanley Cup, he would have been put on a pedestal. He would have been every bit as big as Orr. His style was so completely identified with what the Boston fan likes. It just clicked."

Do yourself a mammoth favor. YouTube Cam Neely. You want goals, you'll get goals. You want hits—no, H-I-T-S—you'll get hits. That man was a hockey player's hockey player.

You hang around long enough in this business and you can get lucky. I was still on the job when the 2011 Boston Bruins made all people in this area of mine very happy by bringing home the Stanley Cup for the first time in thirty-nine years. I just hopped on a moving train. I had nothing to do with covering their exciting first-round conquest of Montreal, decided on a Game 7 overtime goal by Nathan Horton, nor their second-round sweep of the Philadelphia Flyers, the same team that had made a historic comeback against the Bruins a year earlier. By the time the Bruins were lining up to play Tampa Bay in the Eastern Conference Finals the basketball season was over in Boston. The Bruins' win in Game 7 was memorable: 1–0, with no penalties, a game that, Tampa Bay coach Guy Boucher said, "felt like overtime the whole game." You place such a game in that special compartment holding only the most inspiring memories, the ones that reinforce why you are a sports fan in the first place. It really did feel like sixty minutes of overtime, and hockey overtime has a special tension no other sport can match.

The Vancouver Canucks won the first two home games of the finals over Boston, but by this time we all knew that was not going to deter these Bruins, who had lost the first two games of the Montreal series at home only to come back to defeat the hated Canadiens. They held serve at home, and after the Canucks won Game 5 in Vancouver to take a 3–2 series advantage, the Boss told me to stay put there, assuming the Bruins would win Game 6 and come back to Vancouver for the final.

I went to my favorite Vancouver bar, the Lamplighter, to watch and listen to the locals hoot on their team after the Bruins had broken their hearts in Game 6. The Bruins won, of course. And Game 7 was an anticlimax. The Bruins dominated completely, winning, 4–0. Their first Stanley Cup championship for Boston since 1972 represented something special for me, too, as I could then truthfully say I had covered championships in all four mainstream team sports, and within one amazing seven-year span (2004 and 2007 Red Sox, 2005 Patriots, 2008 Celtics).

I won't ever really *get* hockey the way I get baseball and basketball. Hockey has a charm all its own. The penalty box. The Zamboni. The Lady Byng Memorial Trophy. The in-between-period TV interviews with the towels around their necks and the sweat pouring down their cheeks.

The Stanley Cup, out of which a man can actually drink if he wants to. The goalie masks. "O Canada," the greatest of all anthems not named "La Marseillaise." The Great Handshake Line at the end of a playoff series.

I would change the game by doing away with offsides, as I don't understand the point of it. If someone were to stash a guy at the other goal in the hockey equivalent of basket hanging, a team would have to put someone back there with him. After a while, they'd get tired of that and rejoin the other guys. All that happens with offsides is that you lose some very good scoring chances in a game that could use a few more goals. Would there be something wrong with an occasional 8–7 game? And you'd still have your 2–1s and 1–zips. I guarantee it.

I'm sure no one in power will consider a radical change in hockey proposed by a basketball guy. But I'm right about Bobby Orr. Nothing will change that. I'll bet Punch Imlach would agree.

CHAPTER 25

Doc and the 2008 Champs

I can safely say that no one in the Boston media was happier than I when general manager Danny Ainge named Doc Rivers coach of the Boston Celtics in 2004. He had been near the top of my favorite NBA people since entering the league as a rookie in 1983. He had no jock affectations. He was a well-bred, well-educated, just plain well-adjusted young man, a very good but not great player who made it into one All-Star Game. He had been the 1999–2000 Coach of the Year in Orlando, and after that a successful TV color man. He was a pleasure to be around.

Prior to Game 6 of the 1988 Celtics' playoff series with Doc's Atlanta Hawks, I approached him on the floor and told him I considered him one of the best people I had come into contact with during my (then) twenty years covering the league. I thought he deserved to know that. So you're not going to hear me say a bad word about him.

This resolve was put to the test during the 2006–07 season, when the Celtics lost eighteen consecutive games and twenty-three of twenty-four in a five-week stretch in January and February of 2007. Doc was more than a little fortunate that the Celtics brain trust did not take the easy way out and throw their coach to the mob. Very few professional sports coaches survive eighteen-game losing streaks.

So I was not prepared for what transpired the following season. In fact, I must forever live with the fact that I cannot hide from my own words. Not long after Danny Ainge had brought Ray Allen and Kevin Garnett to Boston, thus giving the Celtics, who already had a great player in Paul Pierce, a second historic "Big Three," I dismissed the notion that it was a championship-caliber team, scoffing at the rest of the roster and going so far as to say that no team in the league would trade its fourth- through its twelfth-best players for Boston's. I stuck in a wise-ass remark about the NBA not being a three-on-three league.

Granted, there were additional moves to be made, right down to the waning days of the season when Danny imported veteran Sam Cassell into the mix, but the Big Three turned out to be even better as a unit than I could have imagined and some of the other players, notably point guard Rajon Rondo, were pretty good.

Until you have experienced certain things in life directly, you really can't anticipate them. One of those things is what it's like to have Kevin Garnett on your basketball team. I'm going to employ the time-honored trick of using the dictionary to make my point: *The Scribner-Bantam English Dictionary* defines the word "intense" thusly:

> 1. Extreme in degree; excessive. 2. Intent, ardent, eager.
> Syn: earnest, ardent, intent, fervid, rapt, glowing.

With regard to Kevin Garnett, that gets us about halfway there. The old cliché "He only knows one way to play" applies to him in every way. I am referring specifically to his defense and rebounding. The great contradiction with Kevin Garnett, to me, anyway, is that he has always been far too deferential on offense. He may be the most reluctant first-ballot, superstar shooter in NBA history. He has always been a pass-first, I'll-only-shoot-if-you-insist guy on offense. He seemed not to notice that he had a signature turnaround jumper that most players would have paid a million bucks to obtain had it been placed on eBay.

But he personally gives you a team defense and is one of the best defensive rebounders ever. He is also among the most historic figures in basketball. When he decided to put himself in the 1995 NBA draft, and thus skip college, he was the first player in roughly twenty years to jump from high school to the pros.* Had he failed, that chapter in basketball history might have been concluded, once and for all. But he was terrific.

---

* Bill Willoughby, Darryl Dawkins, and Moses Malone had made the move in the 1970s.

Kobe Bryant came out the next year and the toothpaste had seeped out of the tube, never to return.

His historical relevance doesn't stop there. He was a seven-footer who made it clear he was not going to be a center. A fabulously mobile big man, he had a faceup game, not a back-to-the-basket, generic Tall Guy approach. A few European big men, starting with the legendary Yugoslavian Kresimir Cosic, had played this way, but Garnett made it fashionable for American Very Tall Guys to play in such a manner.

Paul Pierce was Boston's resident marquee player when Garnett arrived in 2007, but he was smart enough to know which way the wind would now be blowing. He was still the captain and the team's best scorer, and very much the local fans' favorite, but he was no longer the team's primary energy source.

Old-timers are pained to hear me say this, but I believe it absolutely—Paul Pierce was the greatest pure scorer in Celtics history. I don't mean he was a better player than either Larry Bird or John Havlicek. But in terms of having the most ways to get the ball into the basket, he's the best Celtic ever. His game has been a strange combination of the 1950s and the twenty-first century, in that he blends the artistry and chicanery of his elders with the three-point shot they often could only have dreamed of. Unlike both Bird and Havlicek, in his extended prime he could always do it on his own—he did not need a pick, he just needed everyone else to get out of his way.

Ray Allen, meanwhile, brought his own brand of intensity, a borderline obsessive-compulsive disorder condition rather than Garnett's eerily primal sizzle. Allen was a programmed military brat who had routines from which he would not deviate. Great shooting being a repetitive act, and Allen being wired to repeat and repeat and repeat, it was hardly a shock that he was one of the great long-distance shooters of all time.

As soon as the season began this interesting trio announced itself as a winning one. Rondo brought yet another fascinating individual approach to the team concept. He made such a startling improvement in his second year that by the end of the season people were saying the Big Three was actually a Big Four.

There is no question that the Celtics were the best team in the league during the regular season. They won their first eight. By Christmas they were 22-3. They wound up at 67-15. But history teaches us that in every professional sport regular-season success is no guarantee of playoff fulfillment. The dynamics are very different; coaching plays a huge role in the course of a seven-game series where matchups can be pivotal.

The 2008 Boston Celtics playoff experience is unique in NBA history because the task became easier, not harder, with each succeeding series. The young, athletic Atlanta Hawks made the first-round series a strict home-court deal throughout. But after playing the Celtics very tough for six games, they were not ready for a prime-time Game 7 on the road in Boston Garden. The Celtics then needed six games to eliminate Cleveland, with Game 6 being a keeper. The subplot was Paul Pierce vs. LeBron James—Pierce had forty-one, James had forty-five—but the big basket was a jump shot by veteran center P. J. Brown, age thirty-eight, whom Danny Ainge had signed at the All-Star break as a big man playoff insurance policy. GMs earn their money in many ways.

The Detroit Pistons, tenacious foes in the late 1980s, fell in a relatively undramatic six games in the Eastern Conference Finals. Which brought the Celtics up against the Lakers in the finals for the tenth time—by far the most times two teams have played for a championship. Up two games to one, in Game 4 in Los Angeles, Boston came back from twenty-four points behind late in the third period to take a 3–1 series lead. Great bench performances by season-long mainstay James Posey and the hot-and-cold Eddie House were instrumental.

What happened on the night of June 17, 2008, somehow felt inevitable. This was a Celtics team unlike any other in my experience, and, I was reasonably certain, unlike any in the team's glorious history. The squad that had played harder and more relentlessly than any of its predecessors, a team that honestly and truly never took a single night off, put a cap on a very special season with a 131–92 destruction of an ancient rival.

It was the first Celtics championship since 1986, their first in the new century, and it represented a new chapter in Celtics history. Even the constituency was relatively new. I wrote after Game 7 ended,

> This was a championship for a Lost Generation of Boston Celtics fans. These are people for whom Bill Russell, the greatest winner in American sports, and Bob Cousy, the legendary "Houdini of the Hardwood," are like figures out of King Arthur's

Tales. These are people for whom John Havlicek, basketball's consummate sixth man, and Dave Cowens, the mercurial red-headed center, are as relevant as comic book characters. These are people for whom even the great Larry Bird is just another guy wearing short-shorts who pops up occasionally on ESPN Classic.

These are people who were too young to mourn fallen soldiers Reggie Lewis and Len Bias. These are people who do not think hard-bodied young women gyrating in the interests of Celtics green is a sacrilege. These are people who could not imagine entering an arena that did not have a Jumbotron and music and fireworks and who could not possibly imagine that, once upon a time, a portly organist named John Kiley stirred the Boston Garden crowd by playing the "Mexican Hat Dance."

These are the people who were either very angry or very sad when general manager Danny Ainge first traded Antoine Walker, a player their elders generally loathed. These are the people who text instant observations to friends in Singapore. And these are the people who hungered for a Celtics triumph they could call their own, one accomplished in *their* building by *their* heroes.

Celtics championship No. 17 belongs to them.

And to Doc Rivers. Eighteen straight losses one year, an NBA championship the next. I thought that was pretty cool.

CHAPTER 26

The Prince of Pessimism

For me, a pessimist is an optimist with experience; I've lived my life that way. So, I think, had Chuck Daly. I've very rarely bestowed a nickname on someone that has stuck, but I did label the late Chuck Daly the "Prince of Pessimism." Which he undoubtedly was. His glass was always half-empty; his inevitable response to any observation was "Whatever." And he was one of the most memorable people I've ever met.

Chuck Daly entered both my professional and personal lives in 1969, when he left a position as assistant coach at Duke to take the head job at Boston College. At the time BC was a player in Eastern college basketball circles, having gone 117–38 in the previous six years under the legendary Bob Cousy. The Cooz had announced his retirement in January of 1969, and his team then ran off nineteen wins in succession before losing to Temple in the NIT Finals.

At that time Chuck Daly was thirty-nine years old, and his coaching résumé included eight years at Punxsutawney (Pennsylvania) Area High School, where he met neither Bill Murray nor anyone else from the cast of *Groundhog Day* (that movie was twenty-four years away), but where the dashing young teacher/coach, always impeccably dressed and in possession of a noted pompadour, had, according to a woman who wrote me a letter during Chuck's prime in Detroit, "all the girls swooning."

Chuck always had his eyes on a bigger prize and would inevitably graduate to coaching college basketball. He was hired as an assistant by

Duke's Vic Bubas in 1963. Duke had such players as Art Heyman and Jeff Mullins, and in 1964 they had the distinction of becoming the first of John Wooden's ten NCAA championship game victims.

The man in charge became a mentor, first to Daly, and then, starting in 1968, to Hubie Brown, another young coach with an extensive high school dossier. "Without question, Vic Bubas is the most organized man I've ever met. I mean, amazingly organized. He was a little aloof, but brilliant. He could get the most out of two hours of practice," Brown told me in a 1984 interview.

"There is no question he was a big influence on me and Hubie," confirmed Daly. "He was the originator of the IBM theory of recruiting. At one point we had a file of eleven hundred folders with at least four letters each that we had to send out to prospective high school recruits, and that was to take four or five kids a year." Basketball truly mattered at Duke, then and now. Mike Krzyzewski did not create something out of nothing: he took something that was good and made it unimaginably great.

Chuck Daly found out immediately that Boston College was not Duke. His first game as head coach of the Eagles was against Boston University, the game being played in BU's Sargent Gym, a high schoolish bandbox seating maybe twelve hundred. And he lost. A fine midsized forward named Jimmy Hayes dropped thirty-five on him, and BC went down to defeat. I was sitting right behind the BC bench, a recent alumnus and a fan still awaiting my chance at the *Boston Globe*. And I distinctly remember looking at Chuck Daly's face as he took it all in—the surroundings and the reality that he didn't even have a team that could beat Boston University—and I was thinking, This is not exactly what Chuck Daly had in mind.

He went 11-13 that first year and 15-11 the second. He had one very good player, guard Jim O'Brien, a brilliant playmaker recruited out of Brooklyn by Cousy, who, of course, had a natural eye for point guards. Chuck would learn that basketball at BC was what Bob Cousy had created in the previous six years and nothing more. BC had been a hockey and football school before the Cooz arrived and now that he was gone it was a hockey and football school once again.

Chuck Daly was not going to be a BC lifer. Basketball mattered too much to him. But I'm grateful to have met him then, or I might have been deprived the friendship of a fascinating human being, and a great basketball coach.

In the spring of 1970, my wife and I were planning to drive to my childhood home in Trenton, New Jersey, to inform my mother that she was going to be a grandmother for the first time. In the course of a conversation I let Chuck know this and he asked if he could get a ride to New York City because he had some recruiting business there. I'm sure Coaches K, Pitino, Williams, Boheim, and Izzo hitch rides with local writers all the time.

During the drive, he told us about a sensational book he was reading by someone named Mario Puzo and it was all about the Mafia. I'll always remember Chuck Daly making us aware of *The Godfather*. When we arrived in the Big Apple, Chuck insisted we come up to see the rich alum's apartment where he would be staying on Central Park South. He then invited us for a meal at the Stage Deli, where he launched into a discourse about the wonders of New York City. When Elaine and I were finally on our way to Trenton I said to her, "I don't think he's long for Boston College."

He wasn't. His two-year record at BC was enough to impress the folks at Penn, where he spent six years maintaining the level of excellence established by Dick Harter. Penn was a serious national team in the early 1970s, recruiting top one hundred players, at least four of whom—Corky Calhoun, Phil Hankinson, Bob Bigelow, and Dave Wohl—played in the NBA. In addition, Bob Morse, a six-eight forward with a deft shooting touch, became an Italian-league mainstay for a decade.

Chuck's entry into the NBA came suddenly. Gene Shue was relieved of duty as head coach of the Philadelphia 76ers in November 1977 and Billy Cunningham replaced him. Billy had been a great player but in all sorts of coaching ins and outs, he was seriously unprepared. The good thing was, he knew it. He already had a classic NBA hand at his side in Jack McMahon, a guard from the fifties, but Billy knew he needed more help than Jack could provide. He turned to Chuck Daly. My guess is that Chuck hesitated for all of one or two seconds before saying yes.

Chuck remained at Billy's side into the early part of the 1981–82 season, and the Sixers were among the NBA's elite, losing to the Lakers in the 1980 finals before becoming victims of a 3–1 Celtics series comeback in the 1981 Eastern Conference Finals. In late fall 1981, the Cleveland Cavaliers were in what could only be described as complete turmoil, thanks to the bizarre stewardship of owner Ted Stepien, whose success in the business world (something to do with Help Wanted ads) was not readily transferable into positive results in the NBA. Stepien had fired coach Bill Musselman with eleven games remaining in the 1980–81 season, replacing him with assistant Don Delaney. Eleven games into the 1981–82 season, Delaney was gone, replaced by Bob Kloppenburg, who was also an interim leader, because Stepien had zeroed in on the man he wanted and gave Chuck Daly his first crack at a head coaching job in the NBA.

The Cavaliers had regressed from mediocrity the year before to true sickbed status by the time Chuck took over. All the X-ing and O-ing imaginable could not mask the fact that the team lacked talent. Chuck coached his Guccis off, but under his guidance the team went 9-31 and with twenty-one games remaining in the season he became more collateral damage as Stepien replaced him with the same Bill Musselman who had been deemed unworthy the year before. Musselman was not just intense, he was Parris Island intense. The Cavs won his first two games before settling into terminal Cavdom. They lost their last nineteen games.

I paid Chuck a visit during his strange three months as Cavaliers head coach. He was living in the Holiday Inn adjacent to Exit 11 on the Ohio Turnpike. Many a beat writer and NBA broadcaster had also lain his or her head down at this particular Holiday Inn, but I doubt any of them had closets vaguely resembling Chuck's.

Chuck Daly believed firmly in the old adage that clothes make the man. His father had been a real-life Willy Loman, a Depression-era traveling salesman (Chuck was born in 1930) who taught his son that dressing well was a necessity. Chuck learned his lessons. There never was, nor will ever be, a better-dressed NBA coach than Charles Jerome Daly. Nor will there ever be a closet at that Holiday Inn so graced by impressive male clothing as his. In it hung a score or more of handsome, well-tailored suits, to go with beautiful shirts, countless neckties, and good-looking shoes. Chuck might have been going down to defeat, but he was looking good doing it.

None of this would have surprised his old Duke coworker. "One day when we were at Duke," Hubie Brown pointed out, "Chuck Daly wanted to clean out his closet. He gave me fifty-two neckties, none valued at less than seven dollars and fifty cents—this was 1969, remember—and he still had three racks of ties left, in addition to the fifty suits and the untold pairs of shoes."

Chuck spent the next year doing some broadcast work while pining away for another job in the NBA. College no longer beckoned. He had lived the NBA life, and that was the one he preferred. At the 1983 NBA meetings we found ourselves standing in the lobby of the Century Plaza Hotel in Los Angeles. I was there for the *Globe* and he was looking for a job. "I'm fifty-two years old," he said, "and I don't have a job. Who's going to hire me?"

Twenty-one years later he would be inducted into the Naismith Memorial Basketball Hall of Fame. The lifeline was extended by owner Bill Davidson and general manager Jack McCloskey of the Detroit Pistons. The team he inherited would have been a success in the Spanish league, since most of its players specialized in matador defense. Though undeniably talented offensively, the Pistons were the kind of squad good teams looked forward to playing.

It took time, and included some personnel manipulation on the part of McCloskey, but Daly gradually molded the Detroit Pistons into a unit that would not only win a lot of basketball games and produce two championships, but that stood for something. It can easily be argued that Chuck Daly's Pistons changed NBA thinking, altering the concept of NBA defense. And they did it without sacrificing offense.

This is an important point, because a number of years later, when the NBA had descended into the mosh pit ugliness of the 1994 Houston–New York finals, Daly, who was then working in a broadcast capacity, was cited as the man who had adversely changed basketball. "Hey," he said, "don't blame me. We scored points. Look it up."

And he was oh so correct. The Chuck Daly 1989–90 NBA champion Detroit Pistons featured Isiah Thomas, Joe Dumars, the inimitable Vinnie "the Microwave" Johnson, Mark Aguirre, and Bill Laimbeer, who had a deadly outside shot. The Pistons averaged 106.6 points per game in 1988–89 and 104.3 the following year. In more recent NBA times, these totals would have led the league.

The Detroit defense was equally fierce. After the Pistons had eliminated the Celtics in the 1988 Eastern Conference Finals, Kevin McHale observed: "They made a commitment to shut down certain aspects of our game, and they did it with aggression and they did it with a lot of different people. We had our chances but the sign of a good defensive team is to stop us when they absolutely had to and they did that. They had a game plan, and they stuck with it. They had the confidence a good team must have."

Similar thoughts were expressed by many vanquished foes over the next two seasons. Those Daly teams were unusual in that when they needed a spark from the bench it was just as likely to be provided by the determined defensive attitude of youngsters Dennis Rodman (pre-tattoos) and John Salley as it was by the offensive pyrotechnics of Vinnie Johnson. All of which put these Pistons teams among the elite squads of all time.

Chuck Daly was now placed in the national spotlight, and he loved it. He was always handy with a quip. He had waited more than a half century to be center stage, and he made the most of his opportunity. As hard as it might have been for those girls back at Punxsutawney Area High to believe, now that he had reached middle age he was even more concerned with looking good. This mania reached a peak one evening when the Pistons were still playing in the Pontiac Silverdome.

The Pistons were heavily promoting a game against the Celtics, telling the world that they would have an all-time record NBA crowd. Barely an hour before game time Chuck made a horrifying discovery. His nightly custom was to wear a casual outfit during the afternoon and pregame preparation before changing into his spiffy game suit. But on this night, of all nights, Chuck Daly discovered he had forgotten his game suit! Assistant coach Dick Versace was dispatched to Chuck's house and then had to battle the record crowd that was clogging up the roadways of Greater Pontiac. Mindful that the only thing that would be a bigger concern to Chuck than not having his proper attire would be an injury to Isiah Thomas, Versace broke out his best *French Connection* driving moves and somehow maneuvered his way through the traffic and into the Silverdome lot as game time approached. He slipped on the grassy hill adjacent to the ramp leading into the stadium, but the suit never touched the ground. No assistant coach has ever performed better under pressure than Dick Versace did that night in Pontiac.

Chuck Daly was a philosophical coach, a necessity for leading a team through an eighty-two-game NBA season culminating, with luck, in as many as twenty-eight playoff games. "Each year invariably presents a new set of problems," he admitted. "You've got to fix and alter your goals. You know what coaching a professional sports team is like these days? It's like being the pilot of a plane. Your job is to get that plane through the season. You don't know where the turbulence is coming from. It could come from the right; it could come from the left. But you've got to get it to the destination."

Chuck was a master fixer, in part because of an acquired physical deficiency. Among many insightful Dalyisms, he observed: "The best asset a coach can have is bad hearing." Chuck was unquestionably vain about his appearance, but he knew better than to allow his ego to interfere professionally. "You are fortunate if they *allow* you to coach them," he quipped. You'd never get any argument from Chuck Daly if you acknowledged the NBA to be the players' league it is.

When the strong personalities on his team did allow Daly to coach them, they discovered he had a lot to offer. The simple secret of coaching is the ability to get players to buy what you're selling, and Chuck, like his father, was an excellent salesman.

When the time came to pick a coach to be in charge of the Dream Team in 1992, Chuck Daly was the perfect selection. This was a job for neither a micromanager nor a camp counselor. It required a secure, self-confident man with a large enough ego to think he actually deserved to boss around the greatest collection of basketball players yet assembled, while simultaneously making them think they were doing what *they* wanted, rather than what the coach wanted them to do.

It is probably true that no one could have messed up the Dream Team sufficiently so that they would not win the gold medal, but it is equally true that no one other than Chuck Daly could have made it as smooth a ride for those guys.

During the week the Dream Team spent in Monte Carlo before heading to Barcelona, one late afternoon at the rooftop pool of the Loews Hotel I was occupying a comfy lounge chair next to the coach of the One and Only Dream Team. Thinking back to the days of losing to Jimmy Hayes, riding in my backseat, and eating at the Stage Deli, Chuck Daly looked at me as we both gazed out onto the Mediterranean and said, "Who ever thought it would come to this?"

CHAPTER 27

Michael v. LeBron

Basketball has one problem on offense that must be solved: there are five men but only one ball. Somehow it must be shared. The issue of who is the greatest all-around player in the game at any given time in some ways revolves around this challenge.

In general, however dominating because of their size, centers don't possess the full range of skills that would qualify them to be considered the best player, though a few have been sufficiently dominant to stake a claim to that title. Bill Russell, for example. He wasn't a shooter or ball handler of note, but his rebounding, defending, passing, and, perhaps his most important asset, thinking were the foundation for five league Most Valuable Player Awards and for his team to win the championship eleven times in his thirteen seasons. As a collegian, he had led the University of San Francisco to a fifty-five-game winning streak and a pair of national championships. He was also the key man as the USA won the 1956 Olympic gold medal in Melbourne.

Perhaps even more impressively, in twenty-one winner-take-all games—contests in which the loser went home, a list that includes every NCAA game he played in, all Olympic medal-round games, and the deciding games of both best-of-five and best-of-seven NBA series—Bill Russell's teams just happened to go 21-0. No one should have any problem saying that if he wasn't the most artistically satisfying player in history, he was clearly the most important.

For me, though, the really juicy issue is who should be considered the Greatest (All-Around) Player of All Time, and I believe there are two contenders: Michael Jordan and LeBron James. You can debate this, of course, but that's what I believe. They are a fascinating pair because, while possessing a similar range of athletic ability, they are very different in background and temperament. In fact, they couldn't be farther apart in how they dealt with the reality of their special gift.

Michael Jordan was essentially unknown outside the state of North Carolina when he entered Dean Smith's starting lineup at the University of North Carolina in the fall of 1981. He had had a normal progression at Laney High School in Wilmington, North Carolina. Yes, he was cut from the varsity as a sophomore, but a vast majority of sophomores are supposed to be on the junior varsity team, and he hadn't yet demonstrated his exceptional talent. By his junior year he was on the varsity, and he started his senior season, but he had no national notoriety. I was paying reasonable attention to high school basketball then, and the first time I was aware of his presence was the first time I saw Carolina play on TV during his freshman year.

Contrast this with the circumstances surrounding LeBron James. He first began to attract attention as a freshman at Saint Vincent–Saint Mary High School in Akron, where he was a star as a freshman, and SV, as the school is known, would win the first of three state championships in the next four years. The only missing title was the one from LeBron's junior year, and that, naturally, served as motivation for a stellar senior season. By his junior season, LeBron was a nationally known commodity.

The shift in the marketplace during the two decades between their high school careers was telling. Whereas Michael Jordan's entire high school experience was limited to the state of North Carolina, LeBron was the classic twenty-first-century high school phenom, showcasing his skills from coast to coast, thanks not only to the opportunity provided by Amateur Athletic Union (AAU) travel in the summer, but also because his high school team was heavily marketed by its own administration during his junior and senior years.

LeBron's senior year was downright surreal. He was on the cover of *Sports Illustrated*, *ESPN The Magazine*, *Hoop*, *Dime*, *Slam*, and for all I know, *Vogue*, *Popular Mechanics*, *Architectural Digest*, *Foreign Affairs*, and *TV Guide*. SV's home games were moved from their typically cramped high school gym to the fifty-five-hundred-seat James A. Rhodes Arena at the University of Akron, and in time even that proved inadequate. He became a conversation staple on all ESPN shows, and when ESPN chose to cover a showdown game between SV and famed Oak Hill Academy, the broadcast team was Dan Shulman, Dick Vitale, Jay Bilas, and Bill Walton, who commented that while he was uncomfortable bestowing so much attention on a high school player, "this is the world we've made."

What most of the outside world did not know was that a man named Kristopher Belman had been working on a documentary film on the subject of LeBron and his teammates and had footage of LeBron dating from seventh grade. *More Than a Game*, released for general viewing in 2008, revealed a touching story of near-brotherly devotion. We learned that LeBron had been teammates with Sian Cotton, Willie McGee, and Dru Joyce II since fifth grade, and that made their eventual success a rarity in today's scholastic world, where all too often the best teams are all-star aggregations recruited by so-called prep schools of dubious academic quality playing national schedules. In this case the best high school team in America was a good old-fashioned neighborhood gang of brothers.

The tricky part was that, while there was camaraderie galore, mere selfless friendship alone was not going to win them any state championships. The difference-maker was LeBron James. The others knew it. He knew it, too, but he was careful not to separate himself from the group. Winning by itself was not his only satisfaction. Winning with his friends was.

The hype became insufferable for some of us. Not knowing anything about what made LeBron tick, I, for one, rejected the opportunity to watch him play. Yes, I knew that Jay Bilas, a man I greatly respect, had declared him "the best high school player of the past twenty years," and that would ordinarily have had my antennae up, but the ceaseless talk of a high school kid turned me off. I reasoned that I had seen every great player of the last fifty years and could easily wait until he went to college or entered the NBA to pass judgment. So I boycotted any and all of LeBron's TV games and tried not to pay attention to clips on *SportsCenter*.

Michael Jordan entered college as someone only an ACC junkie would know. LeBron James came out of high school having already made the acquaintance of Jay Z. And, by the way, Michael Jordan.

* * *

Going to North Carolina ensured that Michael Jordan would have a college career guaranteed to suppress his ego. Even after he hit the shot his sophomore year that made Dean Smith coach of an NCAA championship team for the first time in his career, nobody suggested that Jordan was anything more than just one more in a long line of excellent North Carolina players. Dean Smith's charges were always difficult to evaluate for NBA draft purposes, because some of them were enhanced by the system and some were smothered by it.

Exhibit A of the latter phenomenon had been Walter Davis. No one was prepared for how immediately dynamic he was as the fifth pick of the 1977 NBA draft by the Phoenix Suns. He was a very nice player during his four years in Chapel Hill, averaging 15.7 points a game before playing a significant role as the USA, coached by Smith, won the Olympic gold medal in Montreal in 1976. But Walter Davis began with a bang in the NBA, averaging 24.2 points a game right out of the chute, demonstrating an offensive explosion heretofore unseen. He had a simple explanation. "It's hard to play basketball with a bit in your mouth," he told me.

Michael Jordan followed a similar path into the NBA. He had averaged 17.7 points a game during his three years in college before winning a gold medal under coach Bob Knight in the 1984 Los Angeles Olympics following his junior year. In a few years' time, as he began hiccupping up nightly 30-point games, it became fashionable to quip that "Dean Smith is the only person who could hold Michael Jordan under 20." In the interest of accuracy, let the record show that in Michael's sophomore year he scored 721 points in 36 games—exactly 20 points a game. Of course, it is also undeniable that Dean, obviously recognizing his mistake, saw to it that Michael dropped back to 19.6 points a game as a junior. Michael was a two-time *Sporting News* Player of the Year, but no one was translating that into all-time status.

During the 1984 Olympics, rumors surfaced that Knight was saying Jordan was a lot better than people realized, and would, in fact, be a fantastic NBA player. The rumor quickly became fact. Michael declared for the NBA draft after his junior season and was taken with the third pick by the Chicago Bulls, grateful that Portland had taken center Sam Bowie with the first pick and Houston Hakeem Olajuwon with the second. Jordan began raising eyebrows at every stop in the league. It was clear that he, too, had been playing with the Dean Smith bit in his mouth, and now, unleashed, he was unstoppable.

His first trip to my hoop hacienda took place on January 9, 1985. The defending-champion Celtics defeated Jordan's Bulls, 111–108, but the postgame conversation was all about this rookie named Jordan, in part because of his extraordinary ability, but also because of his precociousness.

"When Michael gets a year or two," observed Dennis Johnson, a future Hall of Famer, "he will probably be the best all-around guard in the league. That is, if he's not by the end of the season. There is a lot that everybody has got to learn when they come into the league. He's just learned it a lot quicker than any other rookie. I got a little timid after I picked up my second foul. Michael recognized it and immediately went right after me. Not many rookies are that smart."

Jordan attributed his game knowledge to his hoop upbringing. "You come out of high school," Jordan said. "You know strictly about offense. But when you get to college, and with the coaches I've had, you learn other phases of the game: rebounding, boxing out, setting good screens, good defensive positioning. On this level, you get to use all that. You may have more one-on-one opportunities, but you have that background of being a fundamentally sound player."

Larry Bird, then in the prime of his career, during which he would win three consecutive MVPs, declared of Jordan, "That's the best player I've ever seen." In 1985, the best player in the league was either Magic Johnson or Bird himself, but Larry recognized immediately that Michael Jordan represented something new and different.

Michael's rookie year commanded attention. He averaged 28.2 points a game. He was, of course, Rookie of the Year and he made second-team All-NBA. And yet his true coming-out party as a deity-in-waiting didn't take place until April 20, 1986, in Game 3 of the first-round best-of-five series between the Bulls and Celtics.

Michael had sustained an injury that limited him to eighteen regular-season games, and he had to battle team general manager Jerry Krause's long-term protection wishes to even get into the lineup for the playoffs. When he got there, he made sure the effort was worthwhile.

He opened up by scoring forty-nine points in a Game 1 123–104 Celtics victory, but the performance was actually quite piggy, the forty-nine points largely the result of some serious ball-hogging. However, what we saw at Boston Garden that Sunday afternoon of April 20 was the official launching of a legend. Jordan scored sixty-three points against the best Celtics team there ever was, and every last one of them came in the flow. The performance reeked of basketball sophistication and team awareness, and is still a reference point of basketball artistry this many years later. People are always surprised when reminded that the Celtics actually won this double-overtime affair, 135–131.

Afterward, the tributes came gushing forth from the victors, who considered themselves fortunate to be in on what they regarded as basketball history. "He was going over the top of guys like McHale and Parish to get his shot off. He's just incredible. It's not only that he does it, it's the way he does it," Danny Ainge said enthusiastically. Larry Bird was hard-pressed to believe what he had seen: "Michael is the most exciting, awesome player in the game today. I didn't think anyone could do to us what Jordan has done in these first two games . . . I think it's just God, disguised as Michael Jordan."

LeBron James did not have the benefit of Michael's renowned college coaching. He had received good high school coaching from both Keith Dambrot (who would leave SV for the University of Akron job) and Dru Joyce Sr., but he reached the NBA without having played in college, and so, unlike Michael, was largely self-taught. Jordan was able to learn through example in a fairly rigid system in which the coach was a dictator, however benevolent. LeBron came into the NBA needing to figure it out by himself. Yet from the start there was never any doubt that LeBron's basketball heart was always in the right place.

He did not have that epiphany game, as Michael did on that Sunday afternoon in Boston. But he came in with a wide range of skill and sound basketball instincts. He was no longer playing with Sian, Willie, and Dru; his teammates were Carlos (Boozer) and Zydrunas (Ilgauskas) and many others because the Cavs ran through eighteen players that season. The one thing that had not changed was his willingness to share. He averaged 20.9 points a game, but also placed twelfth in the league assist table, with the eleven men before him all being guards. He had come into the NBA with a reputation as a six-eight passer who could shoot, and that's exactly what he revealed himself to be. He was as much Magic as he was Larry. Bird had been a pretty good rookie himself, but he had turned twenty-three in December of his rookie year. LeBron turned nineteen in December of his.

By his second year there was no doubt where he was heading, and no one knew it better than teammate Scott Williams, who had played with Jordan for three years in Chicago. "The whole time I've been in the league," Williams said in the fall of 2004, "it's been, 'Who's the next Jordan? AI? Stackhouse? Grant Hill? Vince Carter? This [i.e., LeBron] is by far the one who has the ability and the confidence in his ability to be able to raise his game, no matter what the skill of his teammates, or lack of skill. He is so much more than I expected. He does it in a way that leaves me speechless."

On a particular evening, LeBron led his team to victory over the host Celtics, having fed Ilgauskas for a game-winning basket while being double-teamed before preserving the win by blocking a Paul Pierce shot. He finished with twenty points on nine-for-thirteen shooting, eight assists, six rebounds, and four additional passes to people who got fouled, totaling seven points. After the game I wrote: "As his career progresses, this won't rank among his top 200 games, but it was a performance few people in the NBA could match."

This was in December of 2004. LeBron James didn't win a championship ring until 2012, seven seasons later. Similarly, Michael Jordan didn't get his first ring until his seventh season, long after the time his virtuoso genius had been acknowledged. Though similar in this respect, and although they both revolve around basketball's central fact of life—five men, one ball—what ultimately led to their first championships was very different.

I believe Michael Jordan didn't win until he was willing to acknowledge the constant and necessary presence of his four teammates, and that LeBron James didn't win until he was willing to assert even more individual dominance, not less. Michael had to learn to share; LeBron had to learn to stop sharing so much.

Jordan was competitive to the max and very hard on teammates who did not live up to his rigorous standards. The title of Sam Smith's landmark 1991 book, *The Jordan Rules*, was a play on words emanating from the defensive principles employed by the Detroit Pistons against him.

The effect that Jordan had on the group can best be summed up by the decision of point guard B. J. Armstrong to figure out Michael by taking a book on geniuses out of the library. Jordan finally learned how to calibrate his virtuosity to blend better with the abilities and desires of the mortals with whom he had been fated to play. In time he would pass off for major game-winning playoff baskets by Steve Kerr and John Paxson. The 1988–89 Michael could not have brought himself to do that.

LeBron, by contrast, always wanted to be liked by teammates. What worked in high school he hoped would work in the NBA. He always knew he was the best player, but he didn't have to take thirty shots or demand the basketball to prove it. I didn't initially believe that he ran away from the ball against the Celtics in the 2010 playoffs or the Mavericks in the 2011 finals, but on reflection, he did. Whether someone talked some sense into his head or he looked at the tapes and figured it out himself, the fact is that since the start of the 2011–12 season he has recalibrated and accepted that each night he takes the floor he is the best player on it. He has, thus, reached a rare state of excellence, one known only to a precious few in the history of the game. I call it Game Mastery, meaning that a player is in complete control of his actions and has the technical versatility to execute what his mind is telling him to do. Oscar Robertson was once there, as was John Havlicek. Lord knows both Bird and Magic reached that point, as has Kobe Bryant. Michael Jordan was there for years, starting in 1991. And LeBron will be there until his body fails him.

Did I imply I'd pick a winner? Wish I hadn't done that. If championships alone are the measuring stick, then Michael is probably going to remain the popular choice as the GOAT. But if I can go on aesthetics alone, I know I'd rather watch LeBron. The cake looks good, and I'm eating it, too.

CHAPTER 28

A Good Walk—Always

Sportswriters are always being asked, "What's your favorite sport to cover?" What the questioners usually mean is "What's your favorite sport?" because they assume the answer will be the same. Not in my case. My answer always surprises them. That's because my favorite sport to cover is golf.

The reason is simple: Golf is the last sport television scheduling can't mess up, because it has to be played during the day. Thus, golf is the only sport that enables you to cover it properly, allowing you to write what you want without rigorous deadlines that force the story to be contrived. This would not be true for me if I didn't like or understand golf—if, say, it was NASCAR or UFC. Daylight or no daylight, I wouldn't enjoy it. But I happen to really like covering golf.

I'm not a golf expert. I can't talk shaft stiffness or Stimpmeters. I can't analyze swings in minute detail. But I have attempted to play this fiendish game since I was twelve and I have followed it steadily as a fan and curious sportswriter, have a reasonably good grasp of golf history, and know great from good when I see it.

The rhythm of covering a golf tournament suits me. I like arriving very early. I have seen the first threesome tee off at more than one major, and that means being out there at or before seven A.M. I do it because you never know what may happen. At the 2005 U.S. Open at Pinehurst, that opening threesome included a local player, Jimmy Driscoll of Brookline, Massachusetts, I was curious to follow, and it also contained a relative unknown named Jason Gore, who had a terrific backstory concerning a hectic trip just to get there. He then remained in contention for the entire tournament. I was probably the only writer who had seen him on that first tee, and I felt I had gained an advantage in writing his story.

Covering a golf tournament is about choices—and luck. Unable to be everywhere at once, you must make a decision about which player you're going to watch, and it's not always easy to guess right. You're following someone and then you get word that so-and-so is tearing it up and you think you'd better find out what's going on firsthand. But getting from point A to point B is often a challenge. You finally get where you're going and the guy goes bogey-bogey, and you probably should have remained where you were.

On many courses a notorious hole itself may be the story. You park yourself there and chart the trials and tribulations of the frustrated golfers. It's a very common first-day approach for a columnist covering golf. Some writers never leave the pressroom or tent to cover live action. They watch the in-house television coverage, and if someone has posted a good round they move to the "flash area" for a postround quickie interview.

Now the truth is that on Sunday staying inside is usually the better approach, as, if more than one twosome is in contention, following the action on television will reveal the full story. For me, it was always a difficult decision to make. That famous Tiger Woods miracle hole-out on the sixteenth in Augusta? I watched it on TV and I hated myself for it. I had forced myself inside for the back nine for a reason, but if circumstances allow I would far prefer being on top of the action. I couldn't have been more than fifteen feet from Payne Stewart when he sank that dramatic clinching putt to win the Open at Pinehurst in 1999, and the memory is much more vivid as a result.

I came a little late to golf reporting. There is always a give-and-take in sports departments, and because my fellow columnist Mike Madden had a strong interest in golf and I had my own journalistic druthers, the only times I covered golf were occasional drop-ins at the local PGA tour stop at Pleasant Valley in Sutton, Massachusetts.

I had long had a desire to cover the British Open, or, as they haughtily refer to it, the Open. I loved the looks of those largely links courses. *Globe* sports editor Don Skwar made that wish come true for me in 1997. The site was Scotland's Troon, and I was hooked. Troon has one of those signature holes, the 123-yard par-3 eighth, known as "Ailsa." This treacherous little fellow offers a straightforward proposition: hit the green or you're looking at a double bogey, minimum. It was hardly an original thought, but I did my first Troon column from the eighth hole.

Troon was where I encountered one of the great writing subjects of my career. When a larger-than-life theatrical presence falls into your life, you must take full advantage. And Colin Montgomerie—Monty—was just such a figure. By 1997 the Monty legend was in full bloom. He was in the midst of European Tour dominance. He would win their money title—the "Order of Merit"—eight times. He had come agonizingly close to winning majors, losing playoffs in both the 1994 U.S. Open and the 1995 PGA. As he sat down to converse with the media prior to the Open at Troon he was coming off yet another second-place finish at the U.S. Open. He was also building a reputation as a European Ryder Cup mainstay.

Monty was a confrontational fellow. He had a long-standing love-hate relationship with the British press, and he was regarded as a touchy diva in the States. He had problems with the American galleries and had acquired the nickname "Mrs. Doubtfire," stemming from his humorous physical resemblance to the character portrayed by a cross-dressing Robin Williams in that popular 1993 movie. Monty was also cultivated and capable of being very charming. He was complex and human, and he loved to talk. I always thought I would have enjoyed a dinner or two with him.

The two people I would write most about during my golf coverage days were Monty and Tiger Woods. Of the two, Monty was the far more enjoyable subject. He was always at his preening best during the Ryder Cups. Monty never did win a major (seldom offering much of a challenge in the Open, which was surprising), and he never won a PGA tournament on American soil. But he kicked American players up and down courses on both continents during Ryder Cup play and he was proud of that. He compiled a 20-9-7 record as a Ryder Cup participant and he never lost a singles match, not one. He stands second to Nick

Faldo with a total of 23.5 points accumulated, and put a punctuation mark on his Ryder Cup career by captaining the victorious European side in 2010. Any Ryder Cup history will feature the name Colin Montgomerie in giant boldface letters.

In 2004 European captain Bernhard Langer raised an eyebrow or two by making the then-forty-one-year-old Monty a captain's choice selection. As he met the media a day before the competition, Monty was beaming. "From where I was in my life in April when you saw me at the Forest of Arden on the Sunday after I finished the British Masters, to where I am now, I have come a long way . . . I am so proud of myself that I have managed to get in this stage," he said.

He and Padraig Harrington were being matched against Tiger and Phil Mickelson in the leadoff match of the competition. Monty viewed this in somewhat apocalyptic terms. "We can win that game," he declared. "And if we do win that game, it will have a dramatic effect on the day. So, yes, it is important in many ways, but it would be huge for the European team and everybody here to see we can cope with their top two. It is dramatic, isn't it, but it always seems to happen to me, doesn't it?" Typical Monty—charming hubris.

I wasn't shocked, therefore, when Monty and Padraig prevailed over Tiger and Phil, 2 and 1. The Europeans annihilated the Americans, 18.5–9.5. Monty and Padraig did have "a dramatic effect on the day."

I always rooted for Monty. To me, he was the most compelling character in golf and one of the handful of most interesting people I've come across in any sport. I would have loved for Monty to get that elusive major, but it was not meant to be. His last great chance was in the 2006 U.S. Open at Winged Foot. Most people remember the eighteenth hole on Sunday as the spot where Phil Mickelson threw away his Open opportunity by airmailing his drive to downtown New Rochelle. But there was another egregious screwup on that hole.

Monty hit a good drive, and as he stood over his second shot, a simple approach he had executed a thousand times, he could have become the leader with a par. But he made a fateful decision, switching from a six-iron to a seven-iron, figuring that adrenaline would make his seven the right club. Alas, Monty hit short and right, landing in messy rough. He bogeyed the hole. I tell you, Monty had hit that approach to give himself a birdie opportunity at least 70 percent of the time, maybe more. But not this time. And that was his last chance to win a tournament of any kind in America.

What can I tell you about Tiger Woods that you don't already know? His is the most well-documented career in golf history.

I don't know Tiger. I've never had a one-on-one conversation with him. But I also never had any trouble writing about him. People in my business always complain that he is too guarded and programmed in his public appearances, but I never once came away from a Tiger press conference, whether pretournament or after a round, where he didn't offer some good golf stuff to chew on. I was never quite sure what these golf experts wanted. Tiger never let me down.

I was present for his extraordinary rout of the field at the 2000 Pebble Beach Open, which he won by a record fifteen strokes. Some people are put off by routs of any kind, but I've always been partial to artistic destructions. I love history, and you don't often get a chance to see history made in such overwhelming fashion. It was eerie to look at that leaderboard on Sunday and see one person with red numbers and everyone else far, far behind.

I felt I had to walk the entire final round with Tiger. There was no mystery left in the tournament, of course; the only issue was how low Tiger could go and how large the eventual winning margin would be. Tiger's personal goal was to play bogey-free golf for the whole tournament. I was stationed down the fairway as he arrived at eighteen. People had been waiting there to see him, and they wanted him to hit a typical booming drive. However, caddy Steve Williams handed Tiger an iron on the tee, and as soon as they saw the flash of that iron, people began moaning. (Tiger got his wish.)

My personal Tiger moment came two years later at Bethpage Black in Farmingdale, Long Island, a notoriously difficult public course that had been ridiculously tricked up for the U.S. Open, as is the case with most U.S. Open courses. This is one reason I prefer the Open. No one feels the need to trick up a British Open course; as a rule, the only trickery needed is that provided by Mother Nature. Over here the standard U.S. Open course is often a borderline joke, and the Black course at Bethpage was Exhibit A.

Amid the requisite complaining from many in the field, Tiger shot an opening-round three-under 67. The weather predictions for Friday's round two were dire: cold, wet, and thoroughly miserable. By this time I had been around long enough to know that these conditions would give Tiger a chance to end the drama before the weekend even began. In those days we all acknowledged that Tiger's edge over the competition was his mind and his will, not his raw golfing talent alone. Tiger was the acknowledged master of mind over matter. So I decided I was going to be there when Tiger clinched early.

I did not own appropriate golf rain gear, and by the second hole my khakis were soaked through. I can't recall what I wore for a top, but whatever it was had no hope of surviving.

I spent four-plus miserable hours cold and wet, but the really hard part was keeping notes.

Tiger justified my interest and shot a 68. He was in at 135 for two rounds, three strokes ahead of Padraig Harrington. Tiger with a three-stroke lead going into Saturday was, in those days, a pretty solid lock. He wasn't great on either Saturday or Sunday, with a 70 and a 72. But Bethpage was not a course on which great ground was going to be made up and Tiger was never seriously threatened.

I was always pulling for Tiger to pass Jack Nicklaus in total wins at majors. I respected Jack, but none of his eighteen major championships had come on my watch, whereas plenty of Tiger's were. I was historically invested in Tiger's pursuit of Nicklaus. I often said I wanted to be there when he won number nineteen, and who among us back in the midnineties doubted it would take place?

The one thing I always maintained during his long period of dominance was that Tiger was a perpetual my-dog-ate-the-homework guy. He could never just have a bad day, always offering convoluted explanations for everything that had gone wrong. Few were overly bothered because the next big triumph was always around the corner. After his comeuppance following the events of Thanksgiving 2009, people began to catch on. His excuses for nonperformance got tedious.

Would he already have passed Jack had he not messed up his personal life? Very likely. I know it is fair and logical to say that no one ever consistently putts in his forties the way he did in his thirties or twenties, and great putting is the biggest determinant in winning golf tournaments, majors or otherwise, but I can easily see him having won five tournaments out of sixteen opportunities in the years 2010–13, and that's while factoring in injury.

I could go on and on about what it was like to see him at his peak. Jack Nicklaus still has the greatest career accomplishments of all time, but the peak Tiger was unquestionably the most impressive force ever to walk upon a golf course. It's hard to imagine ever seeing anything to equal the 2000–2008 Tiger again.

When I walked into the *Boston Globe* to start my internship in 1968, I could never have imagined that a golf course happening would be one of my top five writing satisfactions. I am speaking of the events that took place at the Country Club in Brookline, Massachusetts, on September 26, 1999, the third and final day of the 1999 Ryder Cup.

The Americans' prospects did not look good, as they began the day trailing 10–6 in points, with 14.5 needed to clinch the victory. American captain Ben Crenshaw spoke bravely after Saturday's second day about his team's not being out of it, but no team had overcome that large a last-day deficit in Ryder Cup play, which had begun in Worcester, Massachusetts, seventy years earlier.

The Americans were the home team, but this had proved no advantage, and the boys in red, white, and blue had been essentially unlikable because they did not seem to enjoy the concept of team play as did the Europeans. A Golf Channel survey conducted on Friday noted that 58 percent of Americans polled said they were rooting for the Europeans. I agreed with that sentiment and had no expectation of any big drama to unfold during the twelve singles matches that day.

However, when I arrived and looked at a scoreboard, each of the first six singles matches was being won by an American, and that's the way the matches played out. Tom Lehman beat Lee Westwood, 3 and 2. Hal Sutton beat Darren Clarke, 4 and 2. Phil Mickelson beat Jarmo Sandelin, 3 and 2. Davis Love III beat Jean van de Velde, 6 and 5. Tiger Woods—usually indifferent to the Ryder Cup—beat Andrew Coltart, 3 and 2. David Duval beat Jesper Parnevik, 5 and 4.

"We won the first six matches," said Love. "And we won *big*. We dominated. We got the momentum going and we started playing as a team."

That had been the knock on the Americans, that they could not reconcile themselves to the idea that Ryder Cup play is team competition, and team spirit is essential. For this one afternoon, many of the American golfers had become invincible.

"The putts were just going in from all angles," said European captain Mark James. "And the chips. We couldn't do anything to stop it. Perhaps I could have rung up a bomb scare. Maybe that would have stopped it."

Winning those first six matches was a start, but more was needed, and the fourteenth hole was a key juncture. For once I had no problem knowing exactly where to go. It was worth any wait to see the Americans finish off three straight matches there, concluding with a Duval triumph that launched the normally taciturn fellow into a wild jig.

Things came to a head on seventeen. Justin Leonard, playing against Jose Maria Olazabal, was facing a forty-five-foot putt for birdie, with Olazabal well inside him at twenty-five feet from the hole. I was back down the fairway trying to keep tabs on both that match and (naturally, given my affections) the following twosome of Colin Montgomerie and Payne Stewart. Of all people, I saw Michael Jordan seated beside the fairway in a golf cart with an NBC logo and I stopped to watch Leonard's putt with him. What we saw will be discussed as long as the Ryder Cup is contested.

Leonard made that forty-five-foot putt and then all Hades broke loose. Exuberant Americans—players, caddies, even wives and significant others—raced onto the green to congratulate him, displaying an enormous breach of golf etiquette. Olazabal still had a twenty-five-foot putt, and the elegant Spaniard was eminently capable of making it. Yet the Americans had tramped all over his line, and he missed. Leonard had won the hole, making him one up with one hole to go and thus guaranteeing a valuable half point after Olazabal won the eighteenth.

The Europeans were, and remain, livid. Do not bring up this topic in Madrid. The European press denounced the Americans. European vice captain Sam Torrance labeled their actions "disgusting." In addition to the questionable American behavior on the seventeenth, many Euros later complained of rude fan treatment out on the course. Alistair Cooke, the erudite British commentator and writer (and golf aficionado), who I always thought was what I'd like to have been had I ever grown up, was appalled by what had taken place on the seventeenth green. "A day of infamy," he called it in one of his weekly "Letter from America" broadcasts, titling it "The Arrival of the Golf Hooligan."

Following the Leonard/Olazabal drama, Monty maintained his perfect Ryder Cup singles record, beating Stewart and becoming one of only three Euros to win his match. Jim Furyk's 4 and 3 triumph over Sergio Garcia sealed the deal. The final score was USA 14.5, Europe 13.5.

I cannot exaggerate the atmosphere—it was positively un-golflike. The feeling out on the course as those American victories kept being posted and as the roars were being supplanted by other roars was unlike anything I have ever experienced covering golf. I believe somewhere I said it was as if golf had become a contact sport. There was an aura of quasi-savagery in the hearts of the American fans. Those people wanted some Euro blood, and they got it.

For several hours on that September day, the Americans became kids again. Mickelson, Lehman, Love, and Sutton sat together, clapping and cheering for Leonard. No one had ever seen the Americans act like this. The Euros would get revenge thirteen years later, erasing their own 10–6 deficit to defeat the Americans, 14.5–13.5, at Medinah in Chicago. There were no international incidents. The Americans simply hung their heads and went home.

But looking back to that September 26 in 1999, a juicy journalistic bonanza was dropped out of the sky. It was the kind of day that makes sportswriters grateful that we have chosen this means of making a living. Had anyone hit me with an exit fee from the Country Club that day, I would gladly have paid it. And the next guy's, too.

CHAPTER 29

Can't Live Without Music

People who don't know me think I'm all about sports. But music matters to me just as much.

In my next life I wouldn't mind trading places with Jonathan Schwartz. I would like to know what he knows and to have heard what he's heard. Jonathan Schwartz plays music on the radio, so some might say he's a disc jockey. What Jonathan Schwartz has done well in more than forty years on the radio is provide the highest level of musical entertainment for an audience that he has subtly educated to expect nothing but the best. I would argue that he knows more about American popular music, the type of music comprising what has come to be known as "the Great American Songbook," than anyone on earth. He was born into music and show business. His father, the late Arthur Schwartz, was the Hall of Fame songwriter of "Dancing in the Dark," "You and the Night and the Music," and "That's Entertainment!" a great showbiz anthem. His mother, Katherine Carrington, was a singer and actress. Music was everywhere in young Jonathan's life.

Jonathan Schwartz is the Sinatra expert Sinatraologists worldwide consult when a Sinatra issue presents itself. Don't challenge him on that score. I know a lot about sports, but Jonathan Schwartz knows more about music than I know about sports. (And he also knows a lot about sports.) If I had not become a sportswriter I would have been very happy being a junior-grade Jonathan Schwartz, spouting back to my audience a great many of the things I've learned from listening to him on WNEW, New York; WQEW, New York; and for the past several years on SiriusXM satellite radio, and on a new incarnation with his own channel streamed on Internet radio.

As a child of the fifties, my basic musical taste straddles the world of the Great American Songbook—the great Broadway and Hollywood musicals of the 1920s,'30s,'40s, and '50s—and the formative days of rock 'n' roll. I also love mainstream jazz. Those three musical streams are my home bases.

Like most people, I think the old days were better. Every generation thinks what is contemporary is the Greatest Thing Ever Written. I will always maintain that the people who came of musical age between roughly 1920 and 1950 can make a strong case for their music being the best America may ever produce. I realize we're talking art here and it cannot be quantified. But do hear me out on this.

I am of the belief that while the mechanical and scientific side of the brain will always come up with technical advancements, the same is not true of the artistic or creative part of the brain. Artistic creations during the Renaissance have stood the test of time hundreds of years later. Michelangelo finished painting the Sistine Chapel in 1512; is anyone making a case that anything better has ever been achieved? The Taj Mahal is still revered by architectural experts, and it was finished in 1653. Monet's paintings will be a wonder to people in the twenty-second century, and Beethoven's Fifth will be played in perpetuity.

Between 1920 and 1950, songs were being written by the likes of Irving Berlin, Richard Rodgers, Cole Porter, Jerome Kern, Harold Arlen, Harry Warren, Jimmy Van Heusen, Jimmy McHugh, Arthur Schwartz, Frank Loesser, Hoagy Carmichael, Johnny Burke, and Walter Donaldson, to name but a few. Duke Ellington was a musical industry unto himself. Great lyrics were churned out by Oscar Hammerstein, Johnny Mercer, Ira Gershwin, Yip Harburg, Howard Dietz, Sammy Cahn, and more.

Yet to me, the greatest popular song wordsmith was the tortured Lorenz "Larry" Hart. Any man who could write the words to "Thou Swell" (in which he "chooses a sweet Lollapalooza in thee") and "I Wish I Were in Love Again" (the "conversations with the flying plates") and "I Didn't Know What Time It Was" ("I wanted love and here it was shining out of your eyes") stands apart. The hundreds of great songs these men and women produced in that one thirty-year period have enriched my life beyond measure. Love was examined up, down, inside, out, sideways, frontward, backward, and then reexamined.

Jazz has also captured my heart. My three jazz icons are Count Basie, Zoot Sims, and Buddy Rich. I may have trouble naming the greatest sports experience I've ever known, but I know for sure that the most fulfilling nights of entertainment I've ever experienced were those listening to Buddy Rich's Big Band blow us out onto Route 1 at a club called Lennie's on the Turnpike in Peabody, Massachusetts, back in the 1960s and '70s. I would go anywhere in those days to hear that band, just as my wife Elaine and I go to great lengths nowadays to hear John Pizzarelli and his great quartet. I could also listen to Louis Armstrong's version of "Just One of Those Things," accompanied by Oscar Peterson, ten times a day, every day.

I was eight going on nine when the Top 40 transition was taking place. Songs like "Shrimp Boats" were giving way to "Rock Around the Clock." The transition on the pop charts was gradual, and instrumentals such as "The Poor People of Paris" or "Cherry Pink and Apple Blossom White" still got airplay and occupied spots on the Top 40 alongside Elvis, Little Richard, and Bill Haley.

The rock takeover was finished off by the Beatles, who became to the sixties music audience what Bing Crosby had been to people in the thirties, Sinatra in the forties, and Elvis in the fifties. The Beatles themselves had an ear for all kinds of music. Paul McCartney's rendition of "Till There Was You" on the *Meet the Beatles!* album is as sweet and poignant a version of that great song from *The Music Man* as I've ever heard.

Many of the early rock greats paid homage to the Great American Songbook. Fats Domino laid down a version of "My Blue Heaven" that ranks with anyone's. Even Little Richard submitted a rousing version of "Baby Face." But if one song can epitomize what rock is all about, one song that has the beat, the sound, the feel, and the subject matter that most defines what rock was saying to its audience, it is "Be My Baby" by the Ronettes. The quintessential rock song must be about love. In this case it's "Here I am; take me. I'm yours." Who can't relate to that? Say what you want about Phil Spector, the man knew what he was doing when he got inside the studio.

Thanks to my friend Ron Della Chiesa, whose name and voice are familiar to generations of Boston-area radio listeners, I had some opportunities in the 1980s to program as much as an hour of music on WGBH radio in Boston. I could follow Sinatra with Screamin' Jay Hawkins singing his immortal "I Put a Spell on You." I have seldom had more fun.

For decades I have fantasized about having my own weekly radio show on which I would combine sports and music. I would take calls, but the conversation would be restricted to either sports or music. I would play music from the Great American Songbook alongside the best of the past fifty years. Perhaps there would be an album of the week. But I'm afraid I've run out of time on that one. Well, I can dream, can't I?

CHAPTER 30

No Complaints

If your father dies when you're eleven, there's a lot you don't know.

I knew some stuff about Bill Ryan. I knew he had been an assistant athletic director at Villanova, because I had gone to some Villanova football games and many Villanova basketball games. I knew he had once worked for the Sally League Columbus (Georgia) Cardinals because we had spent the summer of 1951 living in Georgia. I knew he had once had some kind of connection with the Trenton Giants of the Class B Inter-State League. I knew he knew major leaguers such as Bobby Hofman, Ray Katt, Al Corwin, Marv Blaylock, and even Willie Mays because I had met them myself in either New York or Philadelphia. I knew he had been in the service and that he and my mother spent their honeymoon at Bear Mountain, New York, near West Point.

I knew that when he died at age thirty-nine it seemed as if half of Trenton came to the funeral.

What I did not know was that during World War II he had been part of an experiment in which he and seven other men were set adrift in the Gulf of Mexico on life rafts. They had volunteered to be guinea pigs to test a device that would make regular seawater drinkable. As he explained in the *Villanovan*, the school paper, in a 1953 interview, "Only myself and a guy from Brooklyn held out the full nineteen days. The others had to be 'rescued.'"

I didn't know that as an army swimming instructor he concluded a water carnival by diving forty feet into a burning pool. He was just my dad, and I knew he had never led a "normal" nine-to-five life. I knew that our entire existence was governed by sports. I also knew he had a real estate license and that when he died he was working for Lit Brothers, a department store, and not a sports team or college. I didn't know why, and I still don't. He should have been working in sports.

What I also did not know was that he never made any real money and that he never could get a real break, one that would put him in a better financial position and also take advantage of his phenomenal people skills. I didn't think anything of the fact that, however well-known he was in Trenton, he, my mom, and I were living in my grandfather's house, even in year thirteen of their marriage. It sure didn't bother me. I had everything I needed. But it had to be a real comedown for this local celebrity to be living in his wife's father's house.

And he *was* just that—a local celeb. From the minute he was discharged from the service in 1945 'til his death of complications following ulcer surgery in 1957, he was seldom out of the local sports news. He organized a successful semipro basketball league. He was a legendary Trenton playground instructor. He worked for the Trenton Giants. He helped start a parochial school basketball league that became a feeder for the Trenton Catholic powerhouse teams of the fifties. (The five-year-old me flipped the numbers on the manual scoreboard.) He worked for the Columbus Cardinals.

He was a complete and thorough people person, especially good with kids. And he was astonishingly generous. "Bill couldn't help it," my mother told *Trenton Times* columnist Harold "Bus" Saidt, a friend of both my parents since high school, who was writing my father's obituary. "All his life he did things for everybody else." In that story Bus observed about my father: "With his death Trenton lost one of the wildest, wackiest, lovable sports promotional geniuses this town ever knew."

Bus Saidt was one of the two leading Trenton sports journalistic voices between World War II and 2000. The other was Joe Logue. Every town of that size, or even nowhere near that size, has a local writer whose wisdom and experience are indispensable and irreplaceable. I remember being so excited when I heard that Joe Logue was coming to my school, Lawrenceville, to cover our game with Peddie during my senior year. I had read his stories for years, but I had never had Joe Logue write about my team. Amazingly I had a good game, and even was included in an action photograph. Joe, of course, knew my dad, and so I surmised he might have had some influence in the photo selection.

Only later did I see what Joe Logue had written upon my father's passing some six and a half years earlier.

> Some guys are born lucky. Right connections open important doors. The big time is their apple. Push button executives pave the steps of opportunity and the climb to the top is quickened. Like giant balloons filled with helium, they ascend, confidently doing a job they were lucky enough to uncover.
>
> It wasn't that way with Bill Ryan. He was a guy with big ideas in a small town. His life was sports, and, like many of us, not being gifted with natural ability, he turned to the other facets of the game that fill the daily sports pages. But nothing came easy. The promotion field was his baby and he handled it like a pro, but lady luck didn't smile . . .
>
> Those of us who cover the sports beat were constantly aware of the former Cathedral High and Rider College student. If the idea appealed to him, there was no containing his enthusiasm. Days and nights blended into selfless hours as the energetic fellow rushed from place to place, pursuing the climax of another promotional dream. They were always big—they were always good.

He concluded: "The train from Philly crosses the Delaware and gives a good view of that sign that reads TRENTON MAKES THE WORLD TAKES. It's not necessarily true, you know. Trenton had a fellow ready for the big time and lady luck didn't smile. Sports could use more Bill Ryans. Unfortunately, none are in sight. There may never be."

Was there a fatal flaw? Was he just plain unlucky? I mean, in the end he wasn't even working in sports. I received no answers then, and I never will because all his contemporaries are gone, and that includes his brothers, Jack and Freddy, who might have provided me with some insight.

My father was actually spoken of locally in terms of Bill Veeck. Therein lies the great "What if?" It is truly inexplicable why Bill Ryan did not become a national name.

My mother pretty much summed it up in that interview with Bus Saidt. "He was always on the fringe of everything," she said. "He never received much credit and he never made any money. I think being so close and so frustrated about what he knew he could do in sports and never receiving the chance might have led to his death."

My career is the flip side. I have been fortunate to be in the right place at the right time on many occasions. I received a *Globe* internship interview when my roommate turned it down. I was handed the Celtics beat at age twenty-three because there was no one else in the department with either the interest or basketball feel to take the job. They got very good after one year and I rode the wave. I lucked into doing a TV show because the guy who bought it was an old friend.

Had someone else taken over the show, he would have hired *his* friends. Some great things have happened to me over which I had zero control.

I think my father would have loved the course of my career. I am, quite frankly, extremely envious of my colleagues who have been able to share their own experiences with their sports-loving dads. My father didn't even live long enough to see me in a Little League All-Star Game, let alone see me play varsity basketball, head off to an Olympics, or coauthor a book with Bob Cousy. I'd like to think he'd have been impressed with *that*.

I was astonishingly fortunate to work for a newspaper whose editor in chief, Tom Winship; executive sports editor, Jerry Nason; and morning and evening sports editors, Fran Rosa and Ernie Roberts, believed in the freedom of writers to cover things with a distinct point of view. This was not the case at many American newspapers. It may not even have been the case at a majority of them. But it was very much the case at the *Boston Globe* in the late 1960s. The *Globe* was known far and wide as a "writer's newspaper," not an "editor's newspaper." As writers, we were allowed to be creative. When we needed reining in, there were wonderful desk men such as Art Keefe to lend advice. But we were always encouraged to swing for the fences with our particular views.

The Old Guard at the paper was often quite amused. One of our colleagues was the acerbic Clif Keane, a figure who would have no place in today's scheme of things, which is modern journalism's loss. Apprised that the bosses were considering having Peter Gammons cover the Red Sox for the morning *Globe* and me cover the team for the evening *Globe*, Keane sneered, "Oh, that'll be great. Gammons will write about wars and symphonies, and Ryan will complain about the umpires."

The old-timers on the staff when I joined were downright fictional characters. Roger Birtwell was a veteran baseball writer who, when informed I was a native of Trenton, inquired, "Say, is the Hotel Hildebrecht still the-ah? Stayed the-ah when I covered Hah-vud-Princeton in twenty-fo-ah." Roger would often shuffle into the press box at Fenway Park wearing bedroom slippers sometime around the fourth or fifth inning with a request for the gang to "fill [him] in." He had a distinct writing style. I called him the "the Dash King," because no piece was complete without a minimum of a half dozen parenthetical thoughts set off by dashes. I could never get over the fact that Roger Birtwell had covered Ty Cobb, Rogers Hornsby, and Babe Ruth.

John Ahern was another figure out of central casting. John's areas of expertise were hockey, boxing, and yachting. He was a name-dropper supreme, the most frequent reference being Rocky Marciano. He was our man at the America's Cup, which was then regularly held at Newport, Rhode Island, and he was famous for being able to call races in the first thirty seconds. He was equally well-known for having *two* changes of clothing at the Swampscott races, a staple of Boston's yachting summer.

John wore suits most of the time and he always had a snappy fedora. His big advice to me was "Never read your own stuff." This, of course, confounded me, because I was from the Jimmy Breslin School myself. Breslin had famously said that his biggest thrill was sitting next to someone on the New York subway who was reading his column. I've always been my own favorite audience.

And then there was the inimitable Bud Collins. He would eventually resign from a full-time capacity at the *Globe* in order to make a full-time living as a tennis commentator, but when I arrived in 1968 he was a general columnist who simply had an affinity for tennis. He was also a boxing maven with a strong tie to the young Cassius Clay and he practically adored the Celtics. He dubbed the Red Sox "the Olde Towne Team." He was a swashbuckling personal presence, and he took a liking to me. No one could have been more encouraging to a young writer than Bud Collins.

My own contemporaries are among the best sportswriters of all time—the likes of Ray Fitzgerald, Peter Gammons, Will McDonough, Fran Rosa, Kevin Dupont, and Jackie MacMullan are all in the writers' sections of their respective sports Halls of Fame. At one point the *Globe*'s primary beat people on the four major team sports—McDonough, Rosa, Gammons, and me—were all Hall of Famers–to–be—the only time, I'll bet, that has ever occurred on one newspaper. I have spent my entire journalistic career surrounded by all-stars, and don't think that fact doesn't serve as a nice little motivator to keep up your end of the paper's bargain.

I cared deeply about writing a game story that would be along the lines of what a Broadway critic on opening night would write. What did someone miss by not being there or not seeing it on TV? How did the game look and feel? Was there—and this I took great interest in—an element of humor in the contest? Should the game be put into any kind of context, or was it, as the British might say, a "one-off"? And if someone had seen it, could I bring some enlightenment, either by interviewing principals to explain a questionable circumstance or by fleshing it out with my own observations?

One aspect of basketball game writing I emphasized was the role of the officials. I came to realize that in any given game the referees had an influence that made them the equivalent of a good player, if not necessarily a great one. Referees decide who will stay on the court and how the game will be played. They cannot be ignored. I didn't reference the officiating every night, and not all the references were negative. But I was always on the lookout for exceptionally smooth, well-officiated games. In fact, great games—in any sport—are impossible without high-quality officiating.

I believe each set of officials should be given a one-question quiz before every game: "Why am I here?" The answer is simple: "I am here to adjudicate the smooth flow of the game." That's it. A referee must know the rules, but he or she must also be able to exercise common sense and good judgment. Refereeing is not a science. It is an art form. So, yes, I do believe in makeup calls.

A writer must be true to his or her personality. Many have a primary interest in the people who compete, not the competition itself—who wins and who loses is of less importance. I get the people part. I, too, enjoy writing personality profiles about interesting people. But I have never been able to detach myself from the games themselves. My roots are fan based. If I turn on the TV for a sporting event, I inevitably choose a side. If my wife, Elaine, is there, she'll invariably say, "Who are we rooting for?" However, I never had a problem taking off my fan hat to become a writer/reporter when I sat down to the typewriter or computer.

I love sports and I want people to know it. I'd like to think the word people most associate with me is "enthusiasm." Give me a good game, and I'll be happy; as a fan I may regret the outcome, but as a journalist I'll appreciate the drama. That's the way I was when I was eleven, banging out "The Sportster," and that's the way it is today. I strongly suspect my last words will be, "Who won?"

CHAPTER 31

Short Takes

Get in There, Nellie

I once made an NBA substitution.

The Celtics were in Detroit on the afternoon of February 3, 1975, in the process of what would turn out to be an easy 114–100 victory, when coach Tom Heinsohn removed Don Nelson from the game midway through the fourth period. I knew that when he came out Nellie had 9,998 career points. I also knew that since the team was heading to Milwaukee for a game on Tuesday night, Nelson would not reach his 10,000-point milestone at home.

I was sitting in my usual road press seat, next to the Celtics bench. During a time-out I said to Heinsohn, "Tommy, Nellie only needs two for ten thousand. He's not going to get it at home. Why don't you put him back in to get the two points today?" So help me God, Heinsohn summoned Nelson. They ran a play for him, he nailed his jumper, he came out.

Now, I must admit that neither Heinsohn nor Nelson can verify this. But that's not unusual. Principals are often no good with the details. That's why God invented sportswriters. But neither one can refute it, either. If you look up my game story in the *Globe* of February 4, 1975, you will see that indeed Heinsohn did reinsert Nelson into that game and they did run a play and he did make the shot and he did come right back out at the first opportunity. I just neglected to mention who had suggested Heinsohn put Nellie back into the game. I'm sure I wanted to, but I couldn't. Obviously.

Now the truth can be told. I made an NBA substitution.

ME 'N' JOHN

I can't really say I had a relationship with John Updike. Let's just say we had a slight connection.

We met face-to-face just once. I spotted him on an Eastern Airlines shuttle from Boston to LaGuardia in the fall of 1977. I was a huge Updike fan, and when we alighted in New York I just had to introduce myself. I hit about a 9.8 on the Gush-O-Meter, telling him that it was a great source of frustration among sportswriters that the best piece of sportswriting ever was nothing any of us or our writing forefathers had ever done. It was, of course, his legendary take on Ted Williams's final game on September 28, 1960, for the *New Yorker*. No one had ever topped the essay, entitled "Hub Fans Bid Kid Adieu."

"Oh, I know who you are," he said. I knew he resided on Boston's North Shore, but the idea that the great Updike began his day by perusing the sports pages of the *Boston Globe* was a difficult concept to grasp. He then told me, with regard to "Hub Fans Bid Kid Adieu," that a publisher was about to release a limited edition. There would be just five hundred.

"Would you like to have one?" he inquired. I stammered something in the affirmative. He asked me for my address. We shook hands and went on our way. Shortly after New Year's, the little book arrived. It was inscribed as follows:

for Bob Ryan
from an admirer.
John Updike
1/7/78

Yeah, that's what he said. Would he lie?

Let me put it this way. In that age-old scenario whereby the house is burning down and you only have time to save a few precious items, I have narrowed my list down to two. The first is that bound copy of "Hub Fans Bid Kid Adieu"; the second is a photo in which I am standing between Larry Bird and Magic Johnson with each resting a hand on my shoulder. Just about everything else is replaceable.

I had assumed that would be the beginning and end of any contact with John Updike. But one day I received a postcard from him. I would come to learn that this was his preferred means of communication. He said he was working on another Rabbit novel, and he had a basketball question: Who was the fellow noted for breaking backboards? He thought it might be Moses Malone, but he wasn't sure. I wrote back, informing him that he was thinking about Darryl Dawkins.

There would be another postcard. What year, I'm not sure. This time he had a question about the Patriots. He closed by wishing me a merry Christmas (he had actually written it on Christmas Day), adding, "I always read your words in the *Globe*; you tell it like it is, fearlessly."

Gulp. I guess he really did read me.

Fast-forward to 2008. I had always noted September 28 as the anniversary of the Williams farewell homer, and I thought it would be a nice column if I reached out to John Updike for his anniversary reflections. It took a little work, since he was in China, but I was able to get to him when he returned through his friend Roger Angell, and we had a pleasant chat.

"My one effort as a sportswriter," he said of "Hub Fans." "It's had a longer life than I ever would have expected."

On the back of a postcard featuring a crayon drawing on paper of Henry James, John Updike wrote the following response to me concerning the column: "Everybody keeps telling me about your terrific piece on Ted Williams and me. You have made me momentarily famous among people who don't read much. To those who do, you have always been a hero. Many thanks, John Updike."

Four months later he was dead, a victim of lung cancer. Timing, as always, is everything.

The idea that my name is even remotely connected with his is staggering to me. But if you want to Google it up, I won't stop you.

Good If It Goes

Tommy Lasorda once gave serious thought to becoming an NBA referee. Bet you didn't know that.

I was a friend of the late Earl Strom, an NBA refereeing legend. One day he told me the following story. "I've known Tommy for a long time," Earl said. "He's from Norristown, Pennsylvania, and I'm from Pottstown. Years ago, when Tommy was through pitching and was just a scout, he decided he wanted to become an NBA referee. I recommended him to Sid Borgia. Sid knew who Tommy was because he had umpired in the International League and Tommy would yell things at him and then go run and hide.

"Things were a lot different in those days. We used to ride the buses during exhibition season with the players, drink with them and everything. Sid paired Tommy up with Jim Duffy and sent them on an exhibition tour with Cincinnati and Detroit. They were going to play four games against each other in the Midwest somewhere.

"The Cincinnati coach at the time was Charley Wolf. He was a very straitlaced guy. Well, after Tommy and Duffy had worked the first two games, Charley calls up Borgia and says, 'Sid, you've got to send us two more referees. I can't take any more of those foulmouthed guys.'

"Tommy may have worked one more game, and that was the end of his officiating career."

My favorite part is Tommy yelling things at Sid Borgia and then running into the dugout to hide.

ARE WE ON THE AIR?

Live TV is very dangerous.

When you hang that verbal curveball on TV, and the result is a game-losing grand-slam homer, you have no one to blame but yourself. Believe me, I know.

On a Sunday night in early May of 2003, I was sitting on a TV set with longtime friend Bob Lobel, blabbing away on his Sunday night highlight show, as I had done many times before. The subject was Joumana Kidd, wife of New Jersey Nets star Jason Kidd, and her continual desire to get herself on camera during her husband's games. No matter the time of night, she always made sure their precocious toddler son, T. J., was at her side, as if he were a prop. She was beyond obnoxious. I was far from alone in believing that to be true.

But it was definitely not a good idea for me to say, on live television, that "I'd like to smack her." It was hyperbole, pure and simple. My assumption was that everyone would recognize that to be the case, that I didn't really want to lay a hand on her.

Give Bob Lobel credit. He realized the potential gravity of the situation right away. He gave me a chance to retract what I had just said. But noooo. I was on a roll. I said that I had similarly chastised her behavior the year before and why would I have a change of heart now?

Things happened very quickly the next day. The New York press found out what I had said. This was a juicy story. I had already arrived in New Jersey to cover the next game of that playoff series when I was called back to the *Globe* office. I was brought before a panel headed by *Globe* editor Marty Baron. I had definitely screwed up, since I had ignored the fact that Jason Kidd, once upon a fairly recent time, had, in fact, hit Joumana Kidd. It was in all the papers. I must confess that never entered my mind. That did put a different spin on the story.

For my transgression I was suspended for one month, without pay, from my *Globe* duties. But it didn't end there. I was also forbidden from appearing on any radio or television show, and from honoring any speaking engagements. I was being shut down completely in a month when I had a lot going on. My verbal transgression wound up costing me more than $20,000 in salary and outside income.

This was quite a media cause célèbre. My friend Tony Kornheiser, no stranger to suspension himself, gave me some important advice. "Read nothing, listen to nothing, and watch nothing," he said. "Nothing!" I followed his advice.

Now I had a month on my hands. The first weekend we went to visit my son Keith and his family in Norwich, Connecticut. My daughter-in-law Kate went online to see what was being written and she reported that many of my women friends in the business had come to my defense, which was gratifying. Some of it was because they knew the real me and recognized hyperbole when they heard it, and some of it was because they didn't care much for Joumana Kidd's act, either. Aside from that, I still don't know to this day who dissed me and who didn't. It's much better that way. Tony was right.

I think I survived this affair with reputation reasonably intact. On occasion I'll get an e-mail from someone referencing me as an advocate of violence toward women, but there is nothing I can do about that. Thanks to Wikipedia, it's always going to follow me to some extent. But how can I complain? I did it.

Postscript 1: Shortly after I did what I did, Doris Roberts, Emmy-winning actress from *Everybody Loves Raymond*, was in town to promote something or other. She was discussing the fact that the show might be nearing the end of its run and it was all up to Ray Romano whether or not the show would continue, which, of course, she hoped would be the case. And how did Doris Roberts sum up her feelings about Ray Romano at that particular point in time?

"I'd like to smack him," she said.

Postscript 2: Jason and Joumana Kidd are no longer married.

Fore!

Dr. Gil Morgan's tee shot on the 420-yard par-4 eighth hole at the Salem, Massachusetts, Country Club bounced and hit a spectator. These things happen, but this was a bit different. The spectator was me, and I wasn't just spectating. I was covering the 2001 Senior Open.

I had a press armband. I was properly located; that wasn't the issue. The issue is that a writer is supposed to cover the story, not be part of the story.

My usual MO in covering a tournament as someone tees off is to station myself toward the green, anywhere from 275 to 325 yards or so from the tee. I can thus observe the flight of the ball. But the eighth at Salem has a severe fairway drop, and if you walk far enough away from the tee you can no longer see the tee box. All of a sudden a shot veering far left of the fairway bounced, kicked left, and headed in my direction. I was unable to get out of the way. The ball came to rest in the rough a few feet in front of a wall. I wasn't sure if Morgan was even going to have a chance at a shot. At that moment I wished I were David Blaine or somebody. I wanted to disappear. On the other hand, I might actually have provided Morgan with a service. Had the ball not hit me, it may very well have gone officially out of bounds.

I was, of course, praying for Morgan to salvage his par. He did have a shot, after all. He took out an eight-iron and hit the ball over the back of the green, settling for a bogey five.

I knew I'd have to fess up. When he completed his round of seventy I approached him to explain what happened and he turned out to be a nice guy. After acknowledging that anything can happen on a golf course, he smiled and said, "Next time try to steer it onto the fairway."

Whew!

Dr. Gil Morgan shot a 71 on Saturday and a 70 on Sunday. He finished second in that 2001 Senior Open to Bruce Fleisher—by one stroke. Did I keep Dr. Gil Morgan from getting into a playoff with Bruce Fleisher or did I give him a chance to squeeze out a scrambling par by preventing that ball from going out of bounds?

We'll never know.

BIG HOUSE GAINES

Bob Knight had given me the best heads-up when I told him I was going to pay a visit to see Big House Gaines. "There isn't anybody in basketball," Knight said, "who if asked to name their five favorite people in the game, or the five people in the game whom they most respect, wouldn't name Big House Gaines. His personality greatly transcends the game. But the best thing I can say about Big House is this: I don't enjoy talking to him; I enjoy listening to him."

I went to see Clarence "Big House" Gaines in 1986, when he was sixty-three and had been head basketball coach at Winston-Salem State University since 1946. The word "legend" is tossed around far too lightly in sports, but if ever there was a coaching legend it was him. Had we never met, I would have led a horribly incomplete journalistic life. His best coaching days, in terms of wins and championships, were behind him. He had won an NCAA Division 2 title with Earl Monroe as his key player in 1967, but by the midseventies the world had changed to the degree that recruiting an Earl Monroe was no longer possible. But he had pitched his tent at Winston-Salem and was never going anywhere else. The gym had been named after him in 1976.

The nickname? He was a six-five, two-hundred-sixty-five-pound freshman at Morgan State. When he got out of a car one day, the school's business manager looked at him and said, "The only thing I've ever seen as big as you is a house."

I spent parts of two days with him. I watched his team play, after which we headed to his office, "we" being Big House, Shaw University coach Warren Reynolds, his sports information director, and me.

"What can you tell me about Fayetteville?" he asked Reynolds.

"Same old stuff," he replied. "They had the one six-nine boy go home at Christmas and another one took his place. Can't tell you much about him."

This was what passed for a scouting report. No video. No scout on the road. It was the equivalent of two affable old guys, each full of respect for the other, swapping tales and exchanging information. Close your eyes and you could picture them at a Fourth of July picnic, sipping iced tea and chatting about the grandchildren.

Me, I listened.

Big House died in April of 2005 a month shy of his eighty-second birthday. We all lost something that can never, ever be replaced.

ONE MOE TIME

Doug Moe was the most casual, most irreverent, most refreshing NBA coaching personality ever. While leading San Antonio against the Washington Bullets in the 1979 Eastern Conference Finals, after putting his team through a less-than-strenuous forty-five-minute practice, he told the media, "My biggest problem right now is that my golf club doesn't allow sixsomes on Thursdays."

Eight years later he was holding court one night before a game between his Denver Nuggets and the Celtics. Unlike most coaches, he always said exactly what was on his mind. If he thought his team was going to win, he'd say so. But on this occasion he said, "If I were you, I'd take the Celtics, the points and the *extra* points." Kevin McHale scored the first eleven points of the game and broke the nose of Denver center Danny Schayes. The Celtics won, 119–105. Too bad none of us had called our bookies.

"YOU'RE FIRED!"

Red Auerbach once asked me the following: "Who's the greatest sixth man in the history of the NBA?"

Geez, I thought. That's pretty obvious.

"John Havlicek."

"No."

"Frank Ramsey?"

"No."

Okay, he's going way retro on me. "Ernie Vandeweghe?"

"No."

"Okay, I give up. Who is it?"

"Chinky Shapiro."

"Chinky Shapiro? Who's Chinky Shapiro?"

"He was the timer in Rochester."

Bada-bing, for sure, but I laugh doubly each time I think of it because Red Auerbach was notoriously tough on his own timer when he did not follow the instincts of either Chinky Shapiro or the legendary Nat "Feets" Broudy, whose deft fingering enhanced the Knicks' chances of winning, or not losing, for many years at Madison Square Garden.

A case in point took place on the afternoon of February 12, 1972. With three seconds remaining the Celtics had a 110–109 lead over the Knicks at Boston Garden. Don Nelson inbounded to Dave Cowens, but before the horn sounded he was fouled by Bill Bradley with one second to play. He made both to give Boston a 112–109 victory, but that wasn't good enough for either Heinsohn or Auerbach, who thought timer Tony Nota had left too much time on the clock. No Chinky, he.

Heinsohn ran to the table, addressing poor Nota as "You SOB!" Red rushed over, waving a finger in Nota's face while saying, "You better get on the ball in the future." When Nota informed Red he had no right to talk to him in that manner, Red blurted out, "You're fired!" The next thing you know, more words were exchanged and Red was throwing a punch at Nota. The two were then separated by a couple of police officers.

Nota was a very well-respected man who had operated the Garden clock for years. He was also a noted local track and field official. You can probably guess the outcome. The firing didn't stick. Tony Nota ran that clock for many years to come.

But you must admit the Chinky Shapiro line is pretty funny.

Johnny and the Zink

Boston-Philadelphia was a staple NBA rivalry from 1959, when Wilt Chamberlain joined the Philadelphia Warriors, until 1987, when Julius Erving retired from the Philadelpha 76ers. In the center of it all were a legendary announcer and a legendary PA announcer.

Johnny Most was the Boston radio voice from 1953 through 1993.

He was more than a mite partisan. Dave Zinkoff was the Philadelphia PA man from the fifties until his death in 1985. He was noted for personalizing baskets. Thus there were 'Dipper Dunks' for Wilt Chamberlain and 'Gola Goals' for Tom Gola, to name two. He loved to draw out names. It was Hal Greeeeeeer! and Julius Errrrrrrving! When the time came, there were "Twooooooo minutes left in this ballgame!"

Most did not like Zinkoff, whom he disgustedly called "Hysterical Harry." This from a man who labeled Washington's Rick Mahorn and Jeff Ruland "McFilty and McNasty,"' (later substituting Bill Laimbeer for Ruland when Mahorn switched teams), and this from a man who informed his audience that the Lakers' Kurt Rambis had "crawled out of a sewer." But when the Celtics were trailing the Philly squad and Zink would let loose with one of his patented drawn-out basket calls, Most would growl, "Hysterical Harry is at it again!"

Believe me: the old days really were more fun.

Mr. October

You could not invent Reggie Jackson. He is entirely sui generis.

During the 2003 American League Championship Series between the Red Sox and Yankees, Reggie Jackson was part of the Yankees' traveling entourage. I have always had a good rapport with him, and I had an idea.

I thought I'd bring my score book from the 1977 World Series and have him autograph his three-homer Game 6 page. I showed it to him and he immediately took the book and ran over to Joe Torre, who was watching the Yankees take batting practice. Reggie was animated, to say the least, as he showed the book around.

He brought it back to me and I handed him a pen.

He signed it "Reggie Jackson" on the top line, with "Mr. October" underneath and the number 44 inside the loop of the "J" in Jackson.

It remains a treasured piece of memorabilia.

Quiz Time

Here's a quiz I used to give over a few beers after a game.

Question: What do these twelve NBA players have in common?

Bobby Jones, Kevin McHale, Michael Cooper, Mitch Kupchak, Vinnie Johnson, Bob McAdoo, Dennis Rodman, Bill Walton, Danny Ainge, Mychal Thompson, M. L. Carr, James Worthy. Very few people ever made the connection. The answer is that each of these players came off the bench in a regular capacity at least one year for one of the four teams that won all the NBA championships in the 1980s.

Walton, McHale, Worthy, and, yes, Rodman are Hall of Famers. McAdoo was both a scoring champ and an MVP. Jones was a truly great player. Kupchak and Thompson were instrumental in their teams' winning titles, Kupchak with the Bullets in 1978 and Thompson with the Lakers in 1987. Vinnie the Microwave was a unique offensive force. Ainge played in an All-Star Game and was a major three-point threat. Cooper was a superior defender and a clutch three-point shooter. Carr could play two positions, once led the league in minutes played, and was a classic glue guy. He's a pretty good twelfth man.

Two points with all this: due to the ravages of expansion, no team could ever again afford to bring people like these off the bench, and I honestly believe this team, in each player's individual prime, could have defeated any of the Michael Jordan Bulls teams.

PS: I left off Keith/Jamaal Wilkes, Artis Gilmore, Scott Wedman, and Jim Paxson. Wilkes is in the Hall of Fame. Many people think Gilmore should be as well. Wedman and Paxson played in All-Star Games. My bench even has a bench. Boy, are those days gone.

Acknowledgments

There would be no book without Andrew Blauner. The project was his idea. I was not at all sure my story would be of general interest, and I can only hope that it is. But Andrew believed in me and sat by patiently waiting for me to get my personal act together before I could sit down at the computer.

Nor would there be a book without George Gibson. We were able to resume a writer-editor partnership after a twenty-five-year lapse, and it was great for me to be reunited with him, in both a professional and, far more important, a personal sense. He was a tough-love editor, but I needed that. I am grateful for his sound judgment and his renewed friendship.

A special thanks is in order to my Comcast TV colleague Gary Tanguay for suggesting the book title. We were chatting before a telecast one evening and somehow or other I mentioned that Lawrenceville School football coach Jack Reydel had nicknamed me, one of his team managers, "Scribe" in deference to my work on the school paper, the *Lawrence*. I told him how the nickname had stuck in the Lawrenceville community down through the years.

"There's your title!" he said. It was a eureka moment. Of course, this also means thanks to Jack Reydel.

As Bill Cosby might say, I started out as a child, and so thanks to my father, Bill Ryan, for transferring his love of sports to his only son, and thanks to my mother, Mary Ryan, for recognizing the need to keep me invested in my father's world after he died when I was eleven.

I owe a great deal to the Mercy nuns of Saint Joseph's School in Trenton, New Jersey. They taught me how to handle our mother tongue, and while I can no longer properly diagram a sentence, I am sure my appreciation for the language and my affinity for both reading and writing was developed in their classrooms. I clearly remember Sister Mary Gabriella, whom we had for third, fourth, and fifth grade, and Sister Mary Sebastian, our eighth-grade teacher, who was pretty hip for a Mercy nun, or any nun.

I could thank just about every teacher at Lawrenceville, starting with headmaster Bruce McClellan. But my life being so sports-centric, the two who helped shape me the most were basketball coach (and French teacher) Ed Megna and his assistant Jim Waugh, a published poet who was the toughest English teacher I ever had. Talk about tough love.

I didn't go to Boston College because Bob Cousy was the basketball coach, but getting to know him and getting to watch his teams play exquisite fast-break basketball helped shape my view of that sport. I also learned a great deal of basketball from Frank Power, the BC freshman coach who became a great friend and hoop mentor. I'm not sure I ever met anyone who loved basketball more, but he was an educator first and a truly great man.

My direct link to a *Boston Globe* summer intern interview was BC sports information director Eddie Miller. And it never would have happened if my roommate Reid Oslin, who had first dibs on the interview, hadn't turned it down because he had other career aspirations.

Now we get to the *Boston Globe.*

Tom Winship was one of the great newspaper editors of the twentieth century, and for some reason he took a particular interest in the *Globe* summer intern class of 1968. Absent his leadership, the *Globe* could never have become the great force it was. Everyone, in every department, benefited from his presence.

Globe sports editors Ernie Roberts and Fran Rosa allowed young writers such as Peter Gammons and myself to be creative and even a little wild. Executive sports editor Jerry Nason was likewise in my corner from day one.

I liked working for all my subsequent sports editors, mainly because they pretty much let me be me. So thanks to Dave Smith, Vince Doria,

Don Skwar, and Joe Sullivan. Joe was the only sports editor I worked for who loved college basketball as much as I do, and knew more about it. He was also the perfect guy to supervise my departure from everyday duty following the London Olympics.

Assistant sports editors are an irreplaceable link in the chain of any sports department. Among the assistants who smoothed my passage over the years were Tom Mulvoy, Robin Romano, Greg Lee, Reid Laymance, Scott Thurston, Greg Lang, and Craig Larson. I hope I'm not forgetting anyone.

I owe a huge debt to the many great copy editors who have so often saved me from myself. The first was Art Keefe, who kept me on the straight and narrow in my early, somewhat undisciplined days. In later years I was in the journalistic TLC with such people as Jim Hoban, otherwise known as "Champ"; John Carney (a.k.a. "Carnak"); Bob Richardson; Pete Goodwin; Marsha Dick; Jim McBride; and Bob Fedas. Many others did their best to prevent me from being an item of interest on every English department bulletin board in greater Boston.

Eternal gratitude goes to Sean Mullin, the *Globe*'s technical whiz, who received far too many frantic calls from me while I was on the road. He bailed me out so many times he really ought to be in the will.

Ernie Santosuosso was a beacon for me in the beginning. He invariably referred to me as "the Trenton Kid." Jack Barry, who was present at the very first Celtics practice in 1946, was a repository of both Celtics and NBA information in addition to being one of the five nicest people ever to walk the earth.

Frank O'Brien's photographs enhanced every *Globe* story they ever accompanied, mine included. He also knew more about sports than most of the writers.

I worked with writing all-stars for more than forty years. I'll compare the *Globe*'s roster of sportswriters with that of any paper in the last fifty years. It includes the one and only Bud Collins, Clif Keane, Harold Kaese, Ray Fitzgerald, Leigh Montville, Bob Sales, Jack Barry, Will McDonough, Kevin Walsh, Dan Shaughnessy, Jackie MacMullan, Peter May, Ron Borges, Sue Bickelhaupt, Joe Burris, Gordon Edes, John Powers, Kevin Paul Dupont, Michael Vega, Joe Concannon, Tom Fitzgerald, John Ahern, Roger Birtwell, Charlie

Pierce, Tony Chamberlain, Bob Monahan, Jim McCabe, Bob Duffy, Nick Cafardo, Peter Abraham, Larry Whiteside, Lesley Visser, Ian Thomsen, Mike Madden, Michael Holley, Fluto Shinzawa, Julian Benbow, Chad Finn, Nancy Marapese-Burrell, Michael Vega, Michael Smith, Marvin Pave, Shira Springer, Bob Hohler, and Amalie Benjamin.

A special mention to the late Jack Craig, and early pioneer of print-oriented radio-TV criticism who was a frequent lunch companion and a relentless booster of mine, not to mention the godfather of my daughter, Jessica. I saved Peter Gammons for last, because on June 10, 1968, we both began our stints as summer interns. I'd say he's done all right for himself.

I drew something from each one of them, as I have from such, shall we say, "friendly local enemies" as Joe Looney, Ed Gillooly, Mike Fine, Steve Buckley, George Kimball, Buck Harvey, Michael Gee, Bill "Jake" Liston, Joe Giuliotti, Chaz Scoggins, and Gerry Callahan.

Peg Carson, Nancy Curley, and Bobbie Nardone were den mothers masquerading as sports department office secretaries for more than a combined fifty years, making life better and easier for us all until a *New York Times* bean counter mistakenly thought we no longer needed their services.

Colleague Jim Greenidge left this earth way too soon. In a previous incarnation as sports information director when Harvard's hockey team was playing in the 1983 Frozen Four at Grand Forks, North Dakota, he declared over a beer: "The only things black in this state are me and the puck."

One of the great aspects of this job is making friends and acquaintances with others in the business. I start with Dick "Hoops" Weiss, the ultimate basketball authority. I've known Mike Lupica since he was eighteen years old and a freshman at BC. How could I ever thank Tony Kornheiser enough for calling me "the Quintessential American Sportswriter"? A shout-out and a hearty thank-you, as well, go to Ailene Voisin, Michael Wilbon, George Vecsey, Sean McDonough, Johnny Most, Gil Santos, Bob Lobel, Upton Bell, Marty Tirrell, John Feinstein, Lee Feinswog, Dan LeBatard, Bill Littlefield, Jack McCallum, Bill Reynolds, Henry Hecht, Peter Carry, Alexander Woolf, Dick Vitale, Bob Costas, Marv Albert, Chick Hearn, Bob Neumeier, Mike Lynch, and Chris Russo.

I have written for *Basketball Times* since 1976. Editor and publisher

Larry Donald was a great friend. John Akers, his successor, is carrying on an important tradition.

Thanks to Tom Glover of the Hamilton Township Free Public Library in Hamilton Township, New Jersey, for invaluable aid in researching the life of my father, Bill Ryan.

At WCVB-TV in Boston I received great support from Phil Balboni, Mike Fernandez, Bobby Clark, Don Gillis, and the inimitable Clark Booth.

Joe Valerio changed my life by putting me on his show *The Sports Reporters* in 1989. This has given me a chance to know and work with the likes of the incomparable Dick Schaap, indispensable Canadian import John Saunders, one-man conglomerate Mitch Albom, Bill Rhoden, Bryan Burwell, Israel Gutierrez, Jemele Hill, and many other superb talents.

I was in on the ground floor of ESPN's *Around the Horn*, and what a break that was! Thanks to executive producer Erik Rydholm and producer Aaron Solomon. Mark Hancock was our demon researcher for many years. Tony Reali makes hosting this intricate show look and sound easy when it is anything but. I have loved working with fellow panelists Woody Paige, Tim Cowlishaw, T. J. Simers, Jay Mariotti, Bill Plaschke, J. A. Adande, Kevin Blackistone, Bomani Jones, Pablo Torre, and Frank Isola.

I have cherished every moment filling in for either Tony Kornheiser or Michael Wilbon on *Pardon the Interruption*, where Matt Kelliher, Frankie Nation, Mike Morrell, Matt Awano, Bonnie Berko, and Myriam Leger (who loves it when I break out my French on the show) make it hum, all under the supervision of the amazing Mr. Rydholm.

This one is hard for me to believe. I have been part of a weekly morning radio show, working with the same cohosts, since 1983. There are many listeners who only know me as the "Mr. Everything" who chats with Loren Owens and Wally Brine each Thursday at seven forty-five. It is a vital part of my life and it functions smoothly because producer Brian Bell is in charge.

People in the United States don't know I have had a Canadian radio life. Thanks to Bob McCowan and Ryan Walsh of *Prime Time Sports*.

I have had many important relationships with professional sports teams. It is no secret that my so-called career was launched by the Celtics.

I will be forever grateful to Red Auerbach, Jeff Cohen, Jan Volk, Tom Heinsohn, John Havlicek, Paul Silas, Don Nelson, Satch Sanders, Hank Finkel, Steve Kuberski, Paul Westphal, Bill Fitch, Larry Bird, Kevin McHale and Doc Rivers for giving me great things to write and for treating me with respect off the court.

All media people need the assistance of public relations experts. Among the ones most helpful to me were the late Howie McHugh, Tod Rosensweig, Jeff Twiss, Brian McIntyre, Nate Greenberg, Heidi Holland, Ed Carpenter, Jack Grinold, Terry Lyons, Dick Kelley, Chris Cameron, Howie Davis, Tim Tolokan, Dick Quinn, Dick Lipe, Josh Rosenfeld, Wayne Witt, Bill Needle, Cheri White, Jim Foley, Bob Steiner, Harvey Greene, and the fairly amazin' Dean of Them All, Harvey Pollack.

Many thanks to Terry Pluto for involving me in a successful book project entitled *Forty-eight Minutes*, a chronicle of a 1987 game between the Celtics and Cavaliers. And thanks, as well, to Daniel Okrent for writing *Nine Innings*, a minute exploration of a 1983 Orioles-Brewers game, for it is his idea we, ahem, appropriated for our own project.

The NBA was my meat and potatoes for many years. Helping me negotiate it were Pat Williams, Hubie Brown, Jerry Krause, Jerry Colangelo, Chuck Daly, Billy Cunningham, Pat Riley, Dave DeBusschere, Doug Collins, Chris Wallace, Dr. Jack Ramsay, Frank Layden, Doug Moe, and, of course, David Stern.

I spent a few hours in the world of college sports as well, and at the top of the list of valuable friends are the late Dave Gavitt and his one-time Providence College sports information director, and successor as commissioner of the Big East, Mike Tranghese. Thanks also to Tom Brennan, Frank Sullivan, Jim O'Brien, Gary Williams, Jim Calhoun, and John Calipari.

Some people are difficult to categorize. I am thankful for the friendship and counsel offered me by my broadcast agent, Steve Freyer. I cannot imagine not knowing Dick Johnson of New England's Sports Museum. There is no way my life would have been as pleasurable without knowing Bob Elias, Marty Aronoff, Alan Miller, and James Isaacs.

My late son, Keith, was not crazy about sports, but he had a special place in his heart for college hockey. His sister, Jessica, loves her Boston sports teams and is always good for a spirited Brady-Manning debate. My daughter-in-law, Kate, has done a sensational job raising her fabulous triplets: Jack, who loves the Olympics; Conor, who has his own subscription to *Sports Illustrated*; and Amelia, who loves both ballet and the Red Sox.

Finally, there is my wife, Elaine, who actually claims to have enjoyed (most of) the games I've dragged her to, starting in 1964. To say she keeps me grounded is a rather large understatement.

Index

NOTE: Page numbers followed by an *"n"* indicate a footnote on that page.
NOTE: Throughout the index the author, Bob Ryan, is referred to as BR.

A Note on the Author

Bob Ryan is one of America's most respected sports reporters, writers, and columnists. He retired from daily work at the *Boston Globe* in 2012 after some forty-five years at the paper. He is the author of many books, including *Forty-eight Minutes: A Night in the Life of the NBA*, *The Four Seasons*, *Wait Till I Make the Show: Baseball in the Minor Leagues*, and *The Boston Celtics: The History, Legends, and Images of America's Most Celebrated Team*. He continues to appear regularly on various ESPN shows. He lives in Hingham, Massachusetts.